Praise for Scott Steinberg's
Make Change Work for You

"One of the greatest barriers to progress is fear—of failure, rejection, embarrassment, uncertainty, and confrontation. With actionable advice and empowering examples, *Make Change Work for You* provides the tools we need to succeed in the face of our fears."
—Adam Grant, Wharton professor and
bestselling author of *Give and Take*

"Practical, hands-on, and powerful, Scott isn't afraid to talk about being afraid and how it keeps us down."
—Seth Godin, bestselling author of
The Icarus Deception

"This powerful, practical book is loaded with proven strategies to build your self-confidence, become more innovative, and unlock your creativity."
—Brian Tracy, bestselling author of
The Power of Self-Confidence

"A must read for any working professional—provides the new formula for finding lasting success in your career."
—Dan Schawbel, *New York Times*
bestselling author of *Promote Yourself*

"An eye-opening read that will change the way you look at business. Start competing for tomorrow... today."
—Brian Solis, digital analyst and anthropologist,
and author of *What's the Future of Business?*

"Provides a more personal and practical formula for innovation that's just the prescription for executives looking to break through to the next level."
—Marty Yudkovitz, retired head of
Strategic Innovation, The Walt Disney Company

W9-BWJ-940

"Steinberg provides a one-of-a-kind formula for evolution and growth in an age of constant change. His paradoxical findings, from numerous interviews and research: we deal best with change when we use the tools of both change and constancy, changing ourselves and yet remaining constant in our application of what he calls the F.E.A.R. model—focus, engage, assess, react. It's an eye-opening read."
>—Richard Bolles, author of
>*What Color Is Your Parachute?*

"Provides powerful new insights into the nature of creativity and personal growth."
>—Nolan Bushnell, founder of Atari and
>author of *Finding the Next Steve Jobs*

"Charles Darwin said those who survive are those who adapt. *Make Change Work for You* is a must read for those who want to survive in our rapidly changing world. Clear. Concise. Practical."
>—Gary Shapiro, president and CEO,
>Consumer Electronics Association

Make *Change* Work for You

10 WAYS TO FUTURE-PROOF YOURSELF,
FEARLESSLY INNOVATE, AND SUCCEED
DESPITE UNCERTAINTY

Scott Steinberg

A Perigee Book

PERIGEE
An imprint of Penguin Random House LLC
375 Hudson Street, New York, New York 10014

Perigee trade paperback ISBN: 978-0-399-16677-8

The Library of Congress has cataloged the Perigee hardcover edition as follows:

Steinberg, Scott (Management consultant)
Make change work for you : 10 ways to future-proof yourself, fearlessly innovate, and
succeed despite uncertainty / Scott Steinberg.— First edition.
pages cm
ISBN 978-0-399-16676-1
1. Organizational change. 2. Change (Psychology) I. Title.
HD58.8.S7185 2014
650.1—dc23 2014039886

PUBLISHING HISTORY
Perigee hardcover edition / January 2015
Perigee trade paperback edition / January 2016

PRINTED IN THE UNITED STATES OF AMERICA

10   9   8   7   6   5   4   3   2   1

Text design by Tiffany Estreicher

Most Perigee books are available at special quantity discounts for bulk purchases for sales
promotions, premiums, fund-raising, or educational use. Special books, or book excerpts, can also
be created to fit specific needs. For details, write: SpecialMarkets@penguinrandomhouse.com.

For Z—No skeletons, just keys.

Contents

Everything Changes

Market-leading energy provider Royal Dutch Shell supplies dozens of countries with more than 3 million barrels of oil and 20 million tons of natural gas each year. It isn't the first place you'd expect to find leaders starting a fire—let alone purposefully. But Mandar Apte, head of the company's Empower training program, isn't just tasked with sparking positive change worldwide. He's specifically charged with setting executives' creativity and capacity to innovate ablaze.

Empower classes aren't grounded in traditional business processes and procedures, though. Instead, they revolve around a simple principle: To succeed in increasingly unpredictable and uncertain environments, we can't simply remain static. Rather, we must constantly change, adapt, and strive to fan the sparks of innovation.

But doing this is much easier said than done.

In fact, while preparing hundreds of executives to face tomorrow's challenges, Apte's team has made some surprising discoveries about the common problems modern professionals face. Rather than a lack of time, money, or manpower, many stem from two unlikely sources, he says. Specifically: a lack of risk tolerance and a resistance to change.

Going into Empower training sessions, Apte just *assumes* everyone is capable of being an innovator. In today's hyperkinetic and hypercompetitive world, he argues, we're all forced to constantly adapt and readapt. So he always begins classes by asking a simple question, What's keeping you from being more innovative? Often, he finds, the biggest stumbling block is simply our own sense of perspective.

When we reexamine the difficulties that we confront more closely, we often find several obstacles that prevent us from successfully adapting to and overcoming unforeseen hurdles. These barriers to success include fear, anxiety, insecurity, and others' opinions.

If you've ever run up against these barriers in your own life and business, you're not alone; we all have at one time or another. We all want to reduce stress, be more productive, and better serve our organizations and customers. But to achieve these goals, we must confront the very same issues that Apte outlines, any one or all of which routinely prevent us from realizing our objectives.

Whether we're speaking about individuals or organizations, our perceptions impact our ability to make sound decisions, our willingness to take risks, and ultimately our performance. And all of these factors have a direct effect on our ability to succeed.

But as Shell's Empower program teaches, we all hold the keys to effectively adapt with changing times and get ahead more frequently in life and business as well. Change your outlook, and you can change your future. Rather than look outside at shifting times and trends to do so, as we would in traditional problem-solving scenarios, this transformation process starts by taking a deeper look within.

———

It's no secret that change is all around us, and in business especially it seems that the scope, breadth, and speed of changes taking place today are boundless. This means that throughout your life and organization, the scope, breadth, and speed of changes you should be making to keep up, let alone get ahead, should be equally limitless.

Change in business can take the form of:

- Unstable economic conditions
- Unpredictable operating environments
- Shifting competitive landscapes
- Changing customer needs and expectations
- New tools, trends, and techniques
- Emerging technologies (especially information technologies)
- New communications systems
- Evolving best practices
- Unexpected opportunities and challenges

And that's just to name a few common varieties.

In effect, this rapidly accelerating rate of change (driven by continued advances in IT and personal communications) has greatly compounded the challenges we face. We now cross paths with a rapidly ballooning number of individuals and engage in numerous interactions and cross-reactions as a result of every action we take. The result is an unprecedented and truly radical degree of uncertainty in professional environments. We're quickly discovering that the present is growing more unstable and the future is increasingly difficult to predict.

In short, the world of business is a risky place to be, and looking these risks squarely in the eye—then pushing them out of the way—can seem intimidating. But that's exactly what we must do, even if it means routinely stepping outside the comfort zones we operate in. It's the only way to continually thrive on both an individual and an organizational level.

Hesitate to change or take smart risks, and no matter how pragmatic we believe ourselves to be, we're often unwittingly working at cross purposes. When we allow fears and anxieties to color our decisions and doubts to govern our actions, we often tie our own hands and directly inhibit our ability to grow and innovate.

Happily, because all of these shackles are self-imposed, we all have the power to unlock them the moment we elect to do so. Choose to remove emotion from the equation and put fear in the backseat, and you'll take the first, most powerful step toward future-proofing yourself or your enterprise and begin to tear down the stumbling blocks that stand between you and your ultimate success. Embrace change by taking calculated risks and meaningful action, and you'll put yourself on the path to regular reinvention— the essence of remaining relevant—and create positive, lasting effects on every level.

Nonetheless, many enterprises and professionals still struggle to cope with change, even as others seem to thrive in turbulent markets. As you'll soon discover, the secret to leaders' ongoing success has little to do with individual ability or business environments.

Rather, the source of their continued achievements frequently lies in their own willingness to change, grow, and embrace fresh perspectives.

Are you looking to dive headfirst into tomorrow, spark lasting change, and set yourself on the fast-track to becoming future-proof? Step back and calmly study the challenges before you, then take smart action. When you remove worry and doubt from the decision-making process, you may be surprised just how easy it is to sidestep the obstacles.

This book provides a new approach for making things work—in your personal life, your career, and your business. Apply its principles, and you can consistently find success with just a few simple shifts in thinking, even in the most fast-changing and unpredictable environments.

As will become evident throughout this book:

- Everyone is an innovator.
- Change is your secret weapon.
- Disruption drives learning, growth, and success.
- Relevancy is reinvention.
- Flexibility makes you future-proof.

Put simply, innovation isn't hard. In fact, small changes (*evolutions*) can be every bit as powerful as huge breakthroughs (*revolutions*). Moreover, the same strategic principles that today's most-acclaimed strategic innovators use to produce game-changing advancements can be leveraged to help you positively transform your life, business, and career on every level.

When the average working professionals you'll meet in this

book found their careers stalling out or were struggling to make ends meet, they took simple, practical steps that drove them closer to achieving their goals—then repeated them time and again.

And when the many businesses of all sizes profiled in the following pages found that their industry had become more challenging or that competitors were nipping at their heels, they asserted their leadership position by doing the same as well.

Case in point: When Target wanted to boost its profits, it didn't build more big-box retail outlets. It launched half-size stores in fast-growing urban markets selling half-size packs of paper towels and locally branded merchandise.

When the Danish supermarket SuperBrugsen wanted to differentiate itself and stay competitive in increasingly demanding markets, it simply asked customers what locally branded food products they wanted it to stock.

When medical device manufacturer Medtronic wanted to create growth opportunities, it didn't double down on more cutting-edge defibrillators. Instead, it partnered with hospitals to open on-site laboratories, then—building on the trust it had gained—grew its new business lines even further by providing these partners with IT, support, and management services.

None of these innovations is outside your reach. None of these companies reinvented the wheel either: As we periodically do with our cars' tires to achieve better performance, they simply gave themselves a purposeful realignment. Slight changes in strategy or perspective can often make a big difference.

Throughout this book, you'll learn why courageously embracing change and adapting to shifting environments isn't just crucial but the only proven recipe for lasting success for individuals (whether your career is skyrocketing or stalling) and businesses (whether your market is booming or becoming increasingly risky) alike.

All of us possess the capacity to change, grow, and exert more positive control over our future and do so by practicing small acts of bravery. It all starts with greater awareness, greater flexibility, and greater ability to take action in the face of doubt or indecision.

In later chapters, you'll learn several of life's little secrets:

- Change isn't as difficult as it seems.
- The status quo is no longer a safe bet.
- Cleverness creates competitive advantage.
- Different isn't just good—it's essential.

But most important, you'll discover that courage is a characteristic that we can actively cultivate in ourselves, nurture through repeated application, and consistently put to work to help us more frequently and successfully change and innovate.

Take it from master magician Harry Houdini, who, decades ago, mastered the art of bravery by making dozens of daring escapes from sealed tanks of water or submerged coffins.

"My chief task has been to conquer fear," the illusionist once explained. "The public sees only the thrill of the accomplished trick. They have no conception of the tortuous preliminary self-training that was necessary to conquer fear . . . no one except myself can appreciate how I have to work at this job every single day, never letting up for a moment. I always have on my mind the thought that next year I must do something greater, something more wonderful."[1]

The abilities and opportunities you'll unlock when you find the courage to innovate and make positive changes will appear nothing short of magical as well.

Over the course of this book, you'll discover just how easy it is to tap into these abilities, and that so-called daredevils and mavericks are secretly neither, being far more risk averse than they are risk-takers.

Troubled by growing uncertainty? Dubious about the future? Deeply concerned with rising levels of competition? Prepare to put these problems behind you.

In the pages that follow, I'll show you how to rethink risk, reconsider change, and redefine what it means to be fearless . . . and how to future-proof yourself and your enterprise in the process.

Chapter One

What's Holding You Back?

Twenty-six-year-old Vermonter Melissa Kirmayer Eamer was sick of serving customers clam chowder. After spending five years slinging chow in the restaurant she co-owned with her former husband, she wanted a bigger bite out of life. Every day, Eamer longed for something better. Every day, she felt more stuck.

"I really hit a point where the restaurant business was challenging, but not intellectually challenging," she says. "It was exhausting, but I felt like I was missing something."[1] In retrospect, she discovered that the absent pieces were simply courage and self-confidence.

She was afraid of change. What if she ruined her life? Her career? Her finances? Eamer felt trapped. She convinced herself that there were too many challenges and the stakes were too high in charting a new professional course. Without relevant contacts and work experience, how could she ever make the shift to a new career?

But one day, fed up, she told herself it was now or never: *Something had to give.* She took a long, hard look in the mirror and asked herself, "What's the worst that can happen?" and "What step can I take today to get me started on my path?" Then she took that step.

Eamer had long been interested in the publishing business. So she sent her résumé to several local firms. None responded. Undeterred by this silence, she changed course, offering to work free for six months. This time, two companies agreed. She picked her favorite and signed up. Working at the restaurant by day and the publishing company by night, she tried not to think too far ahead. "I might have been overwhelmed by the challenges if I let myself think about it too much," she explains. "Instead, I took this incremental step."

By the end of the internship, she was hired to a paying position working directly with the CEO, an MBA with impressive business acumen. Inspired, she began studying for the GMAT on top of her two jobs and successfully applied to the University of Michigan's MBA program. Just one catch: Taking the opportunity meant having to leave the restaurant, the publishing company, the husband, and everything she knew behind.

Faced with a host of common fears—change, insecurity, rejection, and so on—she was understandably troubled. ("It was scary. When my sisters showed up to pack the U-Haul to move . . . I said, 'Holy crap, what have I done?'") But that didn't stop her from moving forward. As Eamer explained, she found calm by focusing on the potential opportunity at hand—what lay ahead, not behind her.

"I'd set up all these little tests," says Eamer. "If I passed these hurdles, I'd go on to the next. That reinforced my confidence to see if I could take on bigger challenges."

Up through graduation, and several times since, Eamer has

faced challenges that demanded great change and risk. Each time, she had to conquer her fears, expand her comfort zone, and jump with both feet into each challenge.

Today, she's a technical adviser to consumer business at a large online retailer and has headed up some of its most wildly successful programs; she is also being groomed for senior management. Describing the great leaps of faith she took, Eamer says, "They have made all the difference."

If you want to make a similar difference in your life and business, you too will have to confront common sources of fear, transform uncertainty into opportunity, and take control of your future. And if you happen to lead a team or organization, to consistently effect positive change, you'll also need to find ways to help others break down the barriers that inhibit *their* success as well.

As you'll soon see, getting ahead isn't about being risk free. Instead, it's about being *risk averse*. The dirty secret that many successful organizations and individuals don't share is that relevance is found in ongoing reinvention: To win, you can't avoid but rather *must make* constant gambles. But as with any successful gambling strategy, winning isn't simply a function of playing the game, given the odds we often face. Instead, you've got to be careful and methodical about *where* you place your bets.

The more open you are to change, the more informed you are about challenges faced, and the more relentlessly practical you are about facing them, the closer you'll steadily come to success. Push yourself to change, innovate, and disrupt yourself more often, and respond intelligently and consistently to the results your actions produce, and you'll win far more frequently, with more pronounced impact. It's a principle that working professionals or businesses of any size can put to work to create positive change on every level.

Just ask Starbucks. The world's largest chain of coffeehouses, it's famously "in the people business serving coffee, not the coffee business serving people." Customer service comes first. But the company's consistently willing to put its Arabica beans on the line by routinely rolling out new products and strategies to the public, even before they're error-free or finished.

Why? Because it would rather be first than flawless, make mistakes than miss opportunities, and fall flat than fail to establish market beachheads before its rivals. The company constantly finds new ways to succeed, from successful new store concepts and products to mobile payment solutions and online apps. And via online platforms such as MyStarbucksIdea.com, where shoppers can suggest new innovations, it's also consistently finding ways to slash costs, remove risks, and get customers involved in reinventing the brand.

Whether you're an individual or organization, the lesson Starbucks teaches us is simple. No matter how successful you are, you still face two key choices every day in rapidly evolving business environments: You can look to the future, plan ahead, and prepare yourself to surf the waves of change, or you can pretend they aren't coming and idly float along with the current, treading water until they crash over you.

As you'll soon see, the best way to succeed and keep succeeding over a long-term horizon is to learn to start hanging ten.

Look around you. Change is everywhere. Uncertainty is growing. Risk is rampant. If you want to get ahead, like Eamer and

Starbucks, you too must find the courage to keep pushing forward and evolving. But you can't just change once: To successfully adapt to a changing world on a regular basis, you must continue taking positive action and making consistent changes until the rhythm of change becomes as familiar and comforting as your morning jog.

Change isn't a problem. It's an opportunity and a blessing. With changing environments and expectations come new opportunities. Every time we change, we learn. And every time we learn, we grow, discovering new, more effective ways to get ahead and succeed.

Innovation ranks among the most-quoted business buzzwords today. But you may be surprised by its definition, which is far less well known: "The introduction of something new." Fundamentally, innovation is change, and change *is* innovation. Master one and you've mastered the other. And if you haven't taken a hard look at either your schedule or your priorities lately, pause and do so now. Chances are, you're successfully changing and innovating every day already.

So if we're all fundamentally innovators at heart and capable of achieving success by making small, simple, everyday changes, what's holding us back? The answer: our own fears and misconceptions. But just because these challenges are easily spotted doesn't mean that finding the courage we need to address them is easy; for individuals and organizations alike, the truth is often quite the opposite.

Before we outline key strategies for breaking down the barriers that stand between us and success, let's explore fear and anxiety in greater detail. And how by courageously and constantly confronting them we can successfully change, adapt, and future-proof both ourselves and our enterprises in the process.

What Is Fear?

Technically, *fear* is a negative emotional state—one characterized by a heightened sense of agitation, tension, and alarm—that many animals (including those animals called humans) feel in the presence of danger. This danger doesn't necessarily have to be the fear of physical harm. For example, it can be the fear of making a mistake and losing your job. Alternately, it can be the fear of being embarrassed when asking an executive a "stupid" question or fear that a new product will not connect with customers.

However you define it, this emotion can cause you to avoid taking certain actions that have the potential to benefit you or your company. But as you'll see in the next section, finding the courage to overcome fear can help you overcome the roadblocks that keep your business or career prospects from soaring.

How Fear Affects Us in the Workplace

In a professional context, most jobs don't expose people to imminent or immediate physical danger. But this doesn't mean that the majority of organizations and working professionals don't experience fear; in fact, most feel it all too keenly.

Moreover, there's another brand of fear commonly felt and experienced in the workplace as well: *anxiety*. Anxiety is a negative emotional state in which the threat is not physically present but instead is anticipated or expected.[2] It's an equally frightening reaction, only to an unreal or imagined danger.

Professionals may feel either source of alarm in several common workplace scenarios. Just a few examples:

- Being assigned unfamiliar or challenging tasks
- Assuming new roles or responsibilities
- Pitching prospective clients
- Speaking in front of large groups
- Confronting supervisors, customers, or colleagues

Organizations may experience similar levels of discomfort, especially when facing changing markets, expectations, and competitive environments. This fear can be particularly acute in the wake of shifting trends and innovations. Sample scenarios that may produce corporate anxiety include the following:

- Pursuing new areas or avenues of business
- Facing powerful or emerging rivals
- Addressing changing trends and markets
- Watching sales or market share decline
- Undergoing intense media or public scrutiny

Unfortunately, the fear and anxiety that we experience in the workplace can produce long-lasting, negative consequences.

At their basest level, fear and anxiety can be direct causes of workplace-related stress and discomfort. Each can stymie strategic thinking, hinder our ability to communicate, and decrease overall performance. At their peak, they dangerously impair our judgment, inhibit growth, and stunt development. They may even cause us to overlook or become indifferent to potential opportunities for advancement.

When we let fear and anxiety dominate us, we are negatively affected in a variety of ways:

- **We avoid difficult or uncomfortable situations.** But if we can never confront and overcome these challenges, we can never move past them.
- **We refuse to change as the world changes all around us.** But if we don't greet change forewarned and forearmed, we're often caught flat-footed.
- **We inhibit learning and growth.** But each is crucial to evolution and advancement.
- **We fall back on familiar choices and patterns.** But in a changing world, what worked today won't always work tomorrow.
- **We react instinctively, not out of consideration.** But analyzing challenges and acting objectively as we address them is the surest way to solve problems.
- **We try to change the world instead of changing ourselves.** But our own actions, not those of others, are the only ones we can control.
- **We fixate on the past.** But the present and future are all we can change or affect.

Fear is a tangible and persistent threat. But why does it remain so?

Fear Comes in Seven Flavors

Fear is an extremely complex emotion. This should come as no surprise because humans, like organizations, are extremely complex entities.

But one thing that's especially interesting about fear in the workplace is that it often comes in several shades. Despite appearing to be a single feeling on the surface, workplace-related fears often combine multiple sources of emotional turmoil into a more potent cocktail of confidence-sapping sensations.

For example, a professional preparing to present a paper at an industry conference may be anxious that he will fail at the task, misspeak, and become flustered. These potential stumbles could lead to loss of control and embarrassment, followed by rejection or isolation by the assembled crowd—just some of many underlying sources of his initial worries.

Through research and scores of interviews with leading experts, I uncovered seven sources of fear that frequently mix, match, and combine to create powerful inhibitors to success in the workplace. Let's consider each one in detail.

1. **Fear of failure.** The possibility of being unable to successfully achieve a goal or complete a task set by yourself or others.

Cameras start to flash as the limo door opens and a tall, dapper young man confidently steps out and strides toward his workplace. Smiling at bystanders and nodding to colleagues, we hear a somber voice intone: "I've missed more than 9,000 shots in my career. I've lost almost 300 games. Twenty-six times, I've been trusted to take the winning shot and missed. I've failed over and over and over again in my life. And that is why I succeed."[3]

Just seconds into the Nike commercial, basketball legend Michael Jordan has summarized a crucial life lesson: There's no such thing as failure, only the price of an education. Making mistakes is among the most important ways that we learn. If you're not succeeding at present, you're probably not failing enough.

And yet, making mistakes is the single most common workplace fear today. What could be worse than to fail in a high-pressure business environment? Doubly so knowing that one false step could send us into freefall and potentially drag our careers, accomplishments, and good reputations down with us?

So, instead of stretching and taking risks in your career or learning, growing, and expanding your capabilities and horizons, you (or your organization) don't fully apply yourself. Fear of failure keeps you from taking risks, so you withdraw and play it safe.

This is not how people get ahead in organizations and this is not how organizations develop a competitive advantage in the marketplace. Worse, fear often tricks us into thinking we're playing it smart by sitting still, even as the world changes around us— the greatest risk of all.

With so many complex decisions being made faster and amid growing uncertainty, understand that mistakes are unavoidable. Failure is a routine cost of doing business. In fact, embracing it is the single most commonly recommended piece of professional advice given by dozens of leading authorities I interviewed.

As you'll see in later chapters, successful individuals and organizations don't get ahead in life and business by avoiding failure. Instead, they make a point to fail fast, often, and strategically.

2. **Fear of embarrassment.** The shame and self-consciousness felt when one feels humiliated, unable to live up to expectations, or socially conform.

For mattress industry executive Mark Quinn, newly hired vice president of marketing for Leggett & Platt's $1.7 billion residential home furnishing business, the visit to *Furniture Today*'s Bedding

Conference was shaping up well. Beaming with pride, he basked in the triumphant atmosphere of the company's cocktail party.

At the red carpet gala, Leggett & Platt (L&P) had just unveiled the first episode of *The Virgin Mattress*, Quinn's edgy new online video series, to rave reviews. The clips, which follow fictional couples' efforts to replace mattresses shared by ex-relationships—painted as soiled and creepy—weren't just designed to convince shoppers to replace old mattresses more frequently. For L&P, a 130-year-old manufacturer of bed frames, cushions, and coils, the campaign was also an ambitious attempt to reinvent the company's buttoned-down image.

Backed by extensive advertising and social media promotions, the series was well received by bedding industry insiders; L&P even expected it to go viral. Enthused, Quinn emailed the first episode to the company's 19,000 employees, encouraging all to share the video. It made a splash, but not in the way he intended.

Still at the Bedding Conference, Quinn's phone began to ring off the hook: Colleagues were morally offended by its risqué overtones. Back home in Carthage, Missouri, coworkers were storming around and phoning the CEO, calling for his head.

But it wasn't his marketing instincts that were wrong, Quinn thought, or his belief that L&P needed to radically redefine its image. It was his lack of familiarity with the firm's more conservative corporate culture. So when confronted by the executive team, instead of kowtowing, Quinn stood up for his convictions. With his head on the chopping block, he stood up, stuck his neck out again, and dared colleagues to let the ax fall.

Rather than beg his bosses not to can him, Quinn accepted responsibility for the scandal, demanded a second chance, and actually sweet-talked them into giving him another $100,000. Then he spent the funds remaking *The Virgin Mattress* series and hiring improvisational comedy troupe the Second City for an equally audacious but less racy skit creating a fake rap video promoting L&P's new "hybrid" (part memory foam, part coil) mattresses.

Not only did this latter campaign help drive category sales growth by 35 percent, it introduced the term *hybrid* into industry vernacular.

To those who have felt like Quinn—disheartened, alone, even trapped—don't be afraid to stick to your guns, he says. Fear of embarrassment and lack of self-confidence can prevent us from making crucial decisions or taking necessary risks. Rather than back down, speak up. Instead of doubting, trust yourself. And when others don't believe or care, make them.

L&P could've played it safe, and could've wound up becoming another faceless and ailing manufacturer. Quinn could've accepted humiliation, backed down, and let his work become another footnote in a long line of troubled marketing efforts. Instead, both learned from mistakes and bounced back smarter and sharper. At the time of this writing, years later, both L&P's business and Quinn's career within it are still going strong.

3. **Fear of losing control.** Believing that situations and events have spiraled beyond our ability to command or adapt to them.

This is it—the moment is finally here. Staring at the splashy lookbooks she'd painstakingly assembled, Kyle Smitley couldn't manage to bite back an infectious grin. After a year of sleepless nights scrimping to build a business while attending law school by day, the bubbly twenty-three-year-old was finally ready to explode into the world of high fashion. Lovingly preparing the mailers, addressed to more than 500 clothing boutiques nationwide, she couldn't wait to introduce the world to Barley & Birch, her organic kids clothing brand. "Customers will be knocking down our door," she thought. "Success, here we come."[4]

But despite her best efforts, buyers responded with deafening silence. When a few days passed without calls or emails, Smitley began to worry. When a month had gone by, and she'd received just two orders, she started to sweat—her best-laid plans were spinning out of control, and she wasn't sure what to do about it. Disappointed, broke, and facing increasing stress from juggling a double life as a student and small-business owner, she made the only sane choice she felt she had left. Sitting in class, ignoring her professors, she sent hundreds of emails to parenting bloggers and online journalists, offering free samples.

Within six months, buoyed by a tidal wave of positive press, hundreds of stores around the country were calling, begging to stock Barley & Birch products. What's more, celebrities from Warren Buffett to Sheryl Crow and Jessica Alba were lining up to show their support. All it took was a simple change in strategy and shift in perspective to help steer Smitley's business away from the brink of disaster and back toward success—choices that were well within her ability to execute.

Have you ever felt as if your workday was spinning out of control, and there was nothing you could do to put it back on track?

Maybe a vendor calls to inform you that the chemical your factory needs to produce your bestselling product is out of stock and won't be available again for two more weeks, necessitating an emergency scramble by your purchasing department to scare up a new supplier. Or perhaps your boss tells you on Friday to dump that presentation you've been working on all week and get an entirely different one ready to present to the board on Monday. Or you're on a business trip 3,000 miles away from home to cement a crucial sales agreement when your spouse calls to tell you that your son was involved in a car accident and you need to get to the hospital immediately. In all cases, the fear of losing control over ensuing events can exert a palpable and highly discomfiting influence on us.

We all lose control of our work, our careers, and our lives from time to time, and experiencing the fear of doing so can prove highly unsettling, threatening to trip us up or even paralyze us as we go. Instead of acting, we react. Rather than taking calculated action, we freeze up and sit still.

As a result, we often play it safe and avoid situations that could potentially spin out of control. But when we stop reacting on an instinctual level and start doing so more practically and resourcefully, we benefit. While we can't always control events entirely, we can still help steer them toward more productive outcomes.

As we know, surprises are common in life and business, and disaster can frequently strike, often due to reasons that are not under your direct influence or control. When they do, the experience can prove highly unsettling; it's hard to captain any ship when a storm of uncertainty is raging. And if you can't turn that ship around quickly, self-confidence and self-awareness can shrink rapidly. Anyone who's ever sailed through this kind of tempest is bound to remember it—and the very thought of experiencing one again can become a powerful barrier that impacts your day-to-day productivity and performance.

To be more productive, we can't this ignore these facts: You can't control everything, and there will be days when chaos reigns and there's nothing you can to stop it. But we can always do something to manage it. When those days occur, you need to step back, take a deep breath, and focus your efforts on the things that you *can* control. By taking decisive action, and making more measured responses, you can slowly but surely help steer your ship back on course.

4. **Fear of rejection.** When you, your company, or the products or services you represent are refused, turned away, or avoided by others.

At the age of eighteen, I wanted nothing more than to work in the videogame industry. Unfortunately, that's not what the videogame industry wanted. I called hundreds of publishers, from large corporations to garage shops, happily offering to test their software for free. Of the handful that responded over the years, only three opportunities materialized, and only one is even vaguely memorable. (Infogrames's Alone in the Dark 3—naturally, the worst game in the series.) But it was enough to keep me going.

Fast-forward to 1998: I was desperately seeking a summer internship and called several businesses. I asked for no salary, just a chance to prove myself. Alas, being an East Coaster was a great disadvantage in a field dominated by California companies. With local teens falling over themselves to do the deed for $5 an hour, it wasn't even worth these organizations' time to import a willingly abused understudy.

As luck would have it, though, the industry tradeshow Electronic Entertainment Expo (known as E3) was happening in my town that summer. Visiting it, I discovered, nestled deep in the lowest levels of the smallest convention hall, a little French maker of computer games named Microïds, whose software my grade-school buddies used to download illegally.

Minutes into the random encounter, I had my first internship—and a free three-month stay at their headquarters outside Paris, France. The third week on the job, I'd become the company's head of international public relations. And by the time I returned to school that fall, I was the vice president of product acquisitions, having brought the company three top-rated products from a then-unknown developer (Monolith Productions), later sold to Warner Bros. for millions.

Lesson learned: In business, *no* never means no, only "no for now." You're selling yourself short if you're willing to take either no or dead silence for an answer.

When a supervisor declines our request for a promotion, we naturally question our abilities. When customers don't buy our products, we suddenly find ourselves reconsidering their value. But the reasons behind any given rejection may be due to completely unrelated factors (the organization's budget can't support higher salaries) or even external circumstances (no one can find our kick-ass app in a sea of look-alikes).

Rather than let rejection undermine your confidence, remember: The simple truth is that you're going to hear no far more often in life than you're going to hear yes. So you (1) might as well get used to it and (2) understand that the more no responses you get, the closer you are statistically to getting to yes.

5. **Fear of confrontation.** Experiencing a negative event or having a hostile personal or professional interaction with others.

In many ways, business is all about confrontation. You may be confronting a colleague, a boss, a competitor, a tired company process, or an outdated way of doing business. But the fear of confrontation can be debilitating, and it can throttle new ideas and innovation. It takes courage to confront others, but it is essential for any organization to move forward and progress.

Case in point: As kids' favorite pasta sauce, Unilever's popular Ragú brand enjoyed a special place in children's hearts. But when sales began to stall and rival Prego started outperforming it in taste tests, one ad agency exec had to screw up his courage and tell the firm it needed to cook up a newer, more appealing marketing strategy fast.

Gerry Graf's idea for putting spice back into the sauce's secret recipe was certainly unique: to rebrand childhood as a heart-*wrenching*, not heart-*warming*, experience and cast Ragú as kids' must-have comfort food of choice. But his plan for executing it was equally unlikely: Produce a series of TV commercials featuring tots happily chowing down on the sauce after watching household pets die or accidentally walking in on their parents having sex.

Graf argued with Unilever execs, who were reticent to potentially offend viewers, to follow through. He insisted putting the brand on the line with parents, among today's most demanding audiences, over naysayers' objections. And ultimately, he put both his and his firm's reputation at risk to push through an unproven campaign whose results few could hope to predict.

Amazingly, Unilever was eventually won over. It signed off on making eight TV commercials, backed them with a massive social media push, and aired high-profile spots during the Olympics. This campaign, titled The Long Day of Childhood, went on to win awards, and thirty minutes after debuting, it had actually become one of Twitter's trending topics, alongside the Olympics and a Mars landing by NASA.

As Graf's experiences illustrate, another common obstacle in the workplace is the fear of confrontation. This is the unsettling emotion that you feel when you know that you must overcome resistance or deal with others who are unhappy with you, your work, or a decision you've made. It is also the source of the anxiety you feel when you know you're going up against an intimidating competitor.

At the very least, a fear of work-related confrontations may cause us to not fight for our beliefs, give in too easily, or be anxious about facing situations and individuals by which we are intimidated. At its worst, the fear of confrontation can cause us to freeze up, try to avoid the confronter, or (at the other end of the spectrum) lash out irrationally. None of these choices promotes the advancement of our views, positive decision making, or good outcomes in the workplace.

If you want to overcome obstacles, you have to confront them. Instead of avoiding confrontation, shying away from resistance, or striking out thoughtlessly, a smarter strategy is to step back, take a deep breath, and impartially consider how to best address the problem. If you're staring down a ticking time bomb, defuse the damn thing or be prepared for the blast.

6. Fear of isolation. The feeling of being alone or left to operate on your own without others' support.

As director of innovation for the $42.7 billion high-speed courier service FedEx, which single-handedly invented its industry and employs more than 330,000 people worldwide, Michelle Proctor is tasked with challenging the status quo. Her team's mandate is to discover and exploit game-changing oppor-tunities. The question she finds herself asking every day: "How do you get people to take a risk, let alone a really big risk, and think about our business in different ways?"[5]

"I don't want to say corporations can get comfortable or com-placent," she says. "But even in a culture of innovators and entre-preneurship . . . sometimes you need a shock to the system to really make you think differently about how you're approaching things."

Her biggest challenge as a leader is to get others to speak up and take action without fear of reproach or reprisal. The solution: Create a safe environment in which employees could feel comfort-able failing and feel empowered to speak up, take chances, and pursue original ideas.

"If you're doing your job every day and doing it well, some-times it may be uncomfortable for you to take that risk and do something differently, because we're all creatures of habit," Proc-tor explains. "Showing the organization that it has a team that's dedicated to taking risks, that doing so will be rewarded, and that there is a payoff for taking these risks is important. We're not just looking for quality improvements. We want to hear all [employ-ees'] crazy ideas no matter how crazy they sound, including ways that we can continue to delight our customers and deliver on our brand promise."

Instead of cordoning off innovative individuals or consigning them to toil in solitude, she and her forty-strong team work to *unite* them. Similarly, they work to swell their ranks by transform-ing everyday employees into bold, forward-thinking visionaries.

Why? As she and her colleagues discovered, the sixth source of fear is isolation, or how you feel when you are afraid that you will be ignored and shunned by your peers as a result of choices, appearances, and actions or inaction.

When organizations and teams are functioning properly and support is provided to all professionals involved, we all act more courageously and effectively. Why? Because we know that others are ready to provide assistance when needed or help prop us up when we fall.

When support is withdrawn or withdrawal appears imminent, however, the fear of isolation can cause us to act more timidly, less decisively, and less productively. As a result, our willingness to take chances, take action, and ultimately be accountable for our choices plummets.

Luckily, many modern employers are coming to prize diversity, originality, and self-direction and embrace those individuals who might have at one time been merely tolerated, or shunned.

Conquer the fear of isolation and challenge yourself to think differently, like FedEx and its employees, and you can turn yourself and your organization into powerhouses of creativity, innovation, and success too.

7. **Fear of change and uncertainty.** The process of acting or reacting differently—and the discomfort that accompanies these shifts or surrounding risks and uncertainties.

For employees of Seattle-based video game maker Valve, every day is, almost literally, an adventure.

Imagine, as a new hire, showing up to work with no clue what you'll be working on, with whom, or even how to go about getting started. Now picture discovering that you have no manager to report to, no team you're expected to join, and no immediate goals.

If you've read the sci-fi classic *The Hitchhiker's Guide to the Galaxy*, you may recall the phrase "Don't panic." Valve's staff receives much the same advice, only in the form of an employee handbook stamped "A fearless adventure in knowing what to do when no one's there's telling you what to do." It describes how not to freak out—and with good reason.

The company has no corporate hierarchy: Its organizational chart is a flat line. At Valve, there are no managers, no formal job titles, and no officially assigned tasks. Anyone can start and ship projects. Teams are formed by simply wheeling desks alongside one another. And workers report to only one boss: the customer.

At Valve, 100 percent of employees' time is autonomously controlled, and no one has ever been fired for making mistakes. The result should be total chaos. Instead, the company continues to produce hit after hit, including the bestselling software franchises Half-Life, Counter-Strike, and Portal. A staggering 65 million enthusiasts swear by its Steam online storefront, the gaming industry's answer to iTunes.

Though Valve may be an extreme example, it illustrates a simple point. Most of us prefer our lives to be calmer and more predictable. But we all have the ability to change more frequently and successfully when we embrace constant reinvention.

Change itself often isn't the challenge we face. Rather, it's the uncertainty that comes along with it. Just when you think you've got everything figured out—bam! Everything's changed, and you or your organization has to figure it out all over again.

While change can be an uncomfortable thing to experience, especially on a prolonged basis, it also has a flipside, one rife with opportunity. Not every unknown is bad. As change occurs, opportunities are also forming, including those that are ripe for the taking. As competitive landscapes and customer expectations change, new needs and gaps emerge in the marketplace, both of which you can readily fill.

Don't let yourself be paralyzed by fear of change and uncertainty. Success demands flexibility and adaptation. Leaders of today's most successful organizations don't avoid change. Instead, they empower employees to change, adapt, and lead at every level by encouraging them to participate, speak up, take action, and take risks as they seek out and discuss rising opportunities or concerns, and brainstorm strategies to address them.

To successfully greet change as an individual, you must follow suit. Constantly pursue personal and professional development, acquire new skills, gain additional hands-on experience, and relentlessly nurture your talents and social network.

An organization successfully faces (and anticipates) the challenges of change by building platforms, processes, and systems for sharing and spreading ideas, for collaborating, and for efficiently bringing resources to bear while experimenting in smart ways. Customers are the number one source of innovation, and great ideas can come from anywhere—especially frontline workers who are closest to them.

Change can even be the ultimate source of competitive advantage.

Richard Sheridan, founder of Menlo Innovations, which develops software for a stellar list of clients, including Domino's Pizza, Snap-on tools, and AAA Life, instills a passion for change in employees every day. Two workers share every computer in the office, and their partners and projects shift weekly. Often pairing veterans and interns, this switching system is designed to introduce employees, including the most senior executives, to more cutting-edge approaches and insights. Through direct hands-on experience and mentorship, it also builds greater empathy, added learning, and more effective knowledge transfer into the company.

In addition to making Menlo millions and keeping its capabilities current, its innovative switching system has attracted countless executives from top firms such as Thomson Reuters and Toyota, who visit the business on learning tours hoping to borrow a page from its playbook.

Action Steps

Everyone feels fear from time to time, both our experiences and current situations inform our willingness to change and take risks as well as our overall outlook. In the following chapter, we'll take a look at why this is the case and how, by opening yourself up to change, you can future-proof yourself by learning how to conquer fear and courageously innovate. In the interim, to avoid allowing fear to hold you back and have a negative impact on your actions or decisions, consider taking the following actions:

- **Inoculate against fear of failure.** Allow yourself to fail fast and often—yet also strategically. Every failure is a stepping-stone toward success and a potential game-winning comeback.
- **Immunize yourself against embarrassment.** Begin practicing putting yourself and your organization outside your comfort zones to increasingly large degrees.
- **Counter worries surrounding losing control.** Realize that you can't control everything all of the time. Step back, take a

deep breath, and focus on what you can control, not what you cannot control.

- **Get over rejection.** Get the nos out of the way as soon as you can so you can get to the yeses faster.
- **Handle confrontation.** Deal with it instead of avoiding it.
- **Remove fear of isolation.** Build your own strategies while also building strong work relationships and bridges of trust with your coworkers. Be yourself, but be a part of the team.
- **Handle change and uncertainty.** Don't try to predict the future; instead, study your surroundings as they take shape, and adapt. Design a portfolio of small, smart professional bets to take, bets in the form of changing decisions and actions. Constantly revise these bets as you gain new information. Reassess your environment as it changes, and recalibrate your actions and responses accordingly.

Chapter Two

The FEAR Model

FINDING COURAGE AND SUCCESS

Fortune magazine calls Tim Stevens, former editorial director at AOL, the "nicest guy in technology," and one of the tech industry's most powerful. But he was also once among its most secretly neurotic. However, by finding the courage to step up and effect positive change, he transformed his career prospects, his entire life outlook, and his potential to succeed.

Before 2011, Stevens was just a shy, reserved software programmer with a speech impediment, who did some freelance writing each morning. When the editor-in-chief position opened at the popular technology blog to which he contributed, *Engadget*, he didn't even bother applying. Because he felt neither qualified nor confident (due to his stuttering problem), Stevens nearly derailed his nascent media career before it had begun. But at the insistence of the website's top editor, he submitted his résumé—and promptly got the job.

Unfortunately, once appointed, Stevens found himself unnerved for an even more distressing reason: the job's high profile and the bright spotlight that came with it. Then, more immediately, the fear he felt on being informed that he'd soon be hosting a popular podcast and online video series.

Prone to stammering and stumbling in conversation, Stevens's first order of business was to find someone, *anyone*, to save his microchips. But given the prior show host's last-minute departure, Stevens had no choice: When the cameras rolled, he had to man the microphone. Luckily, his determination to succeed ultimately outweighed his anxiety.

Resolved to make his mark on the Engadget brand, and aware of the visibility boost the online appearances would bring, Stevens screwed up his courage and stepped into the limelight. As in any good Cinderella story, fans responded with enthusiasm. Unfortunately, their reaction was almost universally negative.

Sample responses[1] to his performance ranged from "seriously bored" to "I actually fell asleep on the subway listening to it." One listener described Stevens's work as "the beginning of the end for Engadget." Humiliated, Stevens's self-confidence quickly did a swan dive. But he resolved to learn from the experience.

Refusing to leave a negative impression on his audience, Stevens began to scour viewers' comments, however scathing, seeking meaningful feedback. In hindsight, Stevens describes the experience as "learning in the worst way possible."

Still, he found that he had no choice but to change. With no replacement forthcoming, he could either quit in shame, or become a human punching bag. So Stevens forced himself to face the camera each week and learn by making mistakes, however awkward the experience. Several dozen episodes and hundreds of caustic viewer comments later, his skin has grown noticeably thicker, and his live performances more polished. Today, he's a poised and self-assured speaker who's made dozens of live national TV and radio appearances.

Stevens could have allowed fear to remain an impenetrable barrier to his success—it certainly would have been the easy way out, the path of least resistance. Instead, he realized that he had to change his outlook, plan of attack, and his willingness to confront his fears in order to achieve his career goals. And that's precisely what he did.

The same way Stevens succeeded and found the courage to fearlessly change and innovate, you can too. But you don't have to be as much of a masochist to achieve similar results in your life, your career, and your business.

The Science of Fear

As we saw earlier, change permeates every waking moment of both our personal and our professional lives. But rather than be troubling or intimidating, change can also be electrifying and empowering, depending on how you choose to react to it. Our own outlook clearly determines whether change exerts a positive or negative influence upon us. However, as we also saw, fear can greatly color our perceptions, painting bright opportunity in unwelcome shades of gray.

But in the same way that your refrigerator dispenser can sift impurities from your tap water, we can also filter doubts, misconceptions, and fears from our thoughts. Train yourself to recognize when anxiety and fear are tainting your perceptions, and you can begin purifying them of such influences. The more alert and watchful you are for such inhibitors, the better attuned you'll become to their causes and effects and the better you'll be able to stop responding to them. In other words, the more courageous you'll become, the more receptive to change you'll make yourself, and the more success you'll find as a result.

Naturally, this process is easier said than done. That's because our minds and bodies are preprogrammed to respond quickly and decisively to impending threats, courtesy of age-old survival instincts. These automatic responses can prove highly effective when we're faced with one-dimensional challenges, such as attempting to evade a hungry grizzly bear. They can be far more self-defeating when dealing with complex and highly nuanced scenarios such as determining how best to compete in a fast-changing, overcrowded business environment.

Fear is very real, and unlike the automobile wreck that made you late to work today, it's no accident that it occurs. Feeling fear's emotional tug is the natural result of a carefully engineered sequence of biochemical events, honed over millennia through the forces of evolution. It serves a very useful purpose in any conscious organism, including complex organisms such as organizations. Fear prepares us, both mentally and physically, to deal with dangerous situations.

In the sections that follow, we consider how fear works, how we learn it, and how we can offset its negative effects.

The Shape of Fear

Like any emotion, there is no one single level of intensity when it comes to fear. In its mildest form, fear might be barely perceptible—like the butterflies you feel in your stomach when you're about to undergo your annual performance review or meet with prospective clients. In its most extreme form, fear can prompt equally extreme reactions making you involuntarily freeze in your tracks or actively avoid sources of discomfort. Of course, fear can also reside at any point on this spectrum, depending on how real, intense, and immediate you perceive threats to be.

The best-known reaction to fear is known as the fight-or-flight response. (Note that some researchers have also added a third alternative: freeze.) It is thought that the region of the brain called the hypothalamus initiates this response. In doing so, it activates both the sympathetic nervous system (which acts via nerve pathways) and the adrenocortical system (which acts via the bloodstream). We're preprogrammed to react this way no matter the source of the perceived threat and whether it's real or imagined.

An evolutionary holdover, this process serves several practical functions. Chief among them, it boosts vigilance, awareness, and response times, letting us operate at heightened levels of performance when danger is imminent.

When activated by the hypothalamus, the sympathetic nervous system increases heart rate, releases energy, and heightens blood flow so we're operating at maximum ability. At the same time, the adrenocortical system brings about changes in our physical and mental state to support the fight-or-flight response, boosting vigilance and reaction times.

But while your physical response to fear is pretty much hardwired into you at birth, your psychological response very much depends on your environment and your upbringing.

How We Learn Fear

It is widely believed that humans are born with only two innate fears: a fear of loud noises and a fear of falling. Any others are learned during the course of a person's life, sometimes not long after birth. A toddler may not consider a barking dog to be a frightening thing, for example, until she is bitten by one and feels the pain that accompanies the bite.

As we get older, we learn all sorts of fears and learn them well. In fact, by the time children reach six to twelve years of age, some 40 percent of them will have developed seven or more fears that they find troubling.

While some fears fade as children transition to adulthood, the imprints they leave can be deep. The mere thought of them can produce severe reactions.

A striking 10 to 20 percent of children and adolescents have been diagnosed with anxiety disorder, making it the number one most common mental health disorder in children and teenagers. By the time they reach grade school, nearly a third of children believe themselves to be incompetent, while 20 percent have become reticent about public speaking and new situations. These issues can compound into adolescence and later carry over into the professional world.

As our careers take flight, we also discover new sources of fear: say, when we're reprimanded for speaking up or penalized for taking new approaches and challenging the status quo. We're learning when colleagues are let go for talking out of turn or pioneering initiatives are shuttered for failure to perform. We are learning not to experiment, innovate, or rock the boat. Both our own and others' experiences further inform our outlook.

Like the toddler bitten by the dog, we often behave in a predictable way in the face of perceived danger: once bitten, twice shy. As we conduct our daily business, we may not worry about being unexpectedly dethroned by industry rivals or suddenly laid off. But when unforeseen competitors suddenly storm the market or colleagues are suddenly fired, we may begin to develop lasting fears about these events.

In our lives and work, we learn fear in a variety of ways, including:

- Firsthand experience
- Observation
- The media
- Discussions with coworkers or peers
- Classroom or workplace instruction

Regardless of how we learn fear, once learned, it can exert a powerful influence on our behavior. It can either spur us to action or cause us to become cautious, freeze, or even withdraw in the face of perceived threats. And if there's anything the brain does well, it's to learn. Our brains are sophisticated pattern-recognition machines that are constantly monitoring the world around us and making thousands of decisions each second.

When encountering familiar surroundings and stimuli (such as a clean, neatly ordered office) the brain's cruise-control system serves us well, letting our bodies operate efficiently on autopilot. But when the brain detects anything abnormal—our boss waiting for us at our desk, or a pink sheet of paper in the inbox—our reactions can be equally reflexive. The fight-or-flight response often kicks in, causing us to react unconsciously, just as our mind begins to draw on previous experience vs. present reality to define the preferred shape of these responses.

Unfortunately, this phenomenon can cause us to jump to negative conclusions, based on the meanings we associate with certain mental triggers. (Perhaps our supervisor's there to commend us for our hard work, and the paper's a note of thanks from a colleague.) Worse, it can cause us to take action instinctively and far out of proportion to the context at hand.

How Fear Manifests Itself

Fear can cause people and organizations to react in many different ways. Each depends on how threatening a situation is thought to be, our inherent physical and mental wiring, and what we've learned about fear. At its most negligible level, fear may cause us to shy away from discussion and debate, decline chances for advancement, or become hesitant. At its most pronounced level, fear may prevent us from actively pursuing vital growth opportunities, cause us to make poor decisions, and lead us to avoid pressing challenges that must be confronted. Instead of giving the best of ourselves, we hold back.

To counter fear's influences, we must respond out of reason, not emotion, and insight, not instinct. When we speak of being courageous, really, we're speaking of being cognizant of and adaptable to operating reality. To succeed in your career or business, you don't need to be particularly brave, intelligent, or even all that talented. You just need to be practical, resourceful, and resilient and then practice exercising those qualities on a routine basis.

This then, is the essence of finding courage: being able to impartially assess the scenario you're facing, weigh surrounding opportunities, and consistently move forward, making the wisest decision given the information at hand.

The FEAR Model

Because fear can cause us no end of problems, both in our lives and on the job, we all need to have a quick way to neutralize its negative influences, find courage, and take positive action. Likewise, given the uncertain and risky business environments we inhabit, we also need a framework for addressing new, novel, or pressing challenges— challenges that relentlessly press our emotional triggers.

To make better decisions, ensure optimum productivity, and respond more effectively to any scenario, try using the FEAR problem-solving method.

- **Focus.** When you see a concern or problem headed your way, put it in razor-sharp focus. Study it closely until you're sure you're seeing the challenge objectively. What is it? When will it hit? What is the incoming signal telling you about its ability to wreak havoc? What effect can you expect it to have on you or your organization? How powerful will its effect be? In short, assess its strengths and weaknesses and use this information to effectively prepare to confront it. Let's say, for example, that one of your clients mentions in an online interview that she is unhappy with her current suppliers and will soon seek new sources for the services you provide. This shift could potentially be a huge problem for your company. Learn everything you can about this incoming signal and then quickly prepare to deal with it—by looking either for ways to better solve the client's problems or for new solutions you can deploy elsewhere that can make up for the soon to be lost revenues.

- **Engage.** Don't sit still. Intelligently respond to a problem with a solution. After you've studied a challenge and created an action plan, put it in motion. The future is coming on quick; in response, take action. A problem like your client who announced her displeasure with your services in the media should put you and your business on full, red alert. You cannot *not* respond; you must engage the problem immediately and provide solutions that are responsive to your client's concerns while ensuring that whatever problems precipitated them will never happen again. You might do this by introducing innovative new tools or technologies that the client can't get anywhere else, preventing her from looking elsewhere. Alternately, you may accomplish equally positive results by actively seeking out new clients whose needs you can better serve in different ways.

- **Assess.** As you take action to address your concerns, study the responses you get. What results have your chosen tactics prompted? Are you on the right track? If so, continue. If not, consider the consequences of your actions and what they tell you about how you can make better decisions going forward. For example: Once you engage with your unhappy client and provide her with the solutions you believe she seeks, then determine if your response is having the desired effect. Not sure? Meet with her to find out. If the client is happy and decides to abandon her search for a new supplier—*great*. You've done your job. If not, then circle back and develop new strategies and approaches. Alternately, if you've been reaching out to new partners in new industries, offering to provide similar services, review whether they've embraced these solutions and if business is going according to plan. If so— *great*. If not, maybe it's time to rethink the solution, rethink the audience, or rethink the way you've positioned yourself and your brand.

- **React.** Having learned from the experience, adjust your tactics accordingly. This process may involve minor tweaks to your battle plan or adopting a new strategy entirely. After confronting a problem and seeing the results that your actions produce, learn from this process, repeat, and do better next time. Using our example, execute the new strategies and approaches you developed in the previous step. Keep repeating until you have solved your client's issues or found a welcome home with new clients, and don't stop until every problem or opportunity is resolved to your client's satisfaction.

As you can see, successfully solving problems doesn't have to be a gut-wrenching or emotionally draining process. In fact, it can be far simpler than you think, even in the face of the most daunting or uncertain scenarios.

As *Owner* magazine founder Chris Brogan notes, the best way to get ahead in changing environments is to use "the OODA loop"—a favorite of modern business, law, and military strategists. The basic principle: observe, orient, decide, act. Then repeat. In Brogan's words: "Setting up a fixed game plan means that there are some amazing fax dealers out there selling their heads off . . . but to who?"[2]

Whether dealing with uncertainty or addressing fear at work, you must be constantly vigilant, always on the lookout for new challenges as they arise and then willing to confront them. How well we address and respond to them defines our ability to succeed. Stay aware of your surroundings and filter fear out of the equation, and you can more readily find courage, success, and ways to steer yourself or your business back on course.

Putting FEAR to Work for You

Whether reinventing, repositioning, or rethinking your own personal approaches or your organization's business strategies and models, you can apply the FEAR framework to significant benefit.

Regardless of the situation you find yourself facing, it presents an easily applied and demonstrably more effective approach to overcoming challenges and finding solutions. The beauty of this strategy isn't in its simplicity or ability to be easily replicated, but in its versatility. Whatever business you're in, whatever your level of experience, and whatever scale you're looking to effect positive change on, it presents a more effective formula for innovation.

You don't have to be especially bold or daring to apply it

either—merely systematic and logical. And it's a process you can use to future-proof a business, a brand, or a career in any phase of its lifecycle. As we'll see in later chapters, FEAR is a simple formula that's being applied to groundbreaking success by both everyday working professionals and the world's leading strategic innovators. Whatever your current aim or operating reality, it's a strategy you can start putting to work today to create ongoing success and effect positive change on every level.

Let's take a closer look at this principle in motion.

In the mid-'90s, padlock maker Master Lock, an eighty-year-old corporate institution, faced a mounting threat in the form of value-priced foreign competitors, who threatened to transform its brand-name products from preferred goods into cheap commodities. Against colleagues' advice, corporate president John Heppner chose to reengineer the company's vision radically to address this threat. However, Heppner didn't just respond willy-nilly; he took a deliberate approach to focusing on the problem, engaging and taking action, assessing his situation, and then reacting.

His plan was twofold: (1) to shift Master Lock's strategy away from competitive pricing to superior design.[3] And (2) to rebrand the firm from a hardware manufacturer to producer of premium security products for cars, sporting goods, and retail outlets.

Reorganizing the business into teams focused on identifying new niches the business could serve, Heppner retrained Master Lock's sights on alternative markets. Risks were manifold, including potentially distancing retailers, alienating customers, and eroding brand equity—not to mention pushback from existing players in these markets. Still, he pressed onward, only to see early efforts to market these innovations (such as a new steering wheel lock) become "one failure after another."

Rather than back down, though, Heppner assessed the situation, reexamined his strategy, and recognized a key flaw in his plan. Specifically, the company's decision to attack already established rivals in these new markets head-on. So Master Lock began to narrow its focus, looking for niches with minimal competition, where it could exercise its brand name advantage. The company refocused its efforts toward providing security devices for trailers and towing vehicles, which was then an emerging and fragmented market.

"We realized we could [succeed] more easily . . . because the trailer lock would fill a vacuum for buyers," said Heppner. "Once our credibility was established, we could more easily reenter the automotive category with an innovative steering wheel lock and displace a well-entrenched, brand-name competitor."[4]

Within two years, the business had expanded into most major auto retailers and experienced double-digit growth: a simple example of just how powerful the FEAR model can be in motion.

Such was also the case when two employees of W. L. Gore & Associates—maker of GORE-TEX protective fabric—teamed up to create and market an entirely new product: guitar strings. At the heart of GORE-TEX is a chemical that is closely related to Teflon: ePTFE.

Dave Myers, who was working in the company's medical unit, thought that this ePTFE material would make a good coating for guitar strings, making them more comfortable to play. Myers recruited GORE-TEX associate John Spencer to conduct market research. But after extensive field testing with more than 15,000 guitarists, Spencer discovered that the advantage of ePTFE-coated strings was not that they were more comfortable to play. The advantage was that they maintained their like-new tone for a longer period than regular, uncoated strings. These new strings—soon repositioned and dubbed ELIXIR by W. L. Gore—quickly vaulted to the number one position in sales of acoustic guitar strings.[5]

Myers believed in the project, made choices to bring it to fruition, rallied others to his cause, and tried and explored promising avenues. But he also wasn't afraid to keep his options open and rethink where his efforts were best applied and how. By leveraging the FEAR model to adapt to unforeseen circumstances, he successfully developed a quality product and repositioned it to create commercial success when initial efforts didn't meet with the results he'd intended.

As you can see, the FEAR framework gives us the ability to see situations more objectively, make better decisions, and adapt to unexpected twists and turns of fate. This makes it an invaluable tool for navigating increasingly unpredictable and uncertain environments. Of course, to use it, you've got to be willing to project it onto any given situation, current or future, and respond to the signals it's sending. Inevitably, in changing environments, using this tool will open the door to change and, as a result, many of the fears we met in the previous chapter.

If you want to find success and future-proof yourself or your organization, FEAR can help you draft an action plan. But it can't make you take action. However, finding the courage to adapt in the face of ongoing change is far less challenging than you may think. We'll begin in the following chapter by drafting a new definition of courage for ourselves; in subsequent chapters we'll explore how (by cultivating new habits and success skills) you can put the principles to work transforming your life, transforming your business, and ultimately transforming your ability to succeed at every turn.

FEAR in Action: Questions to Ask

For Brooke Allen, the morning of May 6, 1982, was a tipping point. He'd been out of work for some time, just lost his girlfriend, and was beginning to slip into depression—all while one of America's worst recessions was raging.

But that day, he decided to attend a conference for independent computer consultants, then a rare profession, but one he felt was destined to enjoy a prominent place in the future. Just minutes in, what the first speaker had to say would forever change how he viewed the shape of the unknown. And, quite unexpectedly, the shape of the ever-shifting professional landscape as well.

"There's no shortage of work, this guy tells us," Allen recalls. "When the money dries up, the work piles up—it's all a matter of perspective." As the speaker explained to Allen, you may not know where your next meal, let alone employment opportunity, is ever coming from. But there's always work out there waiting to be done, especially when times are uncertain and budgets are tight, unpredictability be damned.

The real question, as Allen and fellow attendees soon discovered, is simply whether you're willing to step outside your comfortable day-to-day bubble and find it. And, of course, what the associated opportunity cost is—that is, whether performing a task for pennies on the dollar is worth your time, given where completing it could potentially lead.

Allen quickly began to realize that while our precise future may be unclear at any given time, opportunity is always staring us straight in the face. When confronted by the unknown and uncertain—say, unpredictable hiring markets, among the most capricious markets of all—the question isn't *if* chances for advancement exist. It's simply whether we're willing to actively put out feelers, be persistent in our searches, and firmly latch onto these opportunities when they invariably appear.

In the case of the unemployed, for example, Allen notes there is always another potential job or assignment waiting to be had. The question of whether you actually pursue these opportunities and perform the work ultimately isn't one of availability. It's whether you're willing to accept the amount being offered for your time. (And many differing amounts are always being offered, whether in the form of cash, contacts, or growth opportunities.) As Allen soon realized, the future is all ours for the taking. We just have to be willing to reach out and grasp it.

So he quickly took the first, most logical step that came to mind for bettering his situation, and began writing to everyone he knew, looking for potential opportunities.

Shortly thereafter, financial services firm Morgan Stanley responded. The company needed someone who could read software code and write a user's manual. Just one problem: Allen wasn't a talented writer, and Morgan Stanley offered him only a quarter of what he'd hoped to make for the job. Still, he accepted, reasoning that taking the gig could improve his writing skills and suspecting that it could lead to new contacts and opportunities.

Sure enough, two weeks later, the manual was turned in, and promptly returned covered in red ink. Allen's employers told him that he was a crappy writer. But it was also clear to them that he was a great programmer. So they made him a job offer that helped kick-start a lucrative career on Wall Street.

During the many talks he now gives to other prospective job seekers, Allen always emphasizes a key point: The unknown is rife with opportunity, if only you'll pursue it. "Framing is all-important," he says. "Start by making a list of all the things you can do to help yourself, and things people could do for you . . . then get down to work." As you apply the FEAR model to your own life, career, and business, as did Allen—focusing on the challenge at hand, engaging it, assessing, and readapting one's attitudes and approaches—here are some questions you should ask:

FOCUS

- What effect(s) does the specific challenge being faced threaten to have on you or your organization? When and to what degree?
- Is this a new or familiar problem? How so?
- What can you learn about this challenge by looking at it a little closer and from various perspectives?
- Have others faced similar issues? How did they successfully or unsuccessfully deal with them? In what ways can you learn from these prior attempts?
- What's the best way you can respond to this challenge and counter associated sources of discomfort?

ENGAGE

- What's the fastest, most efficient, and/or effective way you can deal with this problem, and how can you begin doing so?

- What resources do you have at your disposal to address the challenge(s), and when, where, and how can you most effectively deploy them?
- Who can you turn to for assistance, support, and/or advice in this endeavor?
- Where is your effort and energy best applied in the near term? The long term?
- Have you taken steps to divide and conquer and broken goals down into approachable tasks and timelines?

ASSESS

- What results did your actions produce?
- In light of negative responses, what have you learned?
- Are the tasks you're attempting and tactics you're taking still the most advantageous and applicable to the problem at hand and its larger underlying concerns?
- Have you clearly defined a strategic vision and communicated it to others? Are you currently executing it?
- If you had to address the problem again, what would you do differently?

REACT

- How can you shift your strategies and approaches to be more successful?
- Where will you begin deploying these changes? How and to what extent?
- Who's actively driving change, and have you allocated him adequate time, tools, and resources to do so?
- What fail-safe and backup plans do you have in place, and which (if any) require retooling or deployment?

- When, how, and in what context is it appropriate to deploy the above changes?

As you can see, successfully changing and innovating becomes far easier when you apply this simple, four-step model. In the following chapters, we'll see its key principles in motion across a variety of industries, individual scenarios, and contexts. We'll also discover ten new habits vital to success that we can cultivate to triumphantly change, innovate, and win time and time again by capitalizing on its key fundamentals.

Action Steps

Fear is something we all have to deal with, but by applying the FEAR model, we can negate the doubts and concerns that debilitate us and courageously change, innovate, and move forward toward achieving our goals. Here are some actions you can take to put its principles to work for you:

- **Acknowledge your fears.** Be positive, and be flexible.
- **Focus on the problems you face.** Determine their timing, magnitude, and potential effects and what you can learn about them by studying these concerns from various angles.
- **Engage.** Take action and don't wait for problems to go away or solve themselves.
- **Assess the situation.** Determine whether your actions are having the desired effect. If not, develop a new strategy.
- **React.** Keep taking action until the problem is defeated.
- **Don't be a perfectionist.** Know that close enough is good

enough and that it's more important to try to learn as you go than to hit the target with every shot.

- **Understand and accept that not everyone is going to like you or agree with what you have to say.** Carry on anyway.
- **Don't fight change in your business.** Instead, lead it by continually leveraging the FEAR model to apply principles of courage and take smart action in the face of changing situations and environments.

Chapter Three

Rule 1: Be Courageous

Robert Biswas-Diener, author of *The Courage Quotient*, has been called the "Indiana Jones of positive psychology" for his experience traveling the globe studying human nature.[1] Among his most surprising findings, he says: "Courage can be learned. The amount of fear you have and the amount of willingness you have to take action are independent of one another. They are not like a seesaw. People think if you push down fear, you'll [become brave] . . . really, all you need is to inflate your willingness to act."[2]

"Fear is very useful and functional," he continues. "It's to signal you about your surroundings and stay alert. But you have to recognize fear as being a messenger—recognize its benefit, tolerate it, and you can learn to control it." The number one training technique he now uses when counseling organizations or executives to be more effective? Improvisation.

Given today's environment of constant change, he argues, there are only two rules of operating reality: never be without a plan and never rely on one.

In Chapter 7, we'll explore in greater detail how to use the art of improvisation to future-proof yourself and your business. But for now, just realize that the first new habit you must cultivate to find success in today's topsy-turvy working world isn't learning to avoid risk completely, but finding the courage to constantly venture forth into uncharted territory, steadily trailblazing and taking unforeseen challenges as they come.

Planning and research offers us general directions in which to walk, Biswas-Diener says. But once we begin on the journey, discovering the courage to keep walking down these paths or take alternate routes is a result of awareness and flexibility. Being highly adaptable and highly mindful aren't just handy traits to possess, he says. They're vital to building or sustaining bravery and ultimately achieving success.

In their research paper "The Construct of Courage," professors Cooper R. Woodard and Cynthia L. S. Pury offer a new definition of *courage* as "the voluntary willingness to act (with or without varying levels of fear) in response to a threat to achieve an important outcome or goal."[3] In other words, you don't have to be *without fear* to succeed; just *relentlessly practical*. It's a definition modern professionals will find they'd do well to adopt.

Biswas-Diener seconds this notion, noting additional findings showing that executives actually ranked as far more courageous than first responders, police officers, and even ROTC soldiers.

"It wasn't that their fear was nonexistent," he says. "It's that their willingness to act was sky high. The day-to-day life of a CEO requires the willingness to make decisions. And I would argue that 100 percent of those decisions are made under conditions of uncertainty."

Rule 1: Be Courageous

Change, risk, and fear are not inherently negative things—in reality, they are vital sources of feedback and continual self-improvement. Being courageous enough to reconsider the messages fear sends, and overcome associated doubts and concerns that we may feel on the job, can motivate us and enable us to succeed in many different ways, including:

- Teaching us more about the challenges we face and how to overcome them
- Spurring us to take smart risks
- Causing us to course correct when a change in strategy is needed
- Prompting us to find new solutions to old problems
- Motivating us to prepare for future challenges and put backup plans in place

When you act courageously—using fear to drive awareness and action—and apply the tools and techniques presented in this book, you will empower yourself to achieve your goals and create positive, lasting change by:

- Leading through times of uncertainty and great upheaval
- Making deep transformations instead of superficial alterations
- Giving your career or enterprise the shot it needs to get unstuck or on the fast-track to success

- Working smarter
- Accomplishing goals faster, more reliably, and with less effort

Become more courageous and you'll become more aware of fear's hidden truth. The only power that fear holds over us is the power we give to it when we allow it to go unchecked or fail to correctly interpret the signals it's presenting.

However, while fear and anxiety can be positive emotions, prompting us to maintain total awareness and effect change when change is needed, too much of a good thing can still be bad. Doubly so when we allow emotion to overcome reason. But by now, you know the secret to controlling fear. We can look courageously to the future, eyes open, and prepare to greet impending challenges by studying them, stripping away their power, and making the changes needed to address them.

To be successful in both life and business, you must be brave, open-minded, and constantly willing to innovate and push forward. But *brave* means many things to many different people, and it's not simply a function of behaving boldly. As we've seen, bravery is at heart a willingness to move forward in the face of adversity, a continuous balancing act that sits somewhere at the nexus of learning, insight, and reaction:

- **Learning** because you are constantly learning new skills and information, learning new ways to address your concerns, and learning about the problems you face. Solutions are always present, if only you could see them from the right angle.
- **Insight** because the better you understand the reality of the scenario you face, possible consequences of the actions you plan to take, and your ability to control these factors, the more

decisive and courageous you can be in making and following through with decisions.

- **Reaction** because you can always gauge the outcome of your choices and then reassess, realign, recalibrate, and revise your actions and approaches, putting yourself in a better, more effective position the next time. Via such acts, you help build your confidence and reserves of courage.

In this chapter, we take a closer look at courage: what it is, where it comes from, and how it affects our lives. We also explore ways to discover and build courage within ourselves and our enterprise. Then we'll see firsthand what courageous careers, individuals, and organizations look like and consider some specific action steps for building courage in our own lives and businesses.

Rethinking Courage

Courage is the antidote to fear and anxiety, and it enables us (and the organizations in which we work) to achieve our loftiest goals and visions. Courage doesn't make fear go away, but it allows us to act in the face of it: the only way to effectively change, innovate, and remain relevant. Let's dig deeply into what courage is and look at the science behind it.

The Traditional Definition of Courage

Turning to the *Oxford English Dictionary*, we find a simple, straightforward, and traditional definition of the word *courage*.

According to this definition, courage is: "the ability to do something that frightens one."

In Chapter 1, we explored the seven major sources of fear—the most common sources of alarm that we are likely to encounter on the job, and likeliest culprit behind the sense of unease that you feel. In the event you've forgotten, the seven sources of fear are failure, embarrassment, losing control, rejection, confrontation, isolation, and change and uncertainty.

The problem with these fears is that in their presence, our immediate reaction isn't to take positive steps to understand and confront them. Rather, it's to avoid, ignore, or discount these emotions—or worse, engage in a variety of negative behaviors, including such self-defeating responses as:

- Anxiety
- Insecurity
- Doubt
- Misinterpretation
- Indecision
- Avoidance
- Paralysis
- Stress
- Defensiveness
- Introversion
- Unwillingness to change, grow, or try new things

Exhibiting any one of these negative behaviors makes it difficult to do your job and for your organization to accomplish its stated goals. But when you add two or more together—especially among a large group or team of individuals—then widespread dysfunction quickly becomes the norm and not the exception. And this is not theory—it's reality. According to the Anxiety and Depression Association of America, 40 percent of Americans experience persistent anxiety and stress during the course of an average day. A whopping 72 percent of those people say that it interferes with their lives. These negative effects influence workplace performance (56 percent), relationships with coworkers (51 percent) and superiors (43 percent), and quality of work (50 percent).[4]

Clearly, fear can affect how we conduct our business and its bottom line. But when you apply the traditional definition of courage—"the ability to do something that frightens one"—to battling fear, it's easy to see that courage is our best hope for defeating the doubts and inhibitions that keep us from achieving our goals or operating at peak performance. These findings certainly make sense on an intuitive level, but what does the research show? Let's find out.

The Science of Courage

The possibility that courage is the cure to fear in the workplace (the single greatest barrier to change and innovation) is no secret. In fact, much research is currently being done on this very topic.

The good news is that the research seems to support what many intuitively feel. Specifically, that being courageous offers the best avenue to defeating fear, including the fear that accompanies changing or taking risks, no matter where it is practiced. Moreover, findings show that consistently exercising acts of courage can cure many of fear's lingering effects. Even if you find yourself stressed out or your self-confidence sapped by daunting situations, applying it steadily and surely over time can alleviate lasting symptoms of duress.

But make no mistake, being courageous does not automatically mean that there is no danger associated with exercising bravery. Indeed, significant and long-term risks can yet be lurking just out of sight. True courage lies in understanding the dangers and risks that one may face, and forging onward anyway.

Award-winning organizational psychologist Monica Worline has conducted a considerable amount of research into courage and how fear affects individuals and organizations. Worline has discovered several interesting findings on courageousness in the workplace which, when coupled with other leading experts' insights, reveal that:

- People who act courageously often don't see themselves that way.
- In organizations, courageous acts are powerful because they break ordinary routines or violate expectations.
- Different people exhibit different degrees of courage at different times and under different scenarios.
- Risk perception greatly affects our willingness to be brave, though our ability to intuitively gauge risks is often questionable.
- Bravery is prone to occurring more frequently when people believe in their chances of success or believe that the consequences of not being brave outweigh the risks associated with doing so.
- Courage has a rousing quality that stirs people and naturally commands their attention.

- Courage also contains an edge of confrontation.
- People who understand how their decisions may affect others are more likely to act courageously.

In addition, courage is contagious. Worline analyzed more than 600 cases of on-the-job courage exhibited in high-tech companies. According to her findings, when managers actively encouraged their employees to challenge them, even the most reticent employees spoke up more, exhibiting more courage on the job. "Being exposed to someone who does those kinds of [courageous] activities actually changes the viewpoint of the person who experiences them," says Worline. "Over time, that observer becomes more likely to do similar actions."[5]

But organizations must actively fight to instill and promote values such as courage and bravery within members. These values aren't simply building blocks but vital keystones of success. Leaders at every level must both ingrain these values in colleagues and exemplify their principles. We can't just talk a good game here; we must also actively practice and exercise these principles and champion and celebrate acts of courage.

You get the drift. Fear is all around us, and it has a negative impact on both us and our organizations. But the solution to our nagging doubts and concerns is all around us too. The solution is courage. We just have to accept it and live it in our daily actions, both on the job and off.

Building Courage

If we hope to successfully change, lead, and innovate on a consistent basis, we must create a new definition of *courage* that goes far beyond the dictionary's. As noted earlier, courage is not about being fear*less*. It's about knowing what to be afraid of, when to be afraid, and to what extent and, more important, what you can do to alleviate fear or turn it to more productive uses.

Constantly calibrating and recalibrating our choices and actions based on feedback from our environment allows us to be more *practical* and more *realistic*. And the more practical and realistic we are, the likelier we are to make wise choices and take smart actions; in doing so, we build and exercise courage, which can be amassed, expended, or depleted like any asset.

This brings us to another key point. A vital part of courage is *resilience*: the ability to bounce back from adversity and learn from mistakes. If you've ever lost your job, stumbled through a crucial sales presentation, or watched new business ventures fail, only to spring back stronger from the experience and succeed a second time around, you've exhibited it. The American Psychological Association notes that this ability is not an inborn trait that we either possess or don't. Instead, resilience is built over time and is slowly, steadily amassed by exercising a range of behaviors and actions that anyone can choose to learn and develop.

Resilience is an "ordinary, not extraordinary" talent, and researchers note that resilient individuals are just as prone to experiencing fear, stress, difficulty, and distress as anyone else.[6] However, confidence, self-control, and the ability to realistically plan and execute problem-solving strategies dramatically boost the resilient person's performance. Literature indicates that the mind is like any muscle. It can be strengthened through routine exercise, and all of us can exercise our mind's ability to build bravery through learning and experience.

One need look no further than professionals operating in

today's toughest environments to see this principle in motion. Thousands of current army and marine corps officers annually participate in the military's Comprehensive Soldier Fitness (CSF)[7] initiative, designed to make soldiers as strong in mind as they are in body. The program offers education in training and leadership and prepares military personnel to cope with the stresses and anxieties of everyday life and careers when they return home from the field.

Grounded in psychological techniques, from positively reframing scenarios to goal setting and dynamic problem solving, resilience-training courses teach vital life skills as much as they prepare recruits for the rigors of combat. Via a combination of classroom instruction, online modules, and high-tech simulations, soldiers aren't just being trained to react smarter under pressure but are also being prepared to more effectively deal with the debilitating effects of fear and anxiety.

The program's core teaching is so straightforward it almost seems laughable. To be precise: Think like an optimist but work like an emergency responder, dealing with whatever the future brings smartly, succinctly, and without hesitation. We can become more courageous when we train ourselves to see that challenges are simply problems to be solved and that failures and setbacks are temporary states that can be overcome.

In an article for *Harvard Business Review*, psychology professor Martin Seligman outlines the concept in simple terms, speaking of two personalities, Douglas and Walter, and how differently they're affected by job loss.[8] Douglas views the situation as a temporary stumbling block, courageously reaches out to contacts asking for help, and shortly lands a new job. Walter blames himself and his lack of ability for his unemployment and spirals into depression. Those who view the world like Douglas, Seligman asserts, enjoy far greater odds of success. More important, we can retrain the Walters to see their problems in a more positive light so they can successfully rebound with greater frequency.

Likewise, leaders can learn to promote courage in the workplace by encouraging others to think more positively and proactively.

In the book *Leadership in Dangerous Situations*, psychologist Paul Lester and cohorts Michael Matthews and Col. Patrick J. Sweeney cite a recent study in which participants were asked to describe a time they acted courageously. When participants were asked to define why they believed the decision they'd made was courageous, the most common response was that they had made *the choice to take action.*

Courage, the researchers say, is the quality that allows someone to pursue valuable goals despite risks. They also note that complex and uncertain situations offer many opportunities to act courageously, if only leaders choose to take them.

Lester and his colleagues suggest three ways leaders can promote courage in colleagues and train others to act on opportunities when they present themselves:

- **Serve as a role model.** Set an example and act courageously so others can learn through observation.
- **Practice being courageous.** Create learning, training, and simulation environments in which courage must be exercised and provide participants with actionable feedback.
- **Provide inspiration and motivation.** Form strong bonds and positive relationships with colleagues and collaborators so they're incited to act, knowing the impact that their choices may have on others.

Marc Shoen, author of *Your Survival Instinct Is Killing You*, suggests that this kind of preparation and training is crucial to building courage, as we're unconsciously shaped by fears throughout the course of our lives. Based on frightening experiences that we associate with specific events and actions, he says, we create involuntary mental triggers. When we're faced with a frightening situation, such triggers stimulate our subconscious into action, which, because it reacts so quickly, often overwhelms the other, more logical parts of our mind.

"Fear is the most overlooked issue in the workplace," Shoen says.[9] "When we experience fears in the workplace, it creates fear-driven decisions. We start taking positions that are more about protecting our losses. We perceive outcomes from negative perspectives more than we do positive ones."

The remedy, he says, is the concept of duality—finding the positive elements of the situations we face, which we can use to associate welcome reactions to the same triggers that prompt negative responses. Shoen trains others to build courage by slowly, cautiously, and voluntarily experiencing the very thing that makes them uncomfortable and helping them find positive aspects of the experience to latch onto. By reframing the scenario, practicing small acts of bravery, and building tolerance, courage is gained.

So if courage is more of a problem-solving process than an emotion and more like a muscle that can be strengthened via exercise than an inborn ability, how do we know it when we spot it? In the following sections, we'll discuss what courage looks like in practice and how you can begin to practice exercising it as well.

What Healthy, Courageous Careers, Individuals, and Organizations Look Like

Facing your fear and conquering it—and then leveraging it to your advantage and to the advantage of your organization—is the essence of courage. Here, we will consider what courage looks like in careers, lives, enterprises, mind-sets, and corporate cultures and why it's vital to begin exercising it.

Careers and Career Plans

We all know someone whose career seems to be charmed. She gets the plum assignments, she is given responsibilities that her colleagues are not, she earns promotions before anyone else. This is no accident. Luck is the place where opportunity meets preparation. Most likely, the person whose career seems to be charmed is actually taking a very active role in ensuring that it's on the right track. And one of the key ways she does that is by being courageous.

Be courageous in your own career by doing the following things regularly, and if necessary, persistently:

- **Instead of waiting for career opportunities to come to you, seek them out.** Look for opportunities first within your organization, and if you can't find the one you're looking for internally, then take your search outside. (If you're waiting for career opportunities to come to you, then you're not being courageous.)

- **Actively push your employer to be assigned new job roles or responsibilities.** When you are granted a new job role or responsibility, do everything you can to learn, grow, and expand your capabilities as you exercise your talents. (If you're not seeking opportunities to learn and grow, then you're not being courageous.)

- **Don't keep a low profile.** Make sure that everyone knows that you are someone who is dedicated and engaged in your job and your business and that you are a top performer. Be humble, but don't be shy. (If you try to keep a low profile, then you're not being courageous.)

- **If you feel your career is stuck, take immediate and deliberate action to steer it back toward success.** You can't assume that someone else is going to notice (or care) that your career progression isn't going according to your plan. (If you're not in the driver's seat, then you're not being courageous.)

- **If you feel you're ready and deserve it, then don't hesitate to ask your boss for a promotion or go ahead and apply for a job that is a step or two up the ladder from the one you've got now.** You shouldn't wait for others to recognize that you're ready to move up; show them you're ready through your own actions and by demonstrating your talents. (If it's been some time since you've done these things, then you're not being courageous.)

- **Make sure you have a plan for your career and career development efforts.** Then once you have a plan, make sure that you take the time to actively pursue it. (If you aren't actively working toward your goals, then you're not being courageous.)

- **If you're not happy with your career or if you want something different, take steps to change your situation.** Find your passion and then pursue it. (If you're not working toward positive change, then you're not being courageous.)

A healthy, courageous career is one in which you are doing the kind of work that you really want to do and that you have a passion for. You also know where you want to take your career, and you have a plan for getting there. Likewise, you don't shy away from opportunities to grow your learning, skills, and experience or take on more responsibility and accountability; instead, you voluntarily seek out these chances. When you have earned a promotion or a raise, you ask for it. When you spot a problem, you call attention to it or fix it. And when challenges present themselves? You make yourself part of the solution, not the problem.

Individuals

To thrive and succeed in this world, our lives also must be infused with courage. Courage gives us the edge that separates us from competitors and helps ensure we achieve the goals that we set for ourselves, others, and our organizations.

Are you courageous in your everyday life? If so, you'll be doing these kinds of things:

- **You are willing to take smart risks.** This means not going too over the top and rarely betting the farm on one decision. Just have a willingness to consistently make small bets that cumulatively add up to big things in your life. You could, for example, decide to try getting a children's book you wrote published or you could buy an inexpensive fixer property as an investment.

- **You are not afraid to push your comfort zone.** If you become too comfortable with the status quo, you miss out on experiences or opportunities that could open up entirely new avenues, including new sources of enjoyment. Attend a city council meeting and speak up about an issue that concerns you or help found a local nonprofit organization that advocates for a cause that you're passionate about.

- **You're always learning, doing, and trying something new.** Doing so keeps you flexible and adaptable. You may even find out that something you've always wanted to do but thought was out of reach is actually possible. Why not take classes at a local university extension program or start a business as a side project?

- **You're routinely looking for ways to leverage existing capabilities in new directions.** You don't always have to be learning something new to make a splash in the world around you either; you can take the knowledge you already have and use it in new ways. If you're handy with graphic design, perhaps you could begin designing a blog site for your current employer or start your own website-building business.

- **You're always seeking opportunities to make contacts and connections.** You look for ways to partner to enhance your capabilities and collectively work to improve everyone's ability to succeed. Life is all about building relationships and making connections with others. Be open to opportunities to meet new people and expand both your point of view and your personal or professional network. If you have children in public school, join the PTA or perhaps attend a Rotary meeting or chamber of commerce mixer.

- **You're constantly hunting for fresh opinions and perspectives.** It's easy to surround yourself with people whose opinions and perspectives match your own. However, seeking out fresh opinions and perspectives can open your mind to new possibilities and opportunities and help you bolster areas where your skills, insights, or capabilities are lacking. Consult with colleagues, consult with peers at industry events, and get out and meet some new people, then ask them what they think.

- **You don't jump to conclusions or allow fear to create distorting effects.** Jumping to conclusions creates barriers between you and whomever or whatever it is you are jumping to conclusions about. It can also lead to misinformation about scenarios, mistakes, or poor judgments. Similarly, if you allow fear to distort your point of view about someone or something, you will also create barriers and limitations when and where you don't need them.

- **You're willing to accept change and the unknown.** In business and in life, it's best to accept that change happens and to welcome it instead of trying to avoid it or pretend it isn't happening. Understand that what is unknown today may be known tomorrow. Plan for both expected and unforeseen scenarios to occur, and prepare accordingly.

- **You prefer to fixate on solutions, not problems.** Be an optimist at heart; look for opportunities instead of issues, solutions instead of puzzles, and the good side of things instead of the bad. Then smartly and decisively approach challenges and experiment with answers, learning as you go. The more flexible and practical you are, the sooner you'll be able to solve any obstacle that you confront.

A healthy, courageous life is one dominated by positive mindsets, firm decision making, and the willingness to transform change or the unknown from sources of concern to sources of opportunity. Likewise, it's also one in which we take on the mantle of leadership, ownership, and accountability; accept a healthy sense of paranoia; and prioritize long-term gain over short-term benefit.

Organizations

Organizations that are healthy and courageous look very different from organizations that are neither. They are more effective and capable of innovation because their people are more engaged, empowered, and motivated. Healthy, courageous organizations are those with the following characteristics:

- **They constantly prepare for bad times in good.** While they don't dwell on what can go wrong, they do make contingency plans in the event something does go wrong. They also build strong reserves of resources and resilience to weather any storm that they may encounter. Likewise, they constantly look for ways to innovate, reinvest in themselves, and expand their learning and capabilities.

- **They encourage employees to find courage and to speak up and take smart chances.** Employees are often afraid to speak up or to rock the boat, concerned that if they offend their managers or make mistakes, they will be disciplined or even fired for their transgressions. When this happens, your organization loses the input and good ideas of a significant portion of your workforce, often including its most informed audience, which puts the company at a competitive disadvantage. By encouraging your people to speak up and take smart chances, you'll gain the benefits of their insight and talent and get their very best as a leader, manager, or enterprise.

- **They embrace failure and experimentation, as long as they are smart and cost-effective.** Instead of punishing employees for failing or experimenting, courageous organizations encourage them to take intelligent, affordable, and productive risks that have the potential to pay off for the company. Then they capture the feedback and insights provided from these efforts and apply them to future endeavors. The more you encourage your people to experiment, the less fear they'll feel and the more smart risks they'll take.

- **They pursue innovation and new avenues of potential growth doggedly and on a consistent basis.** You want your people to be as creative and innovative as they possibly can be, so be sure to reward them for speaking up and sharing ideas. Encourage them to offer new opinions, insights, and strategies. Create ways to recognize employees who come up with useful ideas and applaud them publicly and with great fanfare.

- **They promote the sharing of ideas and resources throughout the organization.** For an organization to function at peak efficiency, information, ideas, and resources must flow freely through every office, department, and building. Use today's communications technology and information-sharing platforms to your advantage and break down the walls that silo information, money, and manpower between divisions, disciplines or departments. Make it a team effort.

- **They partner, ally, or collaborate to fill in gaps or areas where capabilities are weak.** Understand that every organization has strengths and weaknesses. By deploying the right people at the right place in your organization at the right time—or by partnering with outside partners or collaborators to fill in the gaps—you can optimize the company's effectiveness.

- **They celebrate a culture of ownership, leadership, and accountability at every level.** If you treat your people like they are important, creating a culture that encourages an ownership mind-set while offering leadership opportunities and promoting entrepreneurial thinking, they will respond in kind, bringing out their very best effort.

- **They reward positive and courageous behavior.** When employees act in positive and courageous ways, honor them for it. A simple thank-you or pat on the back can work wonders. Alternately, you can integrate such efforts into your existing reward and recognition programs.

- **They make firm decisions despite imperfect information.** Ultimately, organizations depend on leaders to make informed decisions to achieve their goals, and in a fast-changing world we seldom have the luxury of ample time or perfect information. So make firm decisions as soon as you have enough information to

ensure that your choices are well-grounded. Then update and refine strategies based on results as more information is gained and
you continue to move forward.

A healthy, courageous organization is one infused with positive
mind-sets, including a culture in which workers think like both
owners and entrepreneurs. Likewise, it's one in which unknowns
are equated with potential opportunities and long-term goals and
rewards are prioritized over immediate upsides. The more courage
you instill in your enterprise, the more capable of successfully changing, innovating, and future-proofing itself your organization will
become.

Action Steps

While practicing courage doesn't make fear go away, it does enable
us to achieve great things anyway. To counter fear, get the information you need, use it to improve your strategy, and then take
corresponding action. Work past obstacles to find growth and opportunity. The more you shine a light on your fears, doubts, and
worries, the faster you can find their Achilles' heels and the faster
they will dissipate.

All it takes is accepting the unknown and a willingness to
take risks and change, along with the following action steps:

- **Be courageous.** To future-proof yourself or your organization, you cannot allow fear in any of its many different forms to
dissuade you from achieving your personal, career, and organizational goals.

- **Draft a new definition of courage for yourself.** You've read this chapter, and you know what courage looks like for today's most successful people and organizations. Starting today, create a new definition of courage for yourself. First, identify the things that you're avoiding or unwilling to do, then commit to confronting or doing those very things. You'll feel fear, but be confident, courageous, and work through the discomfort. In doing so, you'll put your new definition of courage to work for yourself, reaping the benefits today and long into the future.

- **Learn to live with chronic fear and uncertainty and, through conscious decision making, to counter worries and anxieties that force you to erect self-imposed limits.** Doubt and uncertainty are always present for leading individuals or businesses. They're simply risks to be weighed and mitigated so they cease to act as barriers to action. Bravery comes with the realization that compared to the cost of remaining static, the price you pay for stepping outside your comfort zone is paltry by comparison. Exercise courage, and you can put your fears to rest.

- **Translate anxiety into positive action.** Fear is a saboteur of products, brands, businesses, careers, and even entire markets because it causes you to sit still when you need to be changing. Use anxieties about the incessant remodeling all around you to encourage a culture of participation and experimentation. Challenge the status quo, rethink problems, and incubate new ideas, strategies, and perspectives. Successful leaders encourage teams, employees, and organizations to step forward, to put themselves out there, to fail, and to dare to be different.

Chapter Four

Rule 2: Make Fear Your Friend

Like most performing artists, Damian Kulash wakes up every day scared, unsure of where his next paycheck will come from. Unlike many of his peers, the lead singer of OK Go has sold more than 600,000 records[1] and clocked more than 150 million views on YouTube.[2] (Remember those guys dancing on treadmills? He's the one in red pants.) But despite having racked up a dizzying array of accomplishments, even he walks a narrow career tightrope.

"We've never had a life where we know what our paycheck will look like—even an established band never knows what songs the radio will play," Kulash admits. (As proof, he says, see the act's topsy-turvy bank account.) Which is exactly why, after breaking through and headlining shows nationwide, he and his colleagues toured for thirty-one months straight. "The fear that this was our moment and that we wouldn't be there to take it was so strong . . . that we played for two and a half years without stopping."[3]

Still, Kulash says, you can't let fear stop you from taking the plunge. "It's not that we *don't* worry about how we will pay our rent," he explains. "It's that either you work within a system [hostile to artists] or you make your own." Even after all the fame and success, fear remains a constant source of growth and motivation for the group. Despite the band's many achievements, including running a successful independent record label, Kulash and his colleagues have begun to diversify into apps, advertising work, and video production. "We have to course correct all the time," he confesses, "because we don't have a business model . . . it's essentially a cartoon roadrunner jumping off a cliff."

He refuses to see OK Go as being strictly in the music business. Instead, he sees the band as being in the business of creativity and, therefore, constantly seeks ways to branch out, innovate, and grow its potential opportunities.

"Fear is both your ally and enemy," he notes. "You need the ability to be self-critical, [but also] fearful of making the wrong choices." You can let fear prevent you from adapting to changing environments or you can study fear more carefully and intelligently, as Kulash and his peers have done, and use the warning signals it's sending as sources of insight and motivation that spur you to take action.

"Everything is impossible," he says. "Use fear to make what you're making better. But if it stops you from making something, then it is not your friend."

Rule 2: Make Fear Your Friend

When businesses, brands, individuals, entrepreneurs, students, and those seeking a second act in their careers create self-imposed limits, they are drastically stunting their potential. But barriers caused by fear and doubt can quickly be overcome the moment you realize they exist and decide to demolish or steer around them. Better yet, you can use them as learning tools to help guide strategy, fuel growth, and drive constant adaptation.

Picture what you could accomplish if only you could put aside your worries and doubts, make firm decisions, and take smart risks (read: *change* and *innovate*). The good news is that to do so, you don't have to remove fear from the equation entirely. Rather, you can make it your friend just by being smart about how you react to it—another essential habit that helps lay a lasting foundation for success.

We can calmly examine our fears, learn from them, and overcome obstacles by reframing our perspective. View worries as sources of feedback and associated challenges as puzzles waiting to be solved. When you more closely consider what's triggering your fears and why, you can start solving problems using intelligence, not instinct. Begin to look at fear as a personal radar system, not just a security system. Then you can see past its blaring alarm bells to learn from all those flashing indicators. Confronted by fear, we instinctively want to flee, freeze, or fight. Instead, train yourself to learn from it and then keep learning, as you use the heightened excitement, energy, and insight fear provides to change and adapt strategies and approaches to consistently be more poised and practical.

Remember that fear creates a paradoxical effect in that it causes us to assign a greater sense of importance and impact to challenges and uncertainties. According to Dan Gardner, bestselling author of *Risk: The Science of Politics and Fear*, and risk science pioneer Paul Slovic, people are terrible at perceiving risks. We vastly overestimate negative outcomes and vastly underestimate good ones. (The faster we can call related examples to mind, the likelier they seem.) Under the best of circumstances, our minds already create fun-house mirror effects. Add fear to the equation, and distortions in thinking can go wild. Just a few common samples include all-or-nothing (aka black-and-white) thinking, bias, over-generalizations, and jumping to conclusions.

When this happens, we often miss the obvious truth as well as the solutions that are ready and waiting to help us overcome any challenge. As you assess scenarios you may encounter, don't be blinded to reality and don't give threats great power.

A simple way to regain clarity: When fear begins to send your mind into overdrive, recognize the fear you're feeling. Many of us are so accustomed to feeling fear that we barely even acknowledge its presence. To make fear your friend, notice its arrival and the discomfort it brings. Then, when you feel it, consciously pause and objectively assess your situation. Cultivate a habit of mindfulness, being purposefully attentive to and aware of your surroundings, so you can impartially view situations. Train yourself to instinctively *review*, not react.

The moment you feel your thoughts begin to race, purposefully throttle back emotion. The moment alarm bells begin ringing, consider the plausible reasons and responses and respond deliberately to them, rather than acting hastily or jumping to conclusions.

Instead of falling back on knee-jerk responses, weigh the actual urgency of the situation and look at the bigger picture. Identify underlying sources of your fear and why it's present. Are you responding to a problem or to a symptom? How serious and immediate are the issues you are facing and why do they exist? What can you do to alleviate them?

Take a moment to list the messages you're receiving and why and then think of potential responses. Cross off reactions grounded in emotion, not hard facts. Condense remaining concerns into related categories or single them out for further scrutiny and prioritize all by order of importance. Afterward, draw direct lines between each individual or group of issues, underlying causes, and action steps that help you most directly and rapidly move from problems to solutions. Repeat as needed until complete awareness and insight into preferred responses is gained.

When you start looking at fear as less of an emergency signal and more of an *incoming* signal—one that you should welcome—you'll recognize how much more effectively you'll operate. And, of course, the greater your capability to change and innovate will lead to success.

How We Respond to Fear Defines Its Impact

In Chapter 1, we spoke about the seven leading sources of fear that affect our ability to succeed today. Each can exert tremendous power over our potential and our very perceptions of reality. Fear has an inherent duality that defines our perspective on, and reactions to, any given scenario.

For example, you may be afraid to speak in front of large groups of people, causing you to shy away from speaking opportunities. Or you may willingly accept such challenges and push past your fear, knowing that giving high-profile public presentations will provide you with more opportunities to stand out and opportunities for job promotion. Alternately, you may know that great change is coming, yet doubt your ability to adjust to it or worry that if you do something different in your workplace and make a mistake you may be fired. As a result, you don't take appropriate action. Or you may acknowledge the impending business shifts, take smart risks, and add valuable skills and capabilities to your résumé or organization to make it more adaptable to oncoming changes.

My advice? Rather than waste time worrying that fear is present, worry about how to befriend and capitalize on it to drive more positive outcomes.

As a side effect of negatively responding to fears you may make mistakes or hasty (and faulty) decisions, overreact, miscommunicate, or miss opportunities. Similarly, good responses to fear can enable us to act in ways that get us closer to achieving our goals.

But wait: How could experiencing *any* fear exert a positive effect on our lives?

To find the answer, think back to our earlier discussions about what fear is, the side effects it prompts, and why we feel it. There are some very strong and very beneficial reasons why we need fear. Within a split second after we hear an irate customer or supervisor sputtering in outrage or news of an unexpected sales dip, our minds and bodies go on full alert. When we spot emerging trends or competitors that threaten our capability, credibility, or market position, good fear responses can prompt us to take action. When a sudden work emergency pops up (Jenny forgot to send the sales brochure to the printer—think quick!), it's a good fear response that helps us quickly reprioritize tasks and shift gears midstride.

It's important to note that fear can be helpful to us in many different ways when we choose to channel it to more productive outcomes. On the positive side, fear:

- Alerts us to potential threats and dangers
- Makes us more attuned to our environment
- Drives growth and innovation
- Prompts us to make changes and fix problems
- Promotes dynamic decision making and entrepreneurial behavior
- Fights complacency
- Keeps us nimble
- Makes us creative
- Provides a sense of urgency

Psychologist Cynthia Pury (whom we first met in Chapter 3) says that telling yourself not to be afraid or think about fear doesn't work. Because fear is a highly intense emotional experience, she advises us to acknowledge our fears and the messages they're sending but not to let fear distract us from pursuing our goals.

Recognizing that fear can prompt both positive and negative outcomes in the workplace, we must learn to discern how fear makes us feel and react.

If, for example, you're reticent to start a new business ("I've got too much debt and no time, nest egg, or major clients to speak of"), don't waste time worrying that you're incapable of succeeding. Instead, act on the insights your worries provide by, say, creating a debt repayment plan, automatically setting aside a percentage of each paycheck for savings, and pursuing part-time business opportunities evenings and weekends until you're ready to go full-time. By systematically assessing and addressing the sources of our fears, we can train ourselves to stop engaging in self-defeating behaviors and be more proactive about using what we learned productively.

A Better Approach to Fear Response

As we've seen, how you react to fear will determine both your current and future experiences. Don't simply dismiss fear out of hand. Come to understand how fear is making you feel and react—and why—then alleviate or adapt to it. By making fear your ally, you can use it as a springboard to drive heightened levels of productivity and performance.

Consider the difference in responses we generate when we choose to act courageously and respond more calculatedly in the face of fear from those created when we choose to operate more timidly or on emotional autopilot.

"Having a sense of risk and fear are two separate things," says Pury. "The risk is the likelihood that the bad thing could happen to you, whereas the fear is your emotional response to it."[4] She's found that risk takers often don't report feeling that much fear because they were hyper focused on completing the task in front of them. Instead of stopping to think about the terrible things that could happen, they're busy thinking about which action to take next—a choice others could also make.

If you want to make fear your friend and put it to work for you or your team consistently, here are some simple steps to follow:

- Identify the fear you're experiencing.
- Determine whether the fear is exerting bad or good effects on your behavior.
- If bad, neutralize its source and cease engaging in negative behaviors.
- If good, learn from it and take action.

But if fear is made impotent in the face of rational thought, why do we let it keep us from changing, innovating, and embracing the future? We're so often caught up in the moment or in our emotions that we default to less-than-productive strategies and behaviors. And this process can be habit forming.

As we've seen, you and your organization can benefit from fear's presence, depending on how you choose to react to it. Let's look at several common scenarios that may prompt you to experience any or all of the seven fears outlined in Chapter 1 and how, by embracing and smartly addressing each, you can turn the associated concerns to your benefit.

Facing Tangible Threats

There really *are* threats all around us; it's not just in our imaginations. Our companies are under constant assault by competitors, all of whom wish to surpass us, and steal away our customers and clients. And that's before you count ambitious peers or colleagues who may be trying to climb their way up the ladder of success—and occasionally step over, around, or even on us to get ahead.

Just as new talent is constantly entering the market on an individual level, so too are new competitors on an organizational level ready, willing, and able to knock us off our comfortable perches. According to the Kauffman Foundation in Kansas City, approximately 543,000 new businesses are started in the United States *every month*.[5] All represent potential threats.

By acknowledging the threats and responding more productively to them, the associated fears—such as confrontation, isolation, failure, or loss of control—drive us to keep our eyes and ears open. When your fear-fueled radar detects a threat on the horizon, you can better prepare yourself to meet and thwart it and begin doing so well in advance. You might hear through the office grapevine, for example, that your boss is considering laying off half your department if sales don't dramatically increase soon. A rival in your department may have her eye on your job or a new business may be making plans to siphon away your customers.

Detecting tangible threats in the working world by keeping our antennae up increases our level of attentiveness and sharpens our senses. To detect these threats, we must first consider which have the greatest potential to disrupt or exert negative effects on our careers, businesses, and working relationships. Then we must closely study from where these threats typically originate, under what conditions, and the causes behind them, as well as how we can consistently track and respond to them.

Anticipating these challenges before they have an effect can allow you to plan for and exert a major influence over their potential outcome. Our personal and professional radars are effectively switched to full alert, preparing us to greet *any* challenge the moment it arrives by stepping up our game or goading us to seek out opportunities, including those in other fields, areas, or departments.

As you can see, it pays to stay aware and to always be watching for and be ready to address rising opportunities or challenges. The fears we feel when faced by tangible threats can help us do just that.

A simple illustration: In early 2013, the Burger King Twitter account was "brandjacked" (that is, taken over by hackers) and quickly reworked to give it a McDonald's theme. Then, a tweet was broadcast to the account's 83,000 followers that the company had been taken over by its archrival. According to one observer, this brandjacking "created an all-out crisis for Burger King, damaging their brand and credibility in the market."[6] Security breaches are an omnipresent risk in the high-tech world. However, any organization can build layers of safeguards and crisis response plans into its initiatives long before disasters occur. While no one can say who's to blame, or why, had Burger King's IT team been more concerned with addressing the fears that tangible threats can present, it's possible that this breach may never have occurred.

Operating in Unknown or Uncertain Environments

Fear of change and uncertainty is a common source of concern for most of us, as are worries about experiencing failure and losing control in shifting environments. Aside from the small subset of fiercely practical individuals—often erroneously classified as mavericks, whom we'll meet in Chapter 8—the human species tends to favor consistency and familiarity. When change is rampant and our foundations are shaken, we crave a more routine and comforting reality. But change is a given fact in business and life, and clarity can suffer as a result if we cannot accept it. And we desperately need clarity to successfully evolve and explore changing landscapes.

We may lose clarity when we become too self-absorbed and unwilling to listen to the signals that markets, employees, customers, and others are sending us. Likewise, when individuals or organizations dismiss shifting trends, ignore changing customer needs, or blind themselves to changing competitive landscapes, it's a lack of clarity that's at work. Regain this clarity, and you regain the ability to see the future taking shape and what action steps you can take to successfully greet it (read: *future-proof yourself*).

Ryan Simonetti, cofounder of New York City–based Convene conference centers, notes that it's perfectly natural to question your decisions when operating in an unknown or uncertain environment. But he also says that you can't allow the fear you might feel in this situation to push you off course. According to Simonetti, "There are always moments where you question yourself. The real question is, do you question yourself for extended periods of time or just for a minute?"7 To succeed, he explains, you have to let go of doubt quickly and feel confident in the decisions you're making. If they're incorrect, simply adjust your strategy by making more accurate ones.

"The big thing is admitting failure quickly and redirecting your decision," he confesses. "I think that's something we've done really well since we've started the company. We make decisions quick based on the information presented to us and our intuition. The minute we see something not working, though, we immediately pivot into something else. That is one thing that has helped us get to the point we are at. We admit our mistakes and we correct them immediately."

You must be able to see clearly and see fear's influence at work within yourself and within your organization—and how to capitalize on or counter it. Similarly, you must also be able to figure out how to best adapt to changing environments and markets and where you or your people should apply maximum effort to most readily effect positive change where it can make the biggest impact.

Having to Confront Others

Whether we're confronting a competitor, confronting resistance to change in our organization, or confronting colleagues whose performance levels may lag or hold dissenting opinions, many professional exchanges inherently invite conflict.

But as intimidating as these exchanges may seem, we can greatly benefit from finding the courage to speak up and take action. Fear of confrontation lets us know pressing issues lay before us and when we may be holding back from giving our best efforts because we seek to avoid criticism or potential embarrassment. But by alerting us to these issues, we can gain deeper insights into the causes behind them and better overcome obstacles by learning to attack problems, not symptoms.

For example, when we feel that our voices are going unheard at work or that colleagues or supervisors are constantly trampling on our suggestions, it's not uncommon to lie low and idly stew, hoping the problems will resolve themselves. Some of us may lean toward the other end of the spectrum and consider reading our coworkers the riot act, thereby turning those individuals' own fears about confrontation against them. Neither is a productive solution.

Instead, use your fear of confrontation as a sign to begin setting firmer boundaries. Boundaries aren't barriers, merely guidelines that define our comfort zones, how we interact with others, and how far we're willing to let them push. It's a small leap to speak up more often or be less hasty to back down while not letting someone else steal our ideas or thunder. Put these boundaries in place, and you'll find not only that others will be more conscientious but that they'll start observing the boundaries automatically.

But boundaries must be clearly articulated. Don't assume others are aware of them and don't assume ensuing confrontations need to be calamitous. Taking a neutral tone, you might simply state objective facts by informing others ("We're automatically dismissing this idea") and requesting that things change ("Why don't we consider it?"). If they don't, you might insist further ("We should at least briefly discuss this concept") or suggest an alternative tack ("I'll put together a full briefing, so we've got all the facts to consider before making a final decision"). The key is to address issues on the spot, or as soon as appropriate, and leave others a graceful out. The more clearly, firmly, and rationally you state your case, the more your confidence will grow and less others will seek future confrontation.

Fear of confrontation can also alert us to when it's time to start saying no more often, in both our personal lives and in our careers. If we find ourselves stretched thin and overcommitted, we may need to be more assertive about how we prioritize our time, which projects we take on, and the promises we make to others. We naturally want to please and be liked and grab every opportunity that comes our way. But there's a very real cost associated with each new commitment we take on: We risk overextending ourselves or not leaving sufficient time to pursue bigger and better opportunities that come along.

Before automatically saying yes to a colleague or client, consider what it will take to follow through on the commitment. If you don't like the results, practice saying no to incoming requests or politely declining and suggesting someone else who can help instead if the other party remains insistent. Despite initial discomfort, you may be surprised at how much happier you are in the end.

If you're hesitant to go all in, remember: You can always request more time to think things over or ask about priorities (for example, by showing your boss a rundown of current assignments and where deadline extensions would be needed if you took on another project). Make a point to underpromise and overdeliver, and instead of stretching yourself too thin, leave yourself room to stretch. Little confrontations now can help prevent bigger blowups later.

Action Steps

As we've seen, it's vital to rethink how we react to fear so we can react more positively going forward. Recognize when fear is present, and remember that fear can have positive effects on your work and personal lives. Fear alerts us to potential threats and dangers, it drives growth and innovation, it keeps us nimble, and much more.

We can choose to act courageously or timidly in the face of our fears. Courage is invariably the better course to take. To succeed on the job—and in life—you've got to face your fears, to adapt to a new landscape, and change your behavior. Research and experience shows that making fear your friend is the best way to neutralize its debilitating effects. Use the following points as a cheat sheet for successfully putting fear to work for you:

- **Make fear your friend.** Instead of your enemy, realize that fear is actually your personal warning system, alerting you to both opportunities and threats in your environment.
- **Understand the underlying source of your fear.** Once you recognize fear, identify the signals it's sending and use those signals to make more informed decisions. You will discover

that the fear you feel is not necessarily a bad thing but can have positive effects on you and your organization.

- **Be willing to see the world both objectively and from fresh perspectives.** Encourage yourself and others to take smart risks. If you fail (which, of course, you will from time to time), pick yourself up and try again. Be agile and realign yourself and your approaches and tactics when necessary. Keeping your eyes open and ear to the ground, pay attention to signals being sent by your environment (say, falling sales or rising interest in rivals), thereby preventing your radar from malfunctioning or getting rusty.

- **Become comfortable with fear.** Learn to live with fear as a positive, not negative, emotion, and constantly look for ways to use it as a source of inspiration and motivation. Embrace change, and encourage others to do the same. Become a change leader in your career or enterprise instead of a change avoider.

- **Use fear to heighten your awareness.** This will keep you alert to rising challenges while mobilizing you to take action. Ask yourself and/or your people to constantly examine, and reexamine, the problems they face and to reconsider whether the way it's always been done is still the best way to do it. Make objective decisions grounded in real-world feedback and information. Do this by constantly seeking out the best and most current information about your competition, customers, and marketplace, as well as the latest technologies, tools, and industry trends.

- **Leverage fear to help yourself stay relevant.** Use fear to challenge yourself to keep up to date; to seek out new capabilities, resources, education, and experiences; and to move from thought to action. Be innovative and creative, and constantly seek better ways of doing common tasks and correct areas that may not yet be broken. Surround yourself with people and partners who complement your strengths and offer fresh perspectives. Instead of surrounding yourself with those with similar capabilities and viewpoints, look for those who bolster sectors in which you or your organization is lacking.

- **Let fear drive you to plan for tomorrow today.** Build a strong platform for success by betting against future outcomes, planning to greet them in kind, and hedging your bets by playing multiple solutions. Encourage yourself and your coworkers to play lots of small, smart business and career bets instead of putting everyone's eggs in one basket.

- **Channel your fear into fuel to seek fresh perspectives.** Examine problems from new angles. Ask questions. Be open to novel ideas and solutions. Become proactive instead of reactive as change washes over you and your organization. Empower yourself and/or your people, and encourage and reward yourself or each other, for bringing potential opportunities and issues to light or bringing new trends and tools to attention.

- **Regain the clarity you need to make better choices.** Gather as much objective feedback, data, and information as you can from a variety of different sources. Consistently seek out fresh perspectives that can give you a new viewpoint on your business, your competition, and your industry. Put emotion aside, and study the hard facts and signals your environment is sending you.

- **Don't be afraid to confront others.** While confronting others can be intimidating, when we address problems directly, we can solve them faster, better, and with less difficulty. Use your fear of confrontation to set firmer boundaries in your work, career, and life, and use it as an incentive to more fully explore new avenues of opportunity and prepare yourself for impending challenges.

Chapter Five

Rule 3: Turn Anxiety and Paranoia into Awareness

The world's most famous skateboarder, Tony Hawk, has hurled himself off ramps, down flights of stairs, and into aerial spins so intense that they can crush knee joints on impact. But despite countless bruises and broken bones, he's never scared to get back up on the board, and he's no reckless idiot.

"Our profession is very calculated," he points out. "You may think that guys flying 20 feet above a ramp are throwing caution to the wind. But in reality they've prepared for [the challenge], they're comfortable with it, and they know how to get out of it safely if something goes wrong."[1]

Hawk, a man who's invented more than eighty tricks, keeps two guidelines in mind, whether flying off ramps or handling his multimillion-dollar business: Be aware of the reality of your situation, understand what fear is telling you about it, and know how to use this awareness to adjust your approach. "If you're anxious, plan accordingly," he says. Preparing to greet the potential hazards of completing the trick that would make him a legend, Hawk took four years and hundreds of practice sessions before he feet ready to pull off a 900 (which requires spinning in the air two and a half times).

When attempting to stretch yourself and achieve demanding goals, you can never be too cautious. But you also can't be afraid to test limits or stretch your comfort zone. "Fear can keep you in check, and keep you healthy," Hawk says. "But people who don't have confidence in what they're trying are the ones that fail."

Anxiety can be a source of discomfort. But clearly, it can also be a source of motivation and awareness. To future-proof your career or business, Hawk says, you can even put another common type of anxiety encountered in the business world to work for you: the fear of falling behind (rooted in fear of change and losing control). Instead of agonizing over it, he suggests, use it to keep you changing, adapting, and constantly raising the bar, just as competitors inevitably are. Make it an excuse to remind yourself to never stop innovating, Hawk insists. "Keep challenging yourself, and coming up with new ideas and directions, even if you're successful. It's the best way to stay fresh."

In today's rapidly changing world, prior accolades mean nothing. The faster moving the market (says Hawk's target audience, hyperactive teens), the faster you stand to be forgotten. So when it comes to changing, innovating, and finding the courage to stay ahead of the curve, he asserts, you can't let anxiety hold you back; you've got to use it to drive added insight and added momentum.

But there's also one other key trait related to anxiousness that any savvy businessperson like Hawk (founder of several action sports–related ventures, including Tony Hawk clothing and Tony Hawk Huckjam bicycles) would encourage you to embrace: *paranoia*. Paranoia—the suspicion that others are determined to outperform or outmaneuver you—has the power to continually drive you and your organization to grow and excel. When used constructively, paranoia, like anxiety, can actually serve as a source of strategic growth and a driving force that compels us to deal with potential pitfalls or shortcomings long before encountering them. In Tony's case, barriers to business competition are fairly low because most anyone can build a hip sports event or shoe and market it as the next big thing. As a result, he has to constantly be looking over his shoulder, aware that a serious threat to his business might be coming from any direction, at any time.

Clearly, the more we can channel the anxiety and paranoia we feel toward productive uses, the more we can prevent ourselves from falling behind rivals or changing with changing times and trends. It's up to you to turn the potentially negative emotions of anxiety and paranoia into positive action, however. The best time to do so and to capitalize on the signals these feelings are sending is now, while you still enjoy some measure of competitive advantage.

Rule 3: Turn Anxiety and Paranoia into Awareness

This book is all about finding courage in our careers and enterprises and then leveraging our day-to-day doubts and fears to fuel positive change. But as we have seen, many concerns we face are quite real—while our emotions might sometimes get swept away by them, they definitely aren't figments of our imagination. Likewise, humans, and the organizations they make up, are inadvertently hardwired to subconsciously assign negative triggers to these emotions, especially when they're experienced in the wake of unfamiliar or unknown events. All of these can produce more anxious responses in us and do so on a regular basis.

So it's perfectly reasonable to be anxious when we consider asking our boss for a promotion, when plotting an edgy marketing campaign, or when inventing a new product. Who's to say these efforts will succeed, let alone to the extent we envision, especially if we've encountered related difficulties in the past? And it's also perfectly reasonable to be paranoid when we see competitors tracking and copying our every move, from our entry into new markets to our new product and service introductions. It therefore behooves us to have our professional radars on full alert at all times, ready to spot rising threats or concerns long before they come knocking.

Unfortunately, anxiety and paranoia can often cause us to freeze up when what we should be doing is taking action. This makes sense when you consider that the seven fears that we explored in Chapter 1—fear of failure, embarrassment, loss of control, rejection, confrontation, isolation, and change and uncertainty—are extremely powerful influences and can leave equally powerful lasting impressions.

But the trick to confronting your feelings of anxiety and paranoia isn't to battle them head-on: Fears are intangible, and it's hard to fight ghosts. Rather, the trick is to lift ourselves above the anxiety and paranoia that we feel in our lives and translate the constant noise they're sending into signals whose meanings we can interpret. And, of course, then getting in the habit of taking the messages they're sending and using them to drive greater understanding, greater awareness, and greater capacity to make sound decisions.

Remember, the effects of anxiety and paranoia don't always have to be negative. Both can help inform us, inspire us, motivate us, and make us more acutely aware of what's happening in our environment—both at work, and in our personal lives. Like we discussed in Chapter 2, there are extremely tangible benefits to be realized when we're more vigilant and operating at heightened levels of performance. Most crucially, we can use our sense of anxiety and paranoia to drive us to shore up areas where we're lacking in capabilities, spur us into action where needed, and better prepare ourselves to confront the challenges we face. So it's no surprise that another vital habit for success going forward is learning to transform anxiety and paranoia into awareness.

Using Anxiety and Paranoia to Boost Performance

The emotions we feel when we are anxious or paranoid have many beneficial effects, so long as we process them productively. They help keep us keenly attuned to growing concerns; prompt us to continually innovate, improve, or implement backups and safety measures; and goad us to take action where we might otherwise remain idle. As explained earlier, fear can be a powerful force for good (so long as we respond to it intelligently), helping us keep our ear to the ground, stay abreast of rising threats, and avoid personal or organizational complacency.

Make the right kind of fear, such as many common anxieties and feelings of paranoia, a part of your regular emotional diet and it can serve as a wholesome and nutritional source of energy for any business, brand, or individual. Why? Because it prompts us to keep our capabilities current and drives us to remain flexible, adaptable, and constantly pushing forward.

If, for example, you're anxious that rivals may bump you off your path to promotion, then the anxiety you feel will drive you to work harder, become a more valuable team player, and gain the additional training you need to be a prime candidate for the position. Likewise, your anxiety will push you to constantly look for ways to exceed targets and goals and stay a step ahead of other contenders.

If you're an organization worried that competitors might creep up on you by introducing new products, features, or pricing programs, then the paranoia you're experiencing will keep you up to speed by constantly deploying countermeasures by way of exploring new ideas, opportunities, and markets.

By keeping our antennae perpetually raised in search of potential threats and prompting us to proactively create strategies for dealing with problems before they arise, this sense of urgency actually helps keep us sharp. It reminds us that no head start, lead, or advantage is ever enough. If the race is always being run, while we must appreciate the occasional pit stop and chance to refuel, we must also recognize the value of continuously motoring onward. The only way to win is to always strive to maintain our position at the head of the pack.

Consider the following positive aspects of experiencing anxiety and paranoia on the job:

- **Keeps you attuned to rising concerns.** When you are anxious or paranoid, you become aware of problems of all shapes and sizes, in many cases before they are able to damage your business or your career. Leadership and career expert Kate White describes a situation in her own life where this went a long way. While at one of the routine lunches she enjoyed with her boss at a magazine they both worked for, White noticed that "something odd happened." Her boss yawned while she was speaking, and he seemed preoccupied with other matters. Filing that away in the back of her mind, a few weeks later Kate noticed that her boss had been on a lot more out-of-town trips than usual. Says White, "I connected the dots and saw a clear pattern: My boss had checked out!"[2] So, rather than allowing the status quo to reign supreme or for paranoia to eat her up, White took action. She began spending much more time with the magazine's second-in-command. Sure enough, White's boss resigned a month later to take a position with another company that had been heavily recruiting him, and the second-in-command was soon promoted into his position. Fortunately, White's anxiety had caused her to establish a strong working relationship with her new boss, smoothing her way through the transition at the top and keeping her career on stable ground.

- **Prompts you to innovate, improve, and create backup plans.** When you are paranoid that competitors are breathing down your neck, you are prompted to do whatever it takes to stay a step ahead. For years, Procter & Gamble (P&G) has added innovations and improvements to its Pampers and Luvs brands of disposable diapers in hopes of maintaining its overall lead in sales (and in the hearts of the millions of parents who buy the company's products). But why be so dutiful about improving on an invention as timeless as soiled diapers? P&G had to innovate because its archrival in the Diaper Wars—Kimberly-Clark, with its popular Huggies brand—was constantly sniping at its competitor, waiting for P&G to make a misstep so it could surge into the lead. New water-absorbent gels, hourglass shapes, leakproof waist shields, elastic leg gathers, and more enhancements were developed by P&G diaper scientists, tested, and then incorporated into the company's diapers to keep it ahead of its top rival.[3] At the moment, P&G is in the lead with about 35 percent of global market share versus about 22 percent for Kimberly-Clark.[4] Even still, the company must constantly look over its shoulder, innovating and improving on the disposable diapers it produces to maintain its competitive advantage.

- **Drives forward momentum.** Are you imagining things or is someone really trying to undermine you on the job? Are your accomplishments from last week, last month, or last year enough to keep you at the top of the heap in the eyes of your customers or your boss? If there's one thing you can't do at work, it's rest on your laurels. Instead, you've got to be constantly pushing forward—achieving more, gaining more, and doing more than your competitors or colleagues. Likewise, you've got to be absolutely essential to your clients or your organization because, if you're not, guess who's got a big, fat target on his or her back? You. While it's certainly necessary to rest, recharge, and refuel our batteries on occasion, you can't take an extended sabbatical from your career or your business. The world is constantly turning (especially the business world), and the moment you do, competitors may be waiting to take the opportunity to leave you in the dust. This doesn't mean having to check your smartphone every six seconds, or regularly clock in eighteen-hour days. Take vacations as needed, but don't forget to return. As beauty industry sales executive Billy Lowe, a seasoned veteran of fast-moving markets, explains: "Clients want to know what's new—what's next. By keeping them on their toes, sharing new tips or techniques or things your brand is doing, clients stay interested. Things change from season to season and it keeps clients coming back time and time again."[5]

- **Fuels understanding that success breeds complacency.** Consider the example of Kodak, which reigned supreme over the photography industry for a century, producing billions of dollars' worth of film cameras, photographic film, and photo development supplies each year. Then along came something new: the digital still camera, which Kodak itself invented in 1975—and then promptly ignored. Perhaps if Kodak's leaders had been a bit more anxious about the changing photography marketplace and paranoid about the competitors who were aiming to steal their business, they would have seen the future better—a future in which digital photography would leave the old paper-and-stinky-chemical variety behind in its dust. They weren't attuned to these concerns and they paid the price: filing for Chapter 11 bankruptcy in 2012 after years of decline. As experts note, "Businesses fail either because they leave their customers . . . or because their customers leave them."[6] In this case, Kodak left its customers, ignoring their changing needs to focus on outdated products and processes. In turn, customers left the company in droves, attracted by the convenience, flexibility, and speed of digital photography.

- **Causes you to plan for tomorrow today.** While some say that making plans is difficult or even impossible in these uncertain and fast-changing times, knowing where you are headed—and having a plan for getting there—is more important than ever before. Competitive and unpredictable as the business world has become, you can't afford be without a plan to greet impending changes, and the time to plan is right now. This is true no matter what your organization and industry looks like or what your position is in your company, from the boardroom to the front line. In their book *Great by Choice,* authors Jim Collins and Morten Hansen suggest, "When a calamitous event clobbers an industry or the overall economy, companies fall into one of three categories: those that pull ahead, those that fall behind, and those that die. The disruption itself does not determine your category. You do."[7] According to Collins and Hansen, the companies that succeeded were "10x" companies—businesses that beat their industry indices by at least 10 times. Such companies planned and prepared for unpredictable business environments well before they encountered them, a function of their ongoing anxiety. Say Collins and Hansen, "When it comes to building financial buffers and shock absorbers, the 10x cases were paranoid, neurotic freaks!"[8]

To summarize, there are only two rules of tactics: Never be without a plan, and never rely on it. As we have seen, anxiety and paranoia do indeed pay, both on individual terms and at the organizational level. So how best to harness the paranoia and anxiety we feel and turn them into awareness, then translate awareness into action?

Nurturing Awareness

Your anxiety and paranoia aren't getting the best of you. Markets, opportunities, and expectations are always changing, and new competitors and challenges arising, even as familiar hazards and threats constantly nip at our heels. Being able to detect these potential dangers, discern when and how we should address them, and act as if their presence were imminent at all times (whether true or not) are often a vital determinants of success or failure.

Think of the emotions you feel when you are anxious or paranoid as your personal alarm system: Wise individuals and organizations will create a system of emergency tripwires that kick into action whenever specific sensors are activated.

Set many throughout your life, your career, and your business—quantitative or qualitative measures that let you know immediately when something is at odds with your comfort level or expectation. For example, if you're concerned about a sales department that is lagging, then set a tripwire that alerts you when sales drop by more than 10 percent in a given month. If you're worried about a decline in the value of your profession, set one that alerts you when you hear repeated news of cutbacks and layoffs as attention shifts to new skill sets and solutions.

Warning signs that we must be aware of at the individual or organizational level include:

- Rising demand for new talents and experiences
- Changes in the industry or organizational environment
- Growing awareness of impending events, such as mergers or layoffs
- Increasing priority around new initiatives and developments
- The failure of strategies and initiatives to meet goal targets
- The appearance of new competitors
- A spike in online activity surrounding rivals or rivals' offerings
- Changes in customer tastes or buying habits
- Rising demand for new skills and experiences

Rather than being overwhelmed by or ignoring the anxiety and paranoia these events and occurrences trigger, channel this energy into a productive system of self-assessment. Ask yourself, What are the real concerns we face? How immediate and troubling are they? To what degree do they affect us, and how can we react smartly to these threats? Which ways can we counter these and other problems before they become pressing challenges?

Instead of defaulting to an instinctive response, we must train ourselves to interpret the signals coming in, weigh their importance, and respond deliberately in kind. Rather than overreact and jump to poor conclusions at every indicator, we must become well attuned to tracking developing indicators, gauging their intensity, and understanding the signals being presented.

Individuals do this by keeping their eyes, ears, and minds open and by researching and coming to know new challenges.

Organizations do this through such models as Michael E. Porter's five forces that determine competitive intensity: rivalry among existing competitors, the threat of new market entrants, the bargaining power of suppliers, the threat of substitute products or services, and the bargaining power of buyers when determining what competitive strategies to employ.[9]

So what are some ways to increase the awareness of your people and your organization while productively leveraging their anxiety and paranoia, along with your own?

- **Assume that you and your business are in rivals' crosshairs.** Your competitors may very well be out to take your job, knock your number one product off its perch, or steal away your best employees. But whether they are or are not isn't the actual concern here. It's whether you're acting as if they were and taking steps to counter these issues accordingly. Heavyweight champion boxer Muhammad Ali coined the phrase "float like a butterfly, sting like a bee." When we set lofty goals, high sales targets, or aggressive growth strategies, we're certainly looking to follow the latter advice and pack a punch. But as you go about fighting the good fight, don't forget to also float like the butterfly—stick and move, bob and weave—unless you want to get hit with an unexpected uppercut. Anxiety and paranoia can keep you alert, fast on your feet, and from being boxed in against the ropes.

- **Keep your friends close, and your enemies closer.** If there are people or companies out to get you or your company's products, key employees, or customers, then you've got to identify them and neutralize their threats—threats that anxiety and paranoia can keep you keenly attuned to. But if you've ever heard the phrase "you catch more flies with honey than vinegar," you also know another important truism: The most successful battles are those never fought. Let anxiety be your guide, but don't let it overwhelm you. Rather than drive conflict with peers, let anxiety help you fuel curiosity about both your own and others' capabilities and exercise cautious optimism about what would happen if you brought them together, not drove them apart. Steadily seeking to build strategic alliances with rivals and to partner where your capabilities lack can be every bit as effective a tactical approach to neutralizing threats as confronting competitors head-on. When it introduced its Verismo single-serve coffee brewing system in 2012, Starbucks fired a direct shot at industry rival Green Mountain Coffee, which owns the extremely popular Keurig single-brew system with its ubiquitous K-Cups. However, after Green Mountain announced a partnership with Dunkin' Brands (think Dunkin' Donuts), which sells enough coffee each day in its stores to be a significant threat to Starbucks, Starbucks decided to team up with its rival Green Mountain to introduce a new system: the hybrid KeurigVue single-brew system. This machine couples Green Mountain brewing technology with Starbucks' Vue coffee packs.[10] Both have leveraged their strengths to complement each other's capabilities, and benefited from the joint effort.

▪ **Leverage your paranoia to become more proactive.** Success breeds complacency: Use paranoia to keep from becoming too comfortable and to remain acutely aware of the world around you and potential problems and opportunities. Plan for bad times in good, speak up when anxious about specific topics, and constantly innovate, course correcting in sync with changing markets. It's the only way to keep up. In fact, "only the paranoid survive" was the guiding motto for former Intel CEO Andy Grove (as well as the title of his critically acclaimed book on business management). By training his team to stay anxious about competitors, emerging trends, and how well the firm was staying up to date with changing business conditions, it kept the company innovating, steadily adapting in time with customer needs, and (by staying in fighting shape) ultimately future-proof. Under his stewardship, Intel rose to become the world's largest chipmaker. If intelligent paranoia does anything, it points out the need to be constantly innovating, repeating, and improving your technique— both in your personal career and in your team and organization. Keep in mind that it's far easier to fall behind and become irrelevant to others than ever before, and an increasing number of companies are doing it far more quickly than in the past. According to research on the S&P 500 Index conducted by Innosight, the lifespan of top companies on the index are shrinking. At the current rate, 75 percent of the S&P 500 will be replaced by 2027.[11] All the more reason to be trying new things to stay ahead of the competition.

- **Be on the lookout for strategic inflection points.** According to Intel's Grove, strategic inflection points are "A time in the life of a business when its fundamentals are about to change." As he further points out, this kind of fundamental change "can mean an opportunity to rise to new heights. But it may just as likely signal the beginning of the end."[12] Such was the case when Xerox, which invented personal computers and the Ethernet, decided that these innovations would never be moneymakers and instead focused its resources on its cash cow photocopying business. While photocopying was good to the company for many years, the enterprise ultimately missed out on an astronomically higher potential level of revenue and profits. It would have been better served had it instead stayed alert and further developed the innovations coming out of its Palo Alto Research Center.

- **Constantly ask questions about your enterprise and test your answers.** Don't assume the status quo is set in stone or sustainable in the wake of coming shifts.

  - What if poor economic conditions cause your customers to reduce their purchases of your products or create the need for you to seek streamlining and cost-cutting measures?
  - What if a competitor cuts prices enough or begins offering innovative new choices and alternatives to increase their market share dramatically at your expense?
  - What if key contacts or colleagues decide to depart or depart without passing on their insights and knowledge?

- **Ask questions on the individual level too:**

  - What will be the net result if your prospects for advancement, business relationships, or performance are minimal?
  - What's the potential impact if you are passed over for a plum assignment or are unable to complete (or complete adequately) a task you've been assigned?
  - How can you course correct or adjust strategy if the talents, skills, and insights you bring to the organization are no longer valued as much as in the past?

- **Reconsider whether data are applicable or accurate.** Be as paranoid about the information you're receiving as the challenges you face. Don't believe everything you see or hear. Anxiety and paranoia help you remain smart and skeptical about interpreting data because facts can easily be manipulated to support any conclusion. Make sure the information you get is replicable and corroborated by many sources (An Experian QAS data quality survey showed that approximately 94 percent of businesses don't trust the accuracy of their data.)

Of course, you've also got to be smart about how you put anxiety and paranoia to work. This requires us to routinely review and reassess how well we're capitalizing on these emotions and whether we're still acting most efficiently and effectively in response to the signals being sent.

You can give yourself a checkup by regularly running impartial systems checks that will verify whether you and your business are operating as smoothly and effectively as you think. Do this by closely reviewing performance and financial data, conducting audits, benchmarking against other working professionals and businesses in your industry, prototyping and presenting unfinished ideas for feedback, using impartial parties to validate your strategies and results, and comparing outcomes to goals.

Similarly, we can't nuke every problem encountered as part of this process. While a bit of healthy anxiety and paranoia is always a good thing, don't go overboard and assign pressing import to every single challenge that you face. According to the Pareto Principle, it can be said that 80 percent of your time will be spent on just 20 percent of your problems. That obviously leaves you with little or no time to deal with the other 80 percent of the problems that you face on an ongoing basis.

Focus on addressing the problems that have the greatest potential to negatively affect your career or business. Understand the opportunity cost associated with every decision, where you can make the greatest impact the fastest and which problems most require your attention. Then assign less import and effort to tackling the rest. If the problems you decide to shed are important enough, then assign them to others within your organization to track or solve. If you look closer, you may also find that many are symptomatic of a larger underlying issue; cure that ailment, and you may quickly and expeditiously find your troubles greatly decreased.

Ultimately, the lesson to be learned from putting paranoia and anxiety to work for you is simple and threefold. By planning for the worst of times during the best of times, we better prepare ourselves to greet the challenges that they may bring. By realizing that success is temporary, not a finite state, we force ourselves to continuously strive to maintain it. And by staying anxious and abreast of both the ever-shifting world around us and emerging threats, we gain the objective insight needed to effectively respond to and neutralize them.

To put it bluntly: We must *always* be anxious and paranoid to some extent. You have to keep your eyes on the road in a rapidly changing world with an equally fast-moving, competitive landscape. But if we manage our fear intelligently, and treat anxiety as a driving force for growth and innovation, we can capitalize on it and channel it toward achieving more positive outcomes.

Action Steps

Complacency in career and company is *out*; turning your anxiety into awareness, and cultivating healthy paranoia of the intelligent kind is *in*. Keep an eye on the prize by constantly scanning your business and career environment, looking for the kinds of changes that may bring you problems or opportunities. You can take the following action steps to address all of these issues:

- **Nurture your awareness of your people and organization.** Accomplish this by converting the anxiety or paranoia you feel into insights and action.

- **Stay closely attuned to your concerns as well as the market and environment that you operate within.** Be aware of emerging challenges and opportunities of all shapes and sizes and whether (and to what extent) they may affect you personally in your career or your business. Be prepared to take evasive action.

- **Innovate, improve, and create backup plans before there's any immediate need to do so.** Your competitors are looking to eat your lunch at any given moment. Always be applying new tactics, new strategies, and new ideas to keep them at bay because you never know when you're going to be on the menu.

- **Constantly be pushing forward.** Always be achieving more, gaining more, and doing more than your colleagues and the competition. Lead change in your department, company, or industry instead of following it.

- **Refuse to become complacent.** Success breeds complacency and complacency breeds opportunity for others to advance. Look to the future: Don't lean on past accomplishments.

- **Plan for tomorrow today.** Tomorrow will be here sooner than you think. Prepare to greet the future before it arrives.

Chapter Six

Rule 4: Transform Failure into Success

Outside of crooked financiers and former child TV stars, Scott Skinger is one of the precious few individuals who can say that they've pissed away millions overnight. But the founder of the Chicago-based computer training firm TrainSignal claims there's a good reason he took his company from $7 million in annual revenue to literally nothing in no time flat, an apparent business failure of significant magnitude: He could see the bigger picture.

Rebooting the fifty-person, decade-old operation (whose instructional DVDs sold for up to $400) into a $49 per month unlimited streaming online video subscription service offering wasn't easy, he admits, and it required what can only be called a near-catastrophic experience. But Skinger says it's precisely this type of pivotal choice that executives will increasingly be forced to make: Today's failure can be a sturdy and oftentimes mandatory, if uncomfortable, launching pad for tomorrow's success. Despite the short-term discomfort associated with change and uncertainty, it's imperative to make decisions that keep your business relevant in the marketplace while best furthering you or your organization's long-term goals, he insists.

Granted, we're all asked to make tough calls, but for Skinger, who'd funded the firm with his own credit cards, reinventing Train-Signal was especially agonizing. By 2012, the company had sold more than $33 million in disks to more than 50,000 clients. Despite a decade of steady growth, however, the firm also found itself in a precarious position.

Demand for capable, cost-effective IT training solutions was growing, but more professionals were turning to online education, even as better-funded competitors began flooding the industry. Ongoing upgrades to popular IT tools also required TrainSignal to revise courses more frequently, a task better suited to digital video than DVD products.

Customer needs were clearly changing; Skinger knew the future lay in online solutions. "But business is going well," he thought, "why create distractions?" Uncertain how to proceed (should he separate, pair, or spin off this new business?) and of the potential financial impact, the firm stood paralyzed, and decreasingly relevant to its customers, in the face of new developments. Falling back on familiar patterns, TrainSignal failed to address these pressing issues and allowed more ambitious Internet-based rivals to gain market footholds.

But eventually, even with profits soaring, Skinger could no longer ignore the truth. As he explained, "to not switch over would be suicide." Facing a similar challenge that movie rental chain Blockbuster confronted when demand for online video soared, TrainSignal had to embrace digital streaming solutions. Given a simple choice (change now and risk immediate failure, or slowly but surely wither away), Skinger made the smarter decision to move forward with the transition.

It's a good thing that TrainSignal followed the course it did. After posting record sales of $850,000 in January 2013, it dropped the DVDs and cut back to zero revenue in February. A drop from monthly sales of nearly $1 million to absolutely nothing a month later would seem a cataclysmic failure in anyone's book. But Skinger had faith that he had taken the right course and that this failure would be just a short stopover on the pathway to newfound success. Sure enough, the company was quickly on track to nearly triple its previous sales within two years. By creating recurring revenue-producing programs, it had also multiplied its value, brand equity, and awareness in the eyes of investors several times over.

As Skinger and TrainSignal discovered, simply being more efficient isn't enough to thrive in today's fast-changing markets. You also have to risk and sometimes even experience failure before you can achieve the success you desire. Like individuals, companies must be dedicated to pursuing both evolutionary and revolutionary change to keep up. But to successfully do so, they have to be willing to do what most others won't: face down common fears, endure the possibility of failure as they make the transition, and steadily push past initial discomfort—eventually turning failure into success and, from there, into competitive advantage.

Rule 4: Transform Failure into Success

Any task worthy of accomplishment will inevitably cause us to experience any one or even all of the seven fears outlined in Chapter 1.

Pursuing these goals requires us to expand our capabilities, comfort zones, and sense of perspective. But as we saw earlier, people and organizations prefer to avoid these sources of fear and operate from places of calm and comfort. This creates an unfortunate paradox. To evolve and grow, we must inherently embrace new prospects. However, we often find these selfsame prospects difficult to embrace because we believe ourselves to be incapable of doing so, or doing so as successfully as we might hope.

Fear of failure is a particularly strong emotion, and it can have a significant impact on people's behavior, whether in their personal or in their professional lives. And for good reason. Not only is failure potentially embarrassing, it also has the potential to distance us from others (that is, isolate us), spark confrontation, and prove emotionally or financially devastating. It's no coincidence, therefore, that among the seven most common and significant fears I explored in Chapter 1, fear of failure takes its place at the head of the line.

Of course, there are very real reasons that we may fear failure in our careers and businesses. If we make a mistake or error on the job (demonstrated to be the most pressing fear among working professionals today), we could be reprimanded, put on probation, or even fired. And if, as the leader of a business, our company, team or division fails, then we and our people may feel the fallout from this failure for years. Entrepreneurs are especially susceptible to these influences: Business start-ups are particularly prone to failure—25 percent will capsize by the end of their first year of business alone.[1]

Truth be told though, every one of us fails from time to time; both individuals and organizations are imperfect. The key is to get past the fear of failure that can dissuade us from taking action and making the decisions that bring us closer to achieving the success we so greatly desire. If you can teach yourself to build your tolerance levels and overcome this fear of pushing forward (including the varying levels of emotional pain it prompts), you'll always be a step ahead.

The more you confront barriers others shy away from, the greater your odds of success. The more you push past them, the greater the rewards you'll reap that lie beyond because they'll be more uncommon and hold more value as a result. A little discomfort today can go a long way toward winning tomorrow: The more others turn away from a goal or task, the more you stand to benefit (and benefit more greatly over a long-term horizon) by completing it. After all, if getting ahead were easy, everyone would be doing it. To succeed and stay future-proof, you've got to bite the bullet and invest in growing your and your organization's comfort zones and capabilities, despite the often painful demands upfront.

Learn to push past the fear of failure, and you can capitalize on areas of opportunity others have abandoned to create winning breakthroughs and create ongoing relevance, on an infinite scale. But to do so, you've got to be more objective when weighing opportunities to pursue, learn to develop greater tolerance for discomfort and—most vitally—be able to dial fear back down to a dull roar.

The former CEO of consumer products giant Kimberly-Clark, onetime army recruit Darwin E. Smith was once told in Officer Training School that he'd never be a leader.[2] And when he inherited the business in 1971, he faced an equally discouraging situation: the bulk of Kimberly-Clark's money was tied up in giant, ailing paper mills, and its corporate culture was going stagnant. But Smith refused to let either himself or the company be defined by these setbacks.

For months, he asked seemingly dumb questions: What drove this business? What could it excel at? Where was its competitive advantage? Then he inadvertently stumbled across Kleenex, a brand name inseparable from its category (think Google or Xerox), which was then only a sideline business for the industrial behemoth. Rather than continue pursuing the same business avenues as his predecessors, Smith decided to take a tip from the success of this promising product and concentrate on new innovations, such as disposable diaper line Huggies (destined to become a multibillion-dollar market leader).

It took tremendous fortitude to do a strategic about-face, throw out a century of corporate history, and sell the mills, but that's exactly what Smith ordered. The possibility of failure was great, and no doubt many of Smith's management team counseled him to take the safer path of a known—albeit sickly—status quo rather than chance failure on a massive scale. Sure enough, the company regrouped around more forward-thinking products, only to see its stock and reputation take a dive as it stretched its comfort zone and expanded away from its core business. But even in the face of seeming defeat, Smith didn't cut and run from this apparent failure in his business strategy, and he didn't allow any fear he felt to push him off his chosen course; he just worked that much harder to transform failure into success. A quarter-century later, Kimberly-Clark had risen to the top of its sector.

When you encounter failure, don't get discouraged and don't resign yourself to ongoing disappointment. Learn from the experience and don't hesitate to try again, using the insights gained as a result to continually improve and do better with future efforts. Refocus your sights, retrain yourself to go from weakness to strength, and give yourself permission to get ahead, and you've got all the qualifications you need to succeed, even if it takes a few attempts. Before there was the history-making social network Facebook, there was Facemash, a site which let students compare how attractive others found them. Before there was Ford's wildly successful Model T automobile, there were models A, N, S, and so on. Try, learn, try again—the formula is simpler than you think.

Remember: You can benefit even from failed attempts to vault yourself forward by boosting your knowledge, skills, and experience and increasing both your visibility and odds of stumbling across unexpected opportunities. Just as there are many ways to win in business beyond financial return, there are rewards to be gained and lessons to be learned from your so-called failures. Lessons such as these:

- Understanding the imperative to break with the status quo
- Recognizing old approaches that no longer work
- Discovering new approaches that do work
- Gaining fresh perspective on problems and opportunities
- Learning how to strategize more effectively
- Comprehending how to better plan for the future
- Identifying where you can most add to your team or organization's value and what stumbling blocks may currently be subtracting from it

But it's not just about learning from failure. It's also about overcoming our insecurities and cultivating the conviction and endurance needed to take continued action when we're confronted by related concerns such as fear of change, isolation, or losing control.

In 2008, executive recruiting firm Korn/Ferry watched its revenue drop 50 percent in just six months. Even as it was laying off staff, instituting furloughs and imposing pay cuts, it decided to expand its comfort zone and core lines of business. Over the cries of distressed managers, who feared the even greater change and uncertainty such choices would surely bring, CEO Gary Burnison began acquiring leadership development and strategic consulting firms.

By the end of 2013, more than 40 percent of KornFerry's revenue came from outside its core recruiting business. And, thanks to fearless expansion into alternate spaces, the company now plays in a $20 billion instead of a $4 billion market.

Accepting sources of trepidation and exerting action where others cannot is precisely how enterprises and individuals create opportunity and gain competitive advantage. But this requires us to rethink how we handle sources of discomfort: Feel the fear and do it anyway.

At a Polaroid eyewear manufacturing plant near Glasgow, Scotland, employee Ian McKeown had a vision. "At the end of each day," he told himself, "I want only people and finished product to leave the plant." In short, he wanted his company to stop producing waste. But given the time and expenses associated with ecofriendly manufacturing, McKeown had to gather the courage to convince his bosses to not only see his vision but to buy into it and take action.

However, that's exactly what he did, despite any concerns for his own job security and mounting instances of failure and rejection. According to McKeown, he heard no many times from management. But he persistently presented ideas for taking less wasteful approaches to manufacturing, packing, and shipping anyway. Eventually executives began to see the light, gradually adopting many of them.[3] His idea to reuse plastic-corrugated boxes have become such a time-, money-, and environment-saving hit that even partners like IBM and Motorola have since followed suit.

Despite the risks associated with not accepting no for an answer, McKeown refused to give in to worries that he might fail in his quest and his career might suffer as a result; he kept moving forward. Using the Japanese concept of "ask why five times," posing pointed questions until colleagues became receptive to change, McKeown stayed on track, potential career fallout notwithstanding. According to *Lean and Green* author Pamela Gordon, McKeown's biggest breakthrough came when he sidestepped his supervisors and pulled aside visiting executives from America, who said, "Why don't we try it?"[4]

What's stopping *you* from asking "why" or "what if" and achieving similar results, even in the face of failure or rejection? That's right—absolutely nothing.

Overcoming Concerns

Concerns that you may not succeed will always be present in every aspect of life and business and become only more pronounced as risk, uncertainty, and competition grow. But just as top innovators do, both you and your organization can learn to thrive on the fear of failure. The key is simply acclimating yourself to such concerns and building both your tolerance and, as we saw in Chapter 3, willingness to take action. The more you're aware of their presence and more ably you comprehend how to counter concerns of failing, the more comfortable you'll be in their midst. In addition, the more effective you'll be at addressing these worries and the more consistently and powerfully you'll be able to push past them to achieve lasting success, regardless of your own initial hesitance or fear of rejection.

Consider the Apple Store. It sells fewer brands than Best Buy, stocks fewer products, and has fewer retail locations. Even as rivals like Sony are shutting down shops, though, Apple continues to expand; in fact, it's the technology field's most successful specialty retailer. But killer high-tech hardware isn't the secret to its success. Rather, it's the chain's relentless desire to understand customers' pain points and offer them meaningful solutions instead of empty sales pitches.

But while it's easy to say this in hindsight, the strategy wasn't a guaranteed successor an easy concept for even Apple itself to embrace. There were numerous concerns to be addressed before the idea could go anywhere—even in a business renowned for thinking differently.

Someone at the company had to put a focus on creating long-term relationships, not short-term profits. Someone had to be willing to fly in the face of traditional store design and implementation. And as genius as those Genius Bars now seem, someone had to fight for the idea of putting customer service stations in every store that would support this mantra. In fact, when the executive heading Apple's retail initiatives heard that his team wanted to take up a significant portion of stores' floor space for help stations? He thought they were insane. Still, someone understood how important it was to differentiate and better serve customers (see: the iPod, iPad, iTunes, and so on) and was willing to keep fighting for their ideas and to overcome colleagues' initial resistance.

This strategy—dare to do things differently, accept that you may not succeed, and keep pushing forward regardless—is notable primarily for the fact it received pushback. Leave it to fear of failure to make even one of the world's most celebrated innovators second-guess a tactic it's already used to devastating effect for decades in business.

But the pressing need to overcome fear of failure isn't just a vital lesson for businesses to learn. Just as leading organizations can prime themselves to succeed at any scale by moving past the fear of falling on their face and building tolerance for challenges and setbacks, so too can individuals.

Golf legend Tiger Woods wasn't born with a gene that makes him hit birdies on every hole. Instead, he spent years being subjected to purposeful heckling and harassment on the green by his father, Earl, to acclimate him to nervousness and pressure.[5] Earl, a former Green Beret, wanted to teach his son fortitude and focus by forcing the budding champion to constantly confront fear and adversity, including the prospect of abject and humiliating failure—any athlete's worst nightmare.

As a result, Woods's determination became so unswerving that he came from behind to win the 1994 U.S. Amateur golf championship, despite trailing deeply coming into the final nine holes. And throughout his career, the more daunting and difficult the scenario, the more comfortable young Woods became on the course. Situations that caused others to crack under pressure actually became a source of competitive advantage for him because he'd spent years acclimating to them. As critics note, he's since become "a dangerous golfer . . . difficult situations bring out the best in him."[6]

By becoming intimately familiar with common fears, preparing to counter them, and acting decisively despite discomfort, his performance and resilience grew while rivals' plummeted.

If you are ready to succeed in the face of an overwhelming fear that you are going to be soundly rejected, or fail in your efforts, take a tip from successful innovators: Instead of reacting instinctively and taking a leap backward or giving up when faced with unexpected hardship or emotional distress, consider the reasons and source of your discomfort and address it. Study fear, confront fear, learn from these exchanges, and respond intelligently in turn (Focus. Engage. Assess. React.) until the pain becomes more tolerable or a cure presents itself.

When auto maker Hyundai was pummeled by a drop in consumer spending during the Great Recession, unlike competitors, it didn't immediately cut prices, says Ivey Business School professor Niraj Dawar. It asked customers and discovered the reason for spending drops was the risk associated with buying automobiles in uncertain times. So instead of giving a knee-jerk response, slashing price tags, Hyundai slashed risks instead, offering a no-strings-attached refund if shoppers lost their job in the next twelve months. The company's sales doubled in January 2009, while the industry's plummeted 37 percent, the biggest drop since 1963.

Similarly, home soda-making products manufacturer Soda-Stream spent $4 million on a Super Bowl ad attacking Coca-Cola and PepsiCo that CBS refused to air, despite SodaStream's contractual obligation to buy TV airtime. So it aired a preexisting ad and released the controversial spot online, which promptly generated 6 billion impressions and far outperformed the broadcast advertisement.

The secret is to train yourself to take setbacks in stride, feed on your worries while becoming smarter about interpreting and addressing them, and grow stronger as competitors falter. In Chapter 2, we explored the many ways fear affects us. To summarize: Fear creates many beneficial effects, including heightened awareness, alertness, and performance. Granted, fear can also prompt very pronounced negative effects as well, including great distress and discomfort. But when you reframe the scenario, reexamine the problem, and rethink your approach to it, anyone can learn to take the pain, and channel the shifts fear causes toward more positive and productive uses.

Here's how you can turn your troubles into sources of strength, opportunity, and action—transforming failure into success in the process:

- **Self-evaluate.** Take a step back from your current situation, consider the source of your concerns, and objectively note how these worries are affecting you. Turn them to your advantage by transforming concerns (oh no, our capabilities are becoming outdated!) into strategic motivators (time to experiment with new ideas and invest in continuing education!). Systematically counter fears, neutralize them, or—if you find legitimate causes for concern—embrace the signals being sent and take steps to remedy the problem.

- **Motivate.** Imagine how good you're going to feel when you reach your goal, whatever it may be. Maybe it's just to raise a minor but persistent work-related issue to your boss or maybe it's to win a promotion or pay raise. The only way to accomplish your objective is to actually pursue it. Get excited about achieving your goal and use the excitement you feel and the energy generated by your fear of not succeeding to spur you to action and drive you across the finish line. Contemplate the many chances and paths you'll have to take to find success. Relish the opportunities and challenges they bring, take calculated risks, and celebrate working through your fears. As we saw before, even if you fail, you can still try again, and grow and learn something from each new attempt.

▪ **Rethink your capabilities.** Assumptions can be dangerous, but we constantly find ourselves making them. But if we must go down this route, let's make some more useful ones instead:

· Assume anything can change.
· Assume you have the power to innovate.
· Assume you are qualified.
· Assume you will figure it out.
· Assume it may take a few tries, whether others like it or not.

The slogan here is simple: Not easy, but *possible*. Make it so. Remember: The ceilings that we see above our heads—the ones that keep us from catapulting ourselves to higher levels of success—are artificial and largely self-imposed.

Consider the story of MSNBC news anchor Mika Brzezinski, who one day discovered that she was earning fourteen times less than her *Morning Joe* television show cohost Joe Scarborough. Instead of accepting the limits that her bosses put into place, Brzezinski fought them, eventually earning a significant pay raise by proving to her employers that she was worth it.[7] Despite the discrepancy, she didn't give up, accept these limits, or leave the show.

Recall that making mistakes is the single most common workplace fear today. We are deathly afraid of failure—so much so that we are the ones who create ceilings with our own fears, doubts, and mistaken beliefs. Each exerts power over us only as long as we are willing to let it. Thinking outside the box is for suckers; the only boxes present are the ones you choose to put in place. All it takes to remove them is preparation, persistence, and a solid plan of attack, not to mention a healthy tolerance for taking the pain that goes along with executing it.

Oh, and if you should happen to encounter a legitimate barrier to success, don't be afraid to take a deep breath, then break out a sledgehammer and start knocking down walls. It's laborious, difficult, and often highly uncomfortable work. (Including the kind that often exposes us to pressing concerns such as confrontation, isolation, and embarrassment.) But as we've seen, as messy an activity as it can be and as incapable of performing it as you may believe yourself to be, your business and career can benefit from this incessant remodeling. You'd be amazed by what can happen when you stop worrying about failing and start swinging away, continuing to dust yourself off and discover what lies behind those surprisingly brittle barriers.

Grit: The New Success Secret

Perhaps more than any other building block for success today, your ability to change, adapt, and ultimately win going forward will be defined by *grit*.

According to University of Pennsylvania research psychologist Angela Lee Duckworth, "Grit is the tendency to sustain interest in, and effort toward, very long-term goals. Self-control is the voluntary regulation of behavioral, emotional, and attentional impulses in the presence of momentarily gratifying temptations or diversions."[8] Exercising grit (and the self-control required to employ it) is the antidote to the fear of failure that can sometimes overwhelm us.

Over the course of six studies, spanning a look at West Point cadets, college undergrads, working adults, and Scripps National Spelling Bee contestants, Duckworth revealed that factors like GPA and IQ had far less impact on success than persistence and perseverance. As Duckworth concludes, "Grit may be as essential as talent to high accomplishment."[9] In other words, our willingness to withstand challenges and hardships and keep moving forward in the face of adversity is an equally important determinant of whether we'll get ahead as education, talent, or experience.

Her findings indicate that:

- From the earliest possible moment, we should be preparing students and professionals to anticipate and deal with failure and misfortune.
- We must encourage pupils and professionals to work with as much stamina as they do intensity.
- Those who demonstrate exceptional commitment to goals should be supported with as many resources as gifted and talented individuals.
- Breadth and depth matter to both organizations and individuals because "The goal of an education is not just to learn a little about a lot, but also a lot about a little."

Haven't yet accustomed yourself to taking the pain that comes with trying, failing, and having to try again and again? Here's the good news: It's possible to cultivate the grit needed to stay the course, overcome challenges, and achieve your stated objectives. By considering the following statements, derived from Duckworth's Grit Scale self-assessment tool, you can gauge your own grit:

- New ideas and projects sometimes distract me from previous ones.
- I have been obsessed with a certain idea or project for a short time but later lost interest.
- I often set a goal but later choose to pursue a different one.
- I have difficulty maintaining my focus on projects that take more than a few months to complete.
- I finish whatever I begin.
- Setbacks don't discourage me.
- I am a hard worker.
- I am diligent.[10]

If you find yourself identifying more with the first four statements and less with the last four, fear not: As we saw in Chapter 3, anyone can build resilience and build their grit along with it. You just have to stay focused and persistent, even if that means repeatedly taking a few shots to the gut.

Try to think of it this way: Roughly 99 percent of leadership is being a punching bag. Remain stoic. Take the hit. Bounce back into place. Occasionally wobble a little bit forward. But you don't have to take every single blow alone or be a masochist to accomplish goals. Teammates, colleagues, supervisors, friends, and family can all help provide a shield against lasting hurt.

The more you teach yourself to spring back into action and steadily work toward goals despite setbacks or misfortunes, the grittier and more successful you'll become.

Overnight Success Seldom Happens Overnight

It may help to remember that creative people—authors, filmmakers, musicians, comedians, artists, photographers—all hone their craft in much the same way: failing frequently and learning as they go. They work hard, they practice hard, they exhibit their work, they get feedback, and they use that feedback to improve their chosen area of expertise... even if it means repeatedly failing, experiencing great discomfort, and having to pick themselves back up again.

Organizations advance in a similar fashion. They design, prototype, and pursue new initiatives, then conduct focus groups, run field tests, gather customer insights, and translate these data into better decisions, using the candid and sometimes painful feedback to take more positive action. Armed with this information, they can enhance and hone their services and strategies, creating the next big commercial hits.

Recognize that overnight victory is primarily the stuff of fantasy. Behind every band that has a hit song, there are years of playing in dive bars for little or no money and grueling road tours in the drummer's '75 Chevy van. In the real world, success often comes in stages, as learning, experience, insight, and resources slowly stockpile and compound. We cannot, and in fact must not, lack the courage to keep pursuing goals, despite failure or hardship, so long as we're continuing to do so intelligently and efficiently, however painful the process of going about achieving them proves. It may help you stay the course to remember that you don't have to build tolerance overnight: You can increase it by undertaking small risks, small leaps of faith, and small goals before making the jump to larger ones.

Before famed director Francis Ford Coppola created his masterpiece *The Godfather*, he had to first work through a number of less critically enduring works, including *The Two Christophers* and *The Bellboy and the Playgirls*. Likewise, before McDonald's Big Mac and Egg McMuffin became super successes, there was the Hula Burger (introduced in 1962) with a slice of grilled pineapple in place of the patty. Burger lovers were not amused, but it didn't stop the McTrain from McRolling.

In fact, the very act of failing and experiencing pain or discomfort can help illuminate the path to the career or business or life choices that have greatest meaning for you, while providing you with the growing resolve you need to achieve them.

Years after graduating from the University of Exeter, Harry Potter author J. K. Rowling was a jobless single mother with a failed marriage. She describes herself then as "the biggest failure I knew." But she came to find this failure liberating. By confronting her greatest fear—the fear of failing completely—and realizing she'd survived, she discovered the determination needed to persevere and create her bestselling book series.

As she explained in a commencement speech at Harvard: "Had I really succeeded at anything else, I might never have found the determination to succeed where I truly belonged. I was set free, because my greatest fear had been realized, and I was still alive . . . and so rock bottom became a solid foundation on which I built my life."

To win, you don't have to succeed with every effort or do so overnight. You just need to train yourself to take the pain that comes as a result of failure, rejection, or underperformance; push past it; and keep success in your sights. The grittier you are, and the more resourceful and resolved, the faster and more frequently you'll get ahead; plus, you'll gain the unique and invaluable talents and resources needed to keep winning and winning over the long haul.

Bouncing Back

Earlier in this book we considered the idea of resilience, which according to the American Psychological Association (APA) is "the process of adapting well in the face of adversity, trauma, tragedy, threats, or significant sources of stress."[11] In other words, resilience is a measure of our ability to bounce back when we pick a battle to engage in and lose. Unfortunately, while we might hope that by picking our battles, we'll win the vast majority of them (and, as we'll see in Chapter 10, we can certainly win more by being more strategic), this isn't always necessarily the case. Not only that but we may also find ourselves bloody and beaten, even after winning a particularly difficult or protracted battle. The ability to pick ourselves up after a stumble and adapt our strategies in the face of failure are crucial capabilities for today's tactician.

Cultivating this capability will go a long way toward helping you future-proof you, your career, and your business. The APA suggests ten ways to build resilience:

- **Make connections.** Accept help and support from friends, relatives, work colleagues, and others. Reach out and help others who are facing challenges and setbacks in their own lives or day-to-day business realities. Apart from purely philanthropic reasons, remember that when fighting battles (especially attempting to rebound from prior losses), it helps to have allies you can call on as well.

- **Avoid seeing crises as insurmountable problems.** Accept that crap happens, but it doesn't have to be a permanent stumbling block. Look beyond your current problems to find new solutions, then apply them strategically.

- **Accept that change is a part of living.** You can't hold on to the anchor of the past, especially when it's sinking fast. Focus on the things you can change, not those you cannot. Then make a point of changing the ones that aren't working for you.

- **Move toward your goals.** Develop small, achievable goals and focus on accomplishing them; set yourself up for success, not failure. Build momentum toward achieving larger goals by accomplishing these smaller tasks. Ask yourself, What's one thing I know I can accomplish today that helps me move in the direction I want to go?

- **Take decisive actions.** Regardless of how difficult the situation you're in may be, make decisions and take action; don't vacillate or stick your head in the sand, hoping problems will go away. They probably won't. Create clearly defined action plans that can help you to go from failure to success, then execute them.

- **Look for opportunities for self-discovery.** When faced with adversity, take time out to look deep within yourself or your organization to assess your priorities and what's important (and what's not) in your life or business. Maybe you can sidestep or defuse a difficult situation or setback by changing your perspective.

- **Nurture a positive view of yourself.** Work on building self-confidence. Be positive about your ability to solve problems. Trust your instincts. Know that you and your business have value and have a welcoming audience. Actively apply these traits and talents as you stay the course, reframing scenarios around solutions you can accomplish, not issues or past mistakes.

- **Keep things in perspective.** While negative events can seem overwhelming when they are occurring, if you step back and look at the big picture, you may find that their importance is actually minuscule. Reassess challenges from a more removed viewpoint; you may find they become more insignificant and easily surmountable as seemingly obvious solutions begin to reveal themselves. Failure is frequently just a state of mind, and one you can easily change by changing your perspective.

- **Maintain a hopeful outlook.** A little bit of optimism goes a long way. Instead of constantly worrying about the bad things that might happen, be optimistic. Think about the good things that can come to pass, visualize success, and then make it happen.

- **Take care of yourself.** Don't forget to take time out of your busy day for the most important person in your life: you. Exercise. Read. Take vacations. Do things that you like to do and that relax you. Rest and recharge your battery: You'll fight harder and better, especially after sustaining losses, than if you constantly hop from one battlefield to another.[12]

So why are these strategies so important? If you want to succeed, you must be able to bounce back from failure and adversity.

Not every setback is a showstopper: You can still lose a battle and win the war. You can't let failure, insecurity, or rejection get you down, beat you up, or otherwise dissuade you from achieving your ultimate goals. Sure, when you fail, you should take a step back—a time-out—to assess what went haywire. But don't remain in this position. Use this time to assess what went wrong and what you can do next time to more effectively achieve your goals.

The U.S. Army knows firsthand the value of soldiers who can bounce back not only from the rigors of combat but also from life's everyday challenges. The organization has created an entire school devoted to teaching resilience: the U.S. Army Master Resilience School (with the motto "Strength Through Resilience"). As the school's website says, "Being Army Strong is about much more than being physically fit; it is about mental and emotional strength, as well."[13]

Market leaders such as Microsoft and Intel fully understand the value of these principles as well. That's because their architects understand the odds against them; realize how many dead ends must be faced before breakthroughs are obtained; and know that those single, rare victories produce such powerful wins that they're worth every stalled attempt. (Not to mention recognizing the value of the learning gained along the way.)

If you're ever within a hundred miles of Waterbury, Vermont, take a few hours out of your schedule to visit Ben & Jerry's ice cream factory. If you do, you'll surely notice the company's flavor graveyard, replete with a white picket fence and numerous headstones. And on each headstone you'll find the name of a Ben & Jerry's flavor that was killed off by the business—in short, a failed product.

Despite the fact that the company has birthed plenty of dead flavors, Ben & Jerry's CEO Jostein Solheim thinks that's just fine. "We celebrate the failures," says Solheim, "because that is how we learn and that is how our organization learns to take risks. One of the strengths of our company is that we are not scared of failure. . . . It's an opportunity to push things further."[14] All these organizations embrace the concept of resilience: They know battles are won by learning to hold the line and by making a well-placed charge. To them, fear has become a simple equation: Pick your battles, wade in knowing the risks, and play fortune's chances. Then bounce back to make the odds work in your favor until you reap the benefits. To succeed, you've got to accept that failure can and will happen from time to time. But just because you've failed doesn't mean that you have to like it; take the steps needed to turn things around and you can drastically improve your situation.

Action Steps

The worries and doubts that we feel due to failure, or the fear of failure, can cause us mental and physical discomfort, and even pain. The more discomfort we feel, the less likely we are to pursue a particular course of action—even if it appears to have high odds of paying off. If you want to achieve your goals, get ahead in life and business, and create competitive advantage, you must be able to do what others won't or can't, and use failures in your life or business as stepping-stones to success. Build your tolerance levels and build your potential: Push past the barriers others turn away from to reap the rewards others miss out on. To turn failure into success and pain into gain in your life, consider taking the following steps:

- **Understand that failure happens and concerns will always be present.** This is true especially as risk, uncertainty, and competition grow. Acclimate yourself to these concerns and embrace them rather than avoiding or hiding from them.
- **Impartially study your fear of failure and rejection.** Acknowledge these concerns and what is causing them. Then confront your fears, learn from your experiences, and strategically respond—growing more familiar with your fears and more inoculated to their effects with each attempt.
- **Evaluate your own response to fear.** Determine why fear is having a negative effect on you, then visualize how good you will feel when you accomplish the goals you seek. Start pursuing them by taking small, positive, and productive actions that you can begin counting as successes. Focus on these successes and use them to build confidence and motivate you to keep racking up more wins. Use them as mileposts you can track to follow your progresses you achieve objectives, and continue setting bigger challenges for yourself.
- **Keep your goals front and center.** Stay excited and motivated to achieve them, and don't get distracted.
- **Push through the pain.** You can do this by realizing that the discomfort will go away, or recede, if you are willing to simply forge ahead despite it.
- **Exercise grit and determination.** Not just in your career, but in your business and personal life as well.
- **Train yourself to deal with adversity.** You can build your adversity muscles by realizing that things will get better and that

you will either achieve your goal or learn valuable lessons in the process, invariably setting yourself up succeed later.

- **Grow your ability to bounce back—both from victories and failures—by building resilience.** Resilience is a key business, career, and life skill, and you can build it within you by keeping things in perspective and nurturing a positive outlook.

Chapter Seven

Rule 5: Master the Art of Improvisation

If you're reading this book at the gym or on your lunch break, you may also have your headphones plugged in and streaming songs from online music services like Rhapsody or Pandora. But those tuning in to hear Kelly Clarkson or Bruno Mars belt out hits via rival Grooveshark are also saving CEO Sam Tarantino's company— and sanity—one chart-topping smash at a time.

In the late 2000s, streaming online music service Grooveshark was considered one of the Internet's most promising start-ups. But by 2012, which Tarantino calls "the year of 10,000 punches," its fortunes had changed drastically. Audience counts had shrunk from 30 to 12 million users.[1] Four record labels were simultaneously suing the company. And just as a kicker, Apple and Google had banned the business's mobile applications at the Recording Industry Association of America (RIAA)'s behest.

Compared with fast-growing competitor Spotify, which enjoyed both skyrocketing awareness and the blessing of music industry giants, Grooveshark was looking pretty bad. As Tarantino told me, "By the beginning of 2012, we had built a team of 160 people, and by April we were down to 45. It was tough."

Oh, and one small added hitch. Despite making $60,000 a year, 233 times less than the average CEO,[2] he was also flat broke.[3]

In the midst of this chaotic tumult, Tarantino could easily have called it quits. He'd encountered just about every unforeseen difficulty a business owner could imagine, including a number of wildly unexpected and potentially fatal mishaps. But he didn't, because while unpredictable events and the disruptions they create can create significant challenges, they're about the only certain thing in business now, especially for entrepreneurs like Tarantino. Moreover, Tarantino says, it's not as difficult as you think to adapt to and address them, and in doing so consistently create ways to bounce back.

The key: embracing the art of improvisation and always using the tools and resources available to create ways to bridge the gap, even if this means constructing solutions out of the unlikeliest materials that come to hand. Of course, to successfully do so, it doesn't hurt to prepare and plan in advance for unexpected surprises, keeping a few alternative escape routes and emergency supplies in stock as well.

"There's a lot of random luck in play [anytime], and it comes in bad and good spurts . . . but there's also seizing upon that luck," Tarantino admits. "Luck hits us no matter what. If you're not prepared for bad luck events, you're screwed. Success is defined [by] being prepared for bad luck events, and taking advantage of good luck events when they come."

Put simply: *Shift happens.*

And before it does, you'll need the flexibility to assess your situation impartially, realistically understand the challenges you face, and then plan and execute an adequate response. After a shift, you'll also have to review the results, adjust tactics accordingly, and try again. Being future-proof means being flexible, greeting change, and innovating your way out of problems by training yourself to put fear on the backburner, make decisions under duress, and make the most of the tools and resources available.

In December 2011, when lawsuits first came down hard, Grooveshark employees started abandoning ship in droves. By January, Tarantino and his partner were fighting. And by February, they'd begun to doubt the viability of their business.

But by March, despite the chaos, the company was back up and swinging. By implementing a web browser–based version of its app, it had found a workaround and was back on mobile devices. More than 3 million listeners were using the program. Today, the company has settled its suits with EMI and Sony Music, employs 85 people, and claims user counts are back up to 30 million.

As Tarantino and his team discovered, doing business is always a form of controlled chaos that can be navigated. Successful tactics are not finite things; they will always be tested by unexpected events, and must be adjusted to adapt to unforeseen twists and turns.

"Failure is a choice . . . if you come up short, then you come up short," he says. Faced by unexpected or unforeseen developments, Tarantino insists, you can't stop. "What we can control is what we do," he says. "Developing new products, and keeping our business at breakeven [level] or higher."

Tarantino and his colleagues took unforeseen change then

improvised and made it work, doing whatever it took within reason to get their business back on track.

Rule 5: The Art of Improvisation

The concept of *improvisation* in life and in business means taking action in a spontaneous and unexpected way. When faced with surprises, it means having to step well outside the box to create less-rigid approaches that are guided by gut feelings and the feedback we receive as we take action. Fear of losing control and fear of failure make us want to keep operating within well-defined boundaries. We may believe it's the easiest way to avoid making mistakes. But if current processes and procedures aren't working, we may inadvertently make additional mistakes in falling back on them, despite the comfort they provide. By improvising new approaches, we can often discover more effective ways to solve problems.

In fact, on a personal level, *Fast Company* says tomorrow's most successful leaders will be members of what it calls "Generation Flux": resilient professionals whose diverse experiences and talents can be adapted to many circumstances. Also on the rise are "T-shaped individuals"—that is, workers who enjoy mastery in one area, but also possess a working knowledge of many other fields. These individuals' competitive advantage isn't based just on intelligence or innate talent. It's their ability to quickly and effectively acclimate to change thanks to the knowledge, skills, and capabilities that they can deploy in fresh and unexpected ways.

In the same way that organizations must perpetually change and innovate to keep pace with changing circumstances and markets, so too must tomorrow's working professional. To deal with impending changes—expected or otherwise—it's essential to improvise.

At Harvard Business School, first-year students are now *required* to participate in a program called Field Immersion Experiences for Leadership Development (FIELD), which provides hands-on job training designed to teach spontaneous leadership through firsthand practice.[4] Preparing students to adapt to changing environments, the program is mandatory because it equips young adults with practical skills they need to succeed in today's ever-changing world (read: improvise and think fast on their feet).

"FIELD allows students to do something real and experience something they wouldn't be able to just by thinking about it," explains Kristen Fitzpatrick, senior director of career and professional development at Harvard Business School.[5] The reason this matters, she says, is that "Students are [increasingly] striking out on their own path and forging opportunities that previously didn't exist. There isn't somebody paving the path before them so they can just follow in their footsteps."

But Harvard students are finding ways to improvise outside the official curriculum as well. When a group of pupils she encountered had no product management experience or software engineering backgrounds, they improvised by creating their own independent study course and produced tangible high-tech products they could point to as proof of experience. Each promptly found employment in these fields.

On an organizational level, businesses assign equal importance to the art of improvisation. Charlie Collier, president of AMC Networks (responsible for smash hit TV shows *Mad Men* and

The Walking Dead) recently stated that when he interviews potential leadership hires, experience and proficiency are a given.[6] Instead, he gauges prospective candidates on how well they can think on their feet, approach unusual challenges, and respond to unexpected difficulties. Collier's intent is to discover "how quickly they can spot opportunities for change early, [be] flexible enough to move strategically toward addressing them, even when they may be outside business-as-usual parameters . . . and how quickly they will be able to adapt and make decisions that will have impact."

Instead of the most-decorated candidates, he looks for:

- Analytical thinkers who can make off-the-cuff decisions
- Creative pros who can strategize like businesspeople
- Finance experts who ask questions when numbers don't add up
- Marketers who can think like designers

As Collier explains, these are the employees who add disproportionate value to an organization—successful improvisers.

But why does improvisation matter so much in day-to-day operations? Because ongoing change is the new operating reality, and in environments in which constant shifts and reprioritizations are the norm, the solutions we seek must be as varied and unpredictable as the changes themselves.

In the business world, multiple solutions frequently exist, street smarts mean as much as classroom learning, and efforts are best tackled as a team. Creativity, spontaneity, and resourcefulness matter most in these scenarios, not the ability to spit back rote solutions or to apply familiar and widely accepted, but often wildly outdated or ineffective, approaches. Because success depends on your ability to be *ingenious*, not *a genius*, improvisational ability often counts for far more than intelligence or academic pedigree.

The more cleverly and creatively you utilize resources, connect dots, and put the pieces of the puzzle together, the better and faster you and your colleagues can get the job done. It's all in how well you improvise.

Playing Without Rules

So if all of us are improvising, why do some appear far more effective at exercising this talent? The answer lies in their willingness to be flexible, to be unself-conscious in their actions, and to roll with the punches.

As seen here and in earlier chapters, most organizations and people naturally prefer to operate within a comfortable and well-defined set of day-to-day rules. Trouble comes when change occurs outside of these fixed and familiar boundaries. The result is a profoundly disturbing and unpredictable state of confusion and disorder, commonly referred to as *chaos*.

But chaos can also bring great opportunities for those who understand it and are prepared to leverage it to their own advantage. Those bound by rigid rules and procedures often struggle when chaos erupts, while those who can improvise new approaches and solutions on the fly thrive and succeed; it's all a matter of perspective. We'll explore chaos (and how to better respond to it) in greater depth later in this chapter.

For now, simply realize that this means that we must constantly improvise to keep up with the unexpected shifts that constantly greet us . . . and that the scope, scale, and speed at which we must improvise should be equally dynamic.

According to leading experts, there are six major types of change:

- **Revolutionary.** A jolt to the larger system that is rapid and potentially deep, followed by a period of disruption
- **Evolutionary.** More incremental, often improvement oriented, and characterized by being continuous and cumulative
- **Transitional.** Moving from a current state to a future state without changing some fundamental paradigms
- **Transformational.** A significant, broad, and deep change that alters fundamental paradigms
- **Strategic.** Change that realigns an individual or organization's mission, environment, market, or strategy
- **Operational.** Altering how individuals and organizations work, including changing processes, systems, workflow, and design

Have you begun planning for these changes, and thinking about how you'll handle them or improvise solutions? If not, you've already got half a dozen reasons to start thinking ahead and getting ready to move fast.

Recently, IBM published a study of making change work, which looked at how more than 1,500 change practitioners, including many market-leading corporations worldwide, successfully dealt with changing environments. Among the most important skills they possessed was the ability to smartly rethink scenarios, revisit solutions, and readjust plans on a recurring basis. According to the study, "No longer will companies have the luxury of expecting day-to-day operations to fall into a static or predictable pattern. *In reality, the new normal is continuous change.*"[7]

To operate in such an uncertain and unpredictable professional environment, we must improvise and innovate, frequently and proactively, and work harder with less. But that's easier said than done. The faster change occurs, the more disorienting it can be. And the impact and implications of the extraordinary conditions in which we now find ourselves operating goes far beyond organizational discomfort. Change affects us in very personal and sometimes very acute ways. The negative effects that change can have on individuals include anxiety, frustration, uncertainty, distrust, heightened stress, fear, and depression.[8]

Individuals and enterprises are now constantly pummeled by change. They're also being hit in increasingly rapid blasts, like the powerful gusts of wind that buffet your home during an intense rainstorm. In such volatile environments, which can produce acute fears about uncertainty, failure, and prospective loss of control, improvisation isn't always an easy concept to embrace. But it's the only sure way to keep the walls from caving in.

In later sections, we'll explore ways that we can improvise, deal with change more readily, and more successfully guard against this tempest. Success begins by being willing to dial back fear, change your perspective, and reconsider your ability to dynamically steer and regain control of any situation.

Understand When Chaos Really Isn't

From the vantage point of your office, the business environment can seem quite confusing, intimidating, and disordered, just as a hurricane might seem if experienced in real time. But, if you were able to step back out of the gale or, even better, fly a few miles above it, you would begin to escape the proximity to the size, power, complexity, and intensity that creates this discomfort. And, for that matter, you'd discover the subtle forces behind the phenomenon.

Look a bit closer, in fact, and you would notice previously invisible physical patterns and spot symmetrical forces at work. What you will discover is evidence that a hurricane is actually an extremely complex and highly ordered system. It is far from the random assembly of rapidly moving and chaotic events that you may witness from the ground.

Corporations, organizations, and the markets in which they compete are also complex and volatile systems. Consider, for a moment, the seemingly random, day-to-day fluctuations of the stock market. One day, prices plunge; the next, stocks suddenly surge upward. Why? No one truly knows for sure; most chalk it up to investors' emotions and the random vagaries of the market. Viewed from a distance, however, the picture looks quite different. Over time, financial markets follow a distinct mathematical order that is so complex that it remains hidden to most of us.

In the 1970s, scientist Benoit Mandelbrot—father of the modern geometry of chaos—used powerful computers to analyze the fluctuations of the price of cotton over a very long period of time. (Cotton is one of the few commodities with more than two centuries of accurate transaction records.) He discovered that these seemingly random fluctuations in market price were not random at all. Instead, they had a discernible order.

Mandelbrot found definite patterns to what were previously considered to be unpredictable day-to-day fluctuations in price. Even more remarkably, when he looked at longer time periods (such as a month) he found that these daily patterns were almost exactly repeated, only on a larger scale. Extrapolating this behavior to modern financial markets, Mandelbrot noted, "The geometry that describes the shape of coastlines and the patterns of galaxies also elucidates how stock prices soar and plummet."[9]

In recent years, Mandelbrot's mathematically derived model has become a valuable tool that leaders use with increasing frequency. It helps them understand how seemingly minor changes in the business environment can metamorphose over time into major events. It also helps them define "zones of probability": boundaries within which the odds of predictability (and therefore the likelihood of making successful decisions) are dramatically enhanced.

The message for individuals and organizations is this: While conditions and events encountered may appear chaotic, irrational, and unpredictable from the inside, when viewed from a distance they are often the exact opposite. Business leaders may not always be able to bring order out of chaos, but they can certainly learn to understand the true meaning of chaos, and readapt their strategy to respond more effectively and capitalize upon it—that is, improvise smart solutions to match.

Every day, for example, United Airlines operates more than 5,600 flights to 374 destinations, ranging from Cleveland to Tokyo.[10] As manager of IT administration for service recovery applications, Jay Hakim observed that unforeseen issues such as electrical storms could cause massive delays, reroutes, or cancellations. Hundreds of employees, who averaged three to five minutes per passenger to correct these issues, were required to get operations back on course.

Then a customer on a delayed flight brought up a good point. Knowing that the plane would be delayed, the company could have started the rebooking process long before it ever landed. In response, the airline instituted United's Customer Automated Reaccommodation System (CARS), designed to automatically and optimally rebook travelers affected by delays or cancellations before touchdown. The system, which takes just three seconds to process each record, served nearly 3 million customers in 2012 alone.[11] One simple shift in viewpoint allowed United to successfully improvise a more capable and cost-effective solution and effectively apply it to the most unpredictable of environments.

Take a step back and look at your problems from a different angle, and you may be surprised at just how effective a change in perspective can be. Four key strategies can help you improvise more effectively and ride the waves of even the most chaotic seas:

- **Embrace unpredictability.** It is impossible to remove uncertainty from any business equation. To best leverage the power of chaos, you need to plan for the worst, hope for the best, and be proactive about preparing for change and applying adaptive strategies when it comes. Disruptions to the status quo don't just upend operating realities, they also create new windows of opportunity; be quick to improvise and act on them.

- **Become a more objective observer.** Be willing to approach challenges with a truly open mind. Pay attention to the finer details that may reveal emerging patterns and trends associated with these changes. Be comfortable taking time to identify the most promising and potentially beneficial aspects inherent in these challenges. Then take necessary steps to ensure that you'll succeed.

- **Be patient.** The underlying opportunities in any given situation often take time to reveal themselves. Don't react out of haste or misguided instinct. Instincts will help provide you with inspiration, but intellect must govern your actions as you go about the improvisational process.

- **Think on your feet.** Once you decide to ride the waves of chaos, you can begin to subtly steer emerging developments in advantageous directions. Via this process, you can flow with and around them versus letting them crash against you. To do so, though, you'll have to take deliberate action and course correct in real time as new events unfold.

Trying to impose order on chaos is ultimately quixotic. Today's most effective leaders don't fight chaos. Instead, they look for (and understand) emerging patterns in their markets, identify and isolate the ones that have the most promise, and manipulate them to their advantage. The more you improvise and work with what you've got, acknowledging the circumstances and tools at hand, the more you enable yourself to go with the flow and channel it toward more productive uses.

Improvising in Your Career

OK, so we know everything is in constant flux, and what tools and techniques it takes to improvise and get ahead in the business world. But how to navigate today's rapidly shifting career landscape? The answer is simple. Chart a course and begin sailing your ship through this sea of uncertainty. Then steer it back on track when incoming currents and tides threaten to carry it away.

Stop looking at a new career path as a road map. Start looking at it as a sea chart instead. Keep navigating however choppy the waters or roundabout the course.

To succeed today in a world of infinite choices and challenges, you must:

- Take existing systems and structures for career advancement with a grain of salt.
- Set aside fears, size up the reality of the scenario sans bias or prejudice, and react accordingly.
- Apply these insights and align the right actions with the right opportunities to drive the results you desire.
- Readjust your course in time with shifting environments and navigate around career hazards when barriers or stumbling blocks threaten to bar your way forward.
- Create your own personal and career development plan and execute it, adapting to changing needs and times.
- Invest in growing your own tools, talents, and capabilities, rather than investing solely in helping others grow their own.
- Accept that career and job shifts can and will happen, and plan and prepare for them before they occur.

The good news: Contrary to what fear and anxiety tell us, we are always in control of the situation.

Consider the example of Pamela O'Leary, whose career came to an abrupt dead end after completing graduate school, an internship at the United Nations, and a congressional fellowship in Washington, D.C. Unemployed and more than $100,000 in debt, she was understandably anxious about her future prospects. However, rather than give up, O'Leary considered her situation, plotted a path to stability, and took action by getting more training and further developing and leveraging her network of contacts.

Within two years, O'Leary was named executive director of the Public Leadership Education Network, a nonprofit that specializes in preparing college women for public policy careers. As O'Leary told *Forbes* magazine, "Was this luck? No way. I have my dream job because all along the way I relentlessly pursued professional development opportunities and established a strong network of colleagues. If you're in a dead-end job or feeling stuck in your career, know that the power to change that is in your hands."[12]

Examples of the power of improvisation at work are plentiful:

▪ Cora Edwards was a poor English immigrant working graveyard shifts in a cold doughnut shop in upstate New York. After taking online courses at Western Governors University (a competency-focused institute founded by nineteen state governors to provide vocational training) and obtaining her master's degree in nursing, she now educates registered nurses herself. "I'm rewriting policy and procedures, formulating different programs, and training other staff members," she says.

- Aspiring twentysomething entrepreneur Steve Espinosa's business prospects had started to stall, until Weblogs cofounder Jason Calacanis posted publicly on Twitter asking if anyone had a ticket for an upcoming Los Angeles Lakers basketball game. Espinoza responded that he did (despite having none), that his seats were great (he quickly searched for and bought some online), and offered to meet Calacanis (they connected two days later). Determined to show Calacanis the value he could provide him, Espinoza got to talking and gladly did some free consulting work; later, Calacanis would invest thousands in his start-up.

- An architect by trade, Richard Saul Wurman became interested in many subjects in his off-hours. He's since become a prolific author, academic, and event organizer. Among other accomplishments, the self-made polymath, who says he has no skill set and is simply curious, founded the popular TED conferences.

- Baby boomer Linda Lombri, a home economics major, was determined to expand into other fields. So she got an MBA at Drexel, and then moved into marketing communications, consumer research, and publications. When she got laid off, she parlayed her communications and project management skills into a second (fourth?) career in self-publishing books.

- Marketing major Adam Witty had no idea what he wanted to do with his life. Then a friend who was a motivational speaker suggested that every speaker needed a book and someone to publish it. Months later, with little experience, Witty hopped a plane and manned a tiny booth at the National Speakers Association convention. He left with thirteen signed contracts and a fast-growing business.

- Joel Massel was a biologist. But he realized that he loved the social aspects of the discipline more than the science. So he put himself through law school, only to realize, six years later, that he was tired of being a litigator. Luckily, between these career shifts, he'd picked up several skills, such as a knack for interpersonal communications, research, and strategic planning. Mixing and matching all of them, he now runs a successful association management business.

So here's how you can look at your career: from the perspective of someone in the captain's chair, or from the rear cabin. You can wait for instructions, wait until you believe you're qualified, and wait until the perfect moment to take a chance. Alternately, you can take the lead, qualify yourself, and set sail for success now, course correcting as you go, creating one opportunity after another by taking decisive and measured action. In other words, you can sit back and passively wait for things to happen or you can improvise; chart a way forward; and by continuing to stay focused and to improvise, watch your prospects soar.

To safely journey through the modern career landscape, you must:

- Choose a logical path forward that best aligns with your core objectives.
- Set foot on it and continuously forge ahead.
- Have the good sense to adapt to changes in its course.
- Veer around obstacles.
- Learn from these encounters.

- Apply insights gained to future ventures.
- Improvise and keep solving problems as you go.

The secret to career success today is to be agile, elastic, and flexible—keeping one's eye on long-term objectives, and making short-term moves that, while seemingly counterintuitive, advance these larger goals. Despite having to take a pay cut, drop in rank, and/or change jobs or industries, by picking up new contacts, training, and insights and by making the right moves—up, down, over, or around—at the right time, you can use the momentum provided to vault yourself farther in the end.

Like many businesses, careers are increasingly fickle and fragile things. According to Siobhan O'Mahony, chair of strategy and innovation for Boston University's business school, the traditional model for professional advancement is predicated on four assumptions:

- Stable organizations in stable environments
- A hierarchy of job positions to ascend
- An intra-organizational focus
- Career mobility within large organizations

O'Mahony and her collaborator, New York University professor Beth Bechky, argue that career planning strategies have not kept pace with changes in the workplace, including the following areas:

- Inter-organizational mobility
- Shorter professional tenures
- Horizontal and lateral career moves
- The growing importance of external hires and labor markets

In the postindustrial world, the pair argues, we're now confronted with a *career progression paradox.*

Specifically, when employers have no knowledge of a person's capabilities or potential, they use prior experience as a screening mechanism. If you're an unknown or unproven quantity, though (say, an aspiring senior leader), that's a problem. How do you demonstrate your talent or ability to expand your core competencies because employers don't know what you can do in the first place? It's a classic chicken-and-egg problem.

The problem is particularly relevant to the growing number of contract and short-term workers, who may be provided less training and education, as businesses don't see them as long-term investments. They are provided with little in the way of career guidance, growth, or development. Likewise, without being provided any experience beyond what's demanded in their contract agreements, it's not hard for them to feel they have a lack of professional options or have reached a career plateau.

Studying these groups, O'Mahony and Bechky found that workers weren't able to resolve the career progression paradox by just embracing the unknown. They did so by willingly diving headfirst into new potential areas of personal and professional growth and opportunity.

The secret to success for these contractors and short-term professionals is not luck, talent, or intelligence but a relentless drive to acquire new skills by taking on assignments that stretch their capabilities. Essentially, to deal with changing and unknown environments, each applied a simple strategy: slowly but surely expanding their toolbox of talents and capabilities to match. To accomplish these goals, contractors wouldn't just seek out jobs that paid the bills. They'd purposefully pursue roles that leveraged competence in existing areas in new ways to convey additional talents and experiences.

For example, IT contractors would take basic skills learned on one software program, purposefully study up on another, faster-growing program, then experiment with using it until they became adept with the latter tool.

Likewise, entry-level film workers would take on jobs (and job responsibilities) in various departments, such as art, wardrobe, and lighting, that required overlapping talents and capabilities. Each helped these professionals gain core vocational skills that, as O'Mahony and Beckhy say, like clay, could be shaped toward more specialized career paths during future assignments.

These types of individuals used four tactics to succeed in uncertain and unknown environments:

- **Differentiating competence**. Performing one's job exceptionally well and building a solid reputation. Workers would distinguish themselves through superior effort and, in doing so, build trust with peers while simultaneously bolstering awareness and respect for their talents.

- **Acquiring referrals**. Extending and drawing on professional networks to leverage credentials in one setting or area to make the jump to new areas, organizations, and industries. Translation: They'd use existing contacts to provide needed recommendations to others for the chance to exhibit their talents to fresh audiences.

- **Framing and bluffing**. Faking it until they made it. Contractors wouldn't just routinely put on a courageous front, they'd also reposition and repackage their talents and experiences so as to link areas of demonstrated competence with those required by new roles and tasks that stretched their skill sets.

■ **Discounting**. Accepting lower pay or making *sidesteps* or *backsteps* (discussed later in this chapter) to grow their skills, experience, contacts, connections, or opportunities. One technical writer said he'd turned down three six-figure offers in a single week to accept a job that paid half as much but that allowed him to become proficient in new technologies and tools.

As you can see, successfully traveling the new career wavelength requires improvisation. Move sideways into a position of equal rank and pay (into an organization that offers more opportunities for advancement or career growth), take a backstep by moving down the ladder and accepting a less prestigious title or less pay (say, leaving a Fortune 500 business to work for a start-up for the chance to gain new skills and hands-on experience, or work in emerging and innovative markets), or take a *slingshot* by making both a sidestep and a backstep while staying focused on your ultimate career target. When you apply the knowledge, experience and skills gained through these moves, you'll leap far ahead.

The only way to know which will work for sure is to study your situation, objectively review your options, and then improvise a solution that helps you best get the job done. Keep doing so over and over again and watch your experience, education, skills, and opportunities grow exponentially with each new effort.

Application Is the New Education

But improvisation isn't just a vital new survival skill for market-leading organizations or modern professionals to possess. Mastering the art of improvisation should be considered imperative for those preparing to take their fledgling steps in the working world as well.

In this fast-moving, overcrowded market, you've got to think differently, because the future belongs to B+ students. Tomorrow, victory doesn't go to pedagogues or perfectionists. It goes to those who apply just enough effort to meet premium standards (a principle that economists refer to as *satisficing*) and devote time that would otherwise be applied toward diminishing returns (what's the practical, real-world difference between scoring an A- and B+ again?) to more productive uses. In short, those who'll win going forward will create more opportunities to improvise and build their own education, experiences, and career paths as they go.

Instead of simply spitting back answers or applying historical solutions (talents that pupils are currently graded on), in the future, savvy individuals will improvise new ideas while delivering just enough effort to earn conventional accolades. Simultaneously, they'll buy themselves additional time—time that can be better spent honing their insights, enhancing their creative capabilities, and crafting more inventive approaches. They'll then generate new opportunities to apply the fresh approaches they've created and to learn in context. In effect, their education begins, not ends, when they leave the classroom.

How is it that self-taught successes continue to amaze us in growing numbers, even as likelier candidates (every mother's beloved straight-A student) continue to face increasing difficulty going forward? Because technological and communications break-throughs have leveled the playing field, and they're constantly seeking new ways to keep up with these changing environments and run rings around rivals by rewriting the playbook. In such a crowded, competitive, and challenging environment, the winning solutions are now the unique (visible), most useful (beneficial), and highest value-adding (irreplaceable). Because the business land-scape has changed and because yesterday's tactics have become so predictable, falling back on the same plays increasingly produces less surprising and less effective results. By being more resourceful and creative, innovators are inventing new ways to win with each passing day, even as rivals struggle to react.

It's not about being smarter or more experienced, it's about being savvier and more resourceful. As a result, traits such as clev-erness, practicality, and leadership are becoming far greater arbi-ters of success than abilities or accolades.

So ask yourself: Why is it we prize innovators above all others, yet do precious little to promote entrepreneurial thinking? Not *every* college student has the capacity to be Mark Zuckerberg (or wants to). But many more *could be* if we gave them the training to do so.

As bestselling author Seth Godin, the author of the educa-tional reform manifesto *Stop Stealing Dreams*, explains, we need to start asking ourselves, What is school for? According to him, vital skills we need—such as learning how to deal with adversity and apply inventive solutions in context—aren't being provided during classroom hours. To gain a more well-rounded education, Godin strongly urges parents to push their kids to take on extra-curricular projects and expand their experiences and comfort zones, while risks are still minimal. But Godin points to a problem with this approach: "Many (young people) aren't taking these opportunities because they're too busy getting an A in classes."[13]

How helpful those A's are remains questionable. Pew Research finds that just 55 percent of graduates believe college was useful in helping them prepare for jobs, while less than half of current students and employers feel it adequately prepares them for the working world.[14]

More so than formal education, said Godin, tomorrow's leaders are winning through the art of improvisation. Nolan Bushnell, founder of Atari and coauthor of *Finding the Next Steve Jobs* (and the man who gave Apple's founder his first gig), seconds this notion. People learn far more from undertaking hands-on projects, pursuing hobbies, and trying new experiments than they do sitting in front of a textbook, he asserts.

As you can see, to succeed in tomorrow's world, we can't just be smart. We also have to be savvy. Doing so requires that we constantly be learning and recalibrating viewpoints and approaches as we go. The goal isn't to be a better student; it's to be a more adaptive, inventive, and practical one.

Teach yourself to improvise, and you can teach yourself to get an A+ in life and business, regardless of what you score on tests or what you've paid for your education. You don't need an MBA. You don't need a PhD. You need a GSD (get stuff done) degree, and all it takes to earn is a willingness to change and innovate, allowing you to readily adapt to and deal with whatever stumbling blocks life throws your way.

Every Challenge Is Just a Puzzle to Be Solved

As anyone in business knows, the path to success is paved with challenges, some of which are more difficult than others. However, even the most difficult challenges can be solved. New products can be developed, competitors can be defeated, customers can be dazzled. Limitations are deceptive—doubly so given our boundless ability to improvise. Each challenge you face in life and business is simply a riddle waiting to be solved. You can solve these puzzles by:

- Weighing the odds and challenges associated with decisions
- Giving yourself permission to experiment, fail, and try again
- Creating an action plan and executing it
- Considering where you're coming up short and why
- Modifying your strategy based on these insights
- Repeating these steps as necessary

Getting to know our fears and the challenges we face and responding productively by improvising countermeasures and solutions are crucial talents for successfully working through conundrums.

The trick to doing so, whether you're an organization or individual, says leadership coach Jake Breeden, is to change your perspective. Shift from one in which you prepare only before encountering challenges to one in which you're in a constant state of alertness and preparation. Whatever life throws at you, be ready to react. Don't let your desire for perfection paralyze you, and don't hesitate to dynamically invent your own response to events as they unfold. There's always more than one right answer, but doing nothing is not one.

Remember the popular 1980s Rubik's Cube toy? Trying to match the colored squares on each side seemed impossible. But it's actually easy once you know the trick. Using the popular layer method, you simply pick one side and one set of pieces and unravel the riddle one layer at a time. Life works similarly. Instead of being intimidated by the larger puzzle, start by focusing on small pieces and then slowly, steadily turn the blocks until they tumble neatly into place.

But here's the kicker: The layer method is just one of many plausible solutions. Take a second look at the challenge before you, the material you're working with, and the resources you can bring to bear, and you may find many ways to unravel the riddle.

As a simple example, ask yourself, How can you be in two places at once? Kurt Kerns, drummer for the gold-selling band Gravity Kills, knows all too well.

With three albums and a thousand shows in four years, Kerns should've been living the rock-and-roll dream. Instead, his band was owed $60,000 in unpaid tour support and outstanding royalties on sales of their records. He was also living on his wife's $24,000-a-year day job.

Then, one day, disaster struck. "The checks just stopped coming," Kerns says.[15] "After selling hundreds of thousands of records . . . TVT [his failing record company] said they weren't giving us anymore and that we had to go home." Worse, Napster had just launched, so radio stations were cutting regular playlist rotations back drastically. He was just turning thirty, with a new baby girl at home.

It wasn't the first time Kerns had faced difficulties: A former tour manager had embezzled $40,000, so Kerns had learned to negotiate contracts, make T-shirts, and hire/fire traveling roadies. But just because the record suddenly skipped a beat again didn't mean it stopped for him. Hanging up his drum kit, Kerns remixed his life, leveraging his love for music, ear for acoustics, and architecture degree into a burgeoning career building high-end performance spaces. Today, he runs V3 Studios, a leading St. Louis–based design firm that caters to clients like Washington University, the city's art museum, and CBS Radio. But Kerns doesn't credit hit records for his success. Instead, he credits a sense of practicality, instilled by his father, a small-business owner, who taught him the art of improvisation. As Kerns points out, whether you're an enterprise or an individual, navigating a successful path through the professional world has become more complex and less certain than ever before. Our journeys have more zigs, more zags, and more ups and downs than any generation has ever seen.

Nonetheless, Kerns insists there's a simple cure for related concerns. Be open to change, learn as you go, constantly course correct, and always live 10 to 20 percent outside your comfort zone. In short, *improvise* and make it work, then keep making it work again and again.

Action Steps

The old rules no longer guarantee success, if they ever did. To future-proof yourself for the long run, you, your teams, and your organization must learn how to freestyle to create new ways of doing things and making things happen. But improvisation doesn't occur in a vacuum; you need to constantly learn new things and prepare yourself to adapt to changes in the environment. To put improvisation to work for you, take the following action steps:

- **Focus on the positive aspects of change in your business or career.** This includes such things as opportunities for growth, learning, and adaptation. Then actively seek them out and do whatever it takes to leverage or put them to work for you.
- **Don't let emotions get in the way.** It's essential that you are able to see the reality of the challenges and scenarios you'll confront and how best to address them.
- **Understand that there is order to what appears to be chaos.** With a simple shift in mind-set or vantage point you can learn to improvise and surf the waves instead of being drowned by them.
- **Embrace unpredictability.** Become a more objective observer, be patient, and think on your feet.
- **Seek out new opportunities for learning and gaining added resources, capabilities, and knowledge.** The more tools you have at your disposal, the more flexibility you'll enjoy and the more effective you will be.
- **Constantly move forward in your career.** Use sidesteps, backsteps, and slingshot moves, improvising as necessary, to keep yourself on a generally upwardly mobile track.
- **Accept that everything is unpredictable.** Strive to control only those variables that are within your ability to influence.
- **Get to know your fears.** You'll be able to react and respond more intelligently on the fly.

Chapter Eight

Rule 6: Play the Odds

If you're looking for a good way to piss off your company's CEO, try second-guessing his or her vision in an email message sent to your coworkers and cc'ing senior leadership—particularly if said CEO is Microsoft founder Bill Gates.[1]

That didn't stop then-twenty-four-year-old J Allard, when he was a recently hired network engineer, from writing a history-making memo, "Windows: The Next Killer Application on the Internet."[2] But penning the document didn't get him fired, it actually got him *promoted*. And it permanently changed high-tech history, persuading the company to embrace connectivity and train its sights on Netscape's Mosaic online browser.

What followed was the stuff of business legend. Microsoft's subsequent shift from selling DOS to giving away Internet Explorer (destined to attain a 95 percent market share by 2003) was a significant sea change in its business strategy. And, of course, Allard meteorically ascended the corporate ranks. But for such a bold gamble, you may be surprised to hear his take: "I saw zero risk in writing that memo."

For most, it may seem a gutsy play. The move could easily have resulted in Allard's public humiliation or rebuke or led to him being ostracized or fired.

But according to Allard, there was absolutely nothing brave about taking this action. Doing nothing would actually have been the *riskier* step.

"When I interviewed at Microsoft, I said, 'A computer on every desk and every home is inevitable now.... the next step in computing is connecting them all together.' But I wasn't making enough traction as an individual contributor then, so I needed to enlist more people. The worst situation for me would have been to feel like I was investing at cross-purposes or that I wasn't doing all that I could to speed us along in our mission. Writing [the note] was *easy*."[3]

From Allard's perspective, here's how the organization could have responded:

1. **People could ignore it.** Outcome: No different from having not written the memo.
2. **People could have argued against what I said and we could have chosen to declare war on the Internet.** Outcome: Clarity that my purpose and the company's purpose no longer aligned. Exit.
3. **People could have been inflamed that I spoke out and reprimanded me.** Outcome: Same as 2.

4. **People could have slowly embraced it and left me out of the picture.** Outcome: Better than 1, 2, or 3.

5. **People could have rapidly embraced it and engaged me to help.** Outcome: Exactly what I wanted.

"Where was the 'risk' in this set of outcomes?" he asked, weighing the odds of each outcome in his mind.

As a result of his convictions and willingness to double down on his vision, Allard wouldn't just be hailed as "Microsoft's Father of the Internet."[4] He'd later be handed the keys to the Xbox (video game system) and Zune (portable music player) divisions.

His story contains valuable choices from which we can all learn. Chief among them: staring down myriad fears and taking the steps needed to put things right, all by playing some very smart bets.

You can do the same and with even less risk. All you have to do is act in an equally calculated way when contemplating any intimidating situation in which you find yourself. Define the challenges you face, quantify possible outcomes, and explore potential recourses. Then play the odds by pursuing the choices you believe will be most favorably received and do so over and over again until you find the success you seek. Your chances of getting ahead are larger than you think.

As Allard eloquently puts it, "When people think about 'risk' or talk about 'career suicide,' I wonder what's in their heads. If you and your employer share a common purpose, and are on the same team and invested in each other, there's no such thing."

Allard urges modern executives to think about fear and risk like cholesterol. As he explains, *healthy risk* can be defined as pursuing an agenda, an idea, or a responsibility beyond your comfort zone but one that you believe you are fully qualified to tackle. (Even though you may need to learn and get some help.) *Unhealthy risk* is when you step into the red zone that anxiety can cause or when you're unqualified to accomplish an objective.

We often shy away from taking any risks, let alone healthy ones, despite their obvious importance, because of the many common fears we face.

Rule 6: Play the Odds

If the risks (and corresponding fears) associated with subjects like change, uncertainty, and failure are primarily a game of chance, get comfortable with the odds and prepare yourself to play them. As the saying goes, "Luck is hard work." If the odds are 100 to 1 against an investment hitting, make 100 investments; if your average closing rate is 10 percent and you're looking to land 20 new sales contracts, make 200 calls. Winners consistently place themselves in the path of opportunity and make probability work in their favor when it presents itself. As Woody Allen put it, 80 percent of success in life is showing up; it's not surprising that another 10 percent is having something meaningful to say when you do. (Our management consulting firm, TechSavvy, has landed its biggest contracts in the same way it's established its most vital customer relationships: simply by picking up the phone.)

Entrepreneurs may be the ultimate gamblers in business. Few seasoned vets truly ever put themselves, their money, or even their investors' money at great risk. But starting a business is itself a risky activity. Each month in the United States, about 543,000 new businesses are started. Of these new businesses, roughly 70 percent survive for two years, 50 percent for five years, and about 33 percent for ten years.[5] That's hardly a sure bet, but entrepreneurs are willing to roll the dice anyway. It's a process that has brought us many of the world's most celebrated firms, from McDonald's to Walmart, the University of Phoenix to Edible Arrangements.

Employees also play the odds on the job every day. Workers count on employers and markets to remain stable enough to provide steady income and benefits. Professionals also play the odds when they pitch new marketing campaigns, undertake new research projects, or explore new markets. Every time workers, from temps and interns up to senior executives, volunteer to take on new roles and responsibilities, they're rolling the dice. But all find the courage to proceed anyway, judging the potential benefits to far outweigh the risks. And these benefits can take many forms: valuable new experiences, contacts, and opportunities to demonstrate that they're meaningful contributors.

The lessons to be learned here are as follows:

- See things objectively.
- Understand the challenges you face.
- Gauge your chances of success.
- Weigh potential losses against potential gains.
- Be willing to take measured risks.
- Seek ways to put yourself in chance's sights.
- Take action when opportunity presents itself.

In other words, never mind common fears like loss of certainty, failure, or rejection and forget others, such as fear of change, embarrassment, insecurity, or isolation. Instead, shake yourself out of that comfort zone: Constantly put yourself in chance's sights, keep making smart bets, and be ready to capitalize on opportunities to advance when they manifest. It's the only sure way to keep getting ahead.

Consider venture capitalists. These wealthy investors have mastered this principle because they have no choice. According to research by Harvard Business School, three out of every four venture capital–backed start-ups fail, and 95 percent never break even.[6] As University of California at Berkeley professor Toby Stuart points out, these firms make many bets, few of which pay off. But despite the small odds of success, the bets that actually hit make a big enough impact to make gambling worthwhile.

On a personal level, you can win by following a similar betting strategy. Modern successes knock on many doors and don't fret failure. As we saw earlier, making mistakes, stumbling, and reacting (read: trying new tactics, approaches, and angles) is how we learn. Some wagers win, others lose; as long as you're intelligent about the hands you play and intelligently diversify, it all evens out in the end. Better yet, winning conditions exist in all scenarios (even if you technically lose, you can still gain crucial insights, connections, and learning from every attempt), and no often means "no for now"—strategies and circumstances change.

Whether you're an individual or enterprise, knock on many doors and sow many seeds. You'll be surprised how many swing open when you play the odds and when you're persistent. It's all about your willingness to make smart bets and keep making them time and again. Rather than spend all your time gathering and hoarding your chips, instead, get ready to gamble.

Risky Is the New Safe

Today, it's safer to take risks than it is to risk playing it safe. If the statement seems counterintuitive, consider the following: Successful organizations are inherently risk takers, despite some commonly held beliefs to the contrary. As they're aware, new products, markets, and opportunities don't create themselves. They're created through decisive action—action that's difficult, if not impossible, to take for those who are hesitant to change and innovate.

Successful individuals are gamblers as well. They constantly work to expand their comfort zone, take measured risks, and tinker with winning formulas, even their own recipes for success.

When faced with challenges or problems, we all understand the need to adapt strategies and solutions to fit shifting challenges and environments. Because like many current cures for potential problems, there's no assurance that these antidotes will work as rapidly or effectively the next time they're applied. As many leaders have learned, the best medicine is, in fact, the one best suited to the problem at hand. In changing times, both professionals and businesses must innovate (gamble), and innovate often, just to keep up with rivals, let alone stay ahead of the curve.

As in tennis, though, you can't win the game by playing defense alone. To score points, you have to constantly take swings at the ball. Similarly, to smash one past competitors, you've always got to be seeking promising openings in the defense. But spotting these openings isn't enough. You must also be willing to act on these chances, always stepping forward—keeping one foot planted in the present and one in the future—while merrily swinging away to be effective.

You and your organization face a similar choice. You can play it safe in the wake of rising competition and diminishing returns, watching the playing field grow steadily tougher. Alternately, you can rewrite the rules of engagement, stack the odds in your favor, press forward, and outperform rivals time and again. Like PepsiCo CEO Indra Nooyi recently told *Fast Company*: "Market growth alone doesn't give you enough tailwind [to continue succeeding and growing] . . . you have to create your own."[7]

But if the prospect of taking risks seems scary, remember: Acting risky and acting reckless aren't the same thing.

We can all borrow a page here from so-called business mavericks. From TV kingpin Ted Turner to hedge-fund manager John Paulson,[8] studies reveal a surprising truth about today's most celebrated risk takers.[9] Successful entrepreneurs aren't the speculators you might imagine. In actuality, they carefully pick and choose their bets. By minimizing risk, maximizing opportunity, and manipulating odds in their favor, many take few chances whatsoever.

We all fight little battles on a daily basis with every action and decision we make. As many business leaders have surmised, it's harder to lose these battles when you weigh the odds, dictate the rules of engagement, and decide when, where, and how they will take place. (A topic we'll discuss further in Chapter 10.)

The most important battle you'll ever fight? Deciding whether to stand up and take action in the face of changing environments (take measured risks) or remain static (pretend you're not gambling, but wind up passively playing the odds anyway). You can gauge your chances, plot a viable strategy, and pick yourself up and run with your ideas. You can play it safe, waiting until others' choices spur you into taking the initiative. But the one thing you can't afford to do is sit still while the world turns, and competitors are in constant motion.

Whatever choices we make, though, realize that we are *always* gambling. You might as well know what you're betting on.

Playing the Odds in Your Career

Following the traditional career path—graduating college, taking graduate classes, getting a job with an established and successful business—may feel safe and comfortable, but thanks to fast-changing odds, there is no guarantee of long-term happiness and success to be found there any longer. Those building their careers today would do well to reconsider the odds and place new bets by seeking the paths less taken and to take the risk of supplementing their experience, skill set, and education with uncommon experiences and wisdom.

Facebook COO Sheryl Sandberg, author of *Lean In*, suggests that the path to the top is now more jungle gym than escalator. But this concept presupposes that rungs exist to climb on and that others have put them in place for you. That's incorrect.

Today, the process of scaling career heights is more like free climbing up a sheer cliff face. To ascend it, you'll have to carve out your own handholds, pioneer new trails, and cling to convenient outcrops for leverage as you climb upward and onward, assessing the odds of success for each move along the way.

You must be prepared to circle around or even double back on your chosen route. As discussed earlier, sometimes you've got to assume a less-advanced job title in a different department (or even take a pay cut) to learn new skills or switch roles or organizations to boost opportunities for advancement. To maneuver around un-expected cave-ins or dead ends, all you can do is keep weighing the odds, considering potential payoffs, and picking the most promising new trail to follow. What's more, the only safety harness available is the one you create yourself. But if you look to the fu-ture, plan ahead and make intelligent bets, you can attach it to the professional equivalent of a bungee cord that can not only save your butt but—as you begin to bounce back—also help vault you to unexpected heights.

Amber Case knows this path well. Your average college senior, she faced the same challenges as many others graduating during the Great Recession. An anthropology and sociology major with little real-world experience, she quailed at the idea of diving head-first into a hostile hiring market. But more worried still of being trapped in a low-paying, dead-end job, and dubious of a graduate degree's ultimate value, she instead decided to transform her life into a self-directed MBA program.

Committing five years to tackling a semester-like timeline of self-imposed challenges, she decided that the odds for success favored bold action. Case bid the academic and working world adieu and then built a personal and professional development cur-riculum designed to systematically eliminate perceived shortcom-ings as well as her doubts and fears.

Although Case saw herself as an awkward introvert, she was determined to fill gaps in her experience and skill set. She declined full-time employment and instead worked about twenty hours a week to make rent while spending eighty hours completing self-directed goals. In her mind, the hands-on learning and contacts she gained would far outweigh the value provided by a routine nine-to-five job.

Risky? Yes. Rewarding? Definitely.

Even as media outlets began to fill with stories of under-employed or jobless twentysomethings, Case watched her own opportunities and self-assurance multiply. After completing every goal on her list ahead of schedule, she proceeded to found and then sell a successful technology start-up. (Not to mention become the youngest-ever member of Lewis & Clark College's board of trustees.) As Case explains, the bets she made weren't nearly as bold or risky as the gambles her classmates elected to play by putting their faith in a broken system.

The only difference between herself and her classmates is, she says, a willingness to embrace the unknown, to play the odds, and to take risks. She had made a promise to herself: *However unfamiliar and uncomfortable any given task or situation seems, it's OK to feel self-conscious and in over my head.* Win or lose, she knew she'd increase her confidence and capabilities by making each attempt.

Years after the financial meltdown, millions of workers, especially young professionals, face hurdles similar to Case and her peers.[10] Not least among them, says the Economic Policy Institute, is an extremely difficult job market defined by skyrocketing competition, shrinking income, and limited advancement opportunities.[11] Due to economic uncertainty, its researchers note, how well students perform academically and how much schooling they pursue appears increasingly irrelevant. As Case discovered, it's practicality that counts.

Despite traditional advice—work hard, study hard, and so on—given by well-meaning advisers, it's time to wake up and realize that the game has fundamentally changed. When you play by yesterday's rules and consider yesterday's odds, you've got a snowball's chance in hell of winning.

Eight New Career Principles

Knowing that careers are no longer linear and predictable, we must be more flexible and calculating when considering the bets we make surrounding them. Recognizing and acting on the following principles can stack the odds in your favor:

- **Good enough is no longer good enough.** To assuage fear, remain competitive, and succeed today, you must be essential, not just a generic cog that can easily be replaced by someone who is more highly motivated or less expensive. For example, you might be the department's expert on reconciling complex regulatory issues, a highly sought-after internal thought leader or mentor, or a crucial contributor to its new products engineering team. If the problems you solve and results you produce are easily documented, measured, and replicated, rest assured that others will be able to perform these tasks better, faster, and cheaper—and diminish their worth. If your expertise can be described and taught in a training manual, you're already irrelevant. To succeed, you must instead see opportunities others haven't. You must solve problems most don't realize exist. And you must create connections waiting to be forged. Rather than a nameless cog in the machine, you must become what author Seth Godin calls a linchpin: a key connector that holds systems together and provides a crucial link in the chain, specifically, one that's fundamentally difficult and expensive to replace, significantly heightening the odds that you'll enjoy an extended tour of duty.

- **Constantly strive to create value, both for yourself and for others you interact with.** Ongoing research, repetition, and self-improvement are crucial to assuaging doubt, reestablishing worth, and remaining competitive. The single most important investment you will ever make isn't in a stock or mutual fund—it's in yourself. For example, rather than being content to write software code as a programmer, you could spend time attending design classes, learning how to build superior user interfaces and more accessible technology, or studying up on marketing, discovering how to best package and present new releases. Or, instead of being a public relations pro content to promote existing campaigns through existing channels, you could be learning from product managers and finding new ways to leverage cutting-edge creative approaches, social media tools, and high-tech platforms to introduce your organization's services to new audiences. The more capable and versatile you make yourself, the greater your odds of succeeding over the long haul, in any business environment.

- **Relevancy, influence, and impact are moving targets; you must change and evolve as well.** Thus you must see farther, working today to cultivate the capabilities, resources, skills, and connections needed to fuel the growth and advancement that will sustain you tomorrow. You could attend industry symposia or conventions to gain the most current information about relevant new technology or to expand your network of industry contacts. Being proactive is vital; you can both become braver and prevent fears from coming true by actively working to stay several steps ahead of the challenges they present. See the future coming, and put yourself in a more advantageous position to get ahead tomorrow by making the choices needed to successfully address the changes it will bring today.

- **Create opportunity, don't wait for it to come to you.** Constant participation, experimentation, and repetition are now essential. Because breakthroughs can come from anywhere, innovation is an ongoing mandate for professionals of every background and experience level, no longer the purview of any lone individual or department. (Though those closest to the problem are frequently best equipped to address it.) The world needs more leaders, not more unskilled labor—in other words, more individuals willing to stand up, try, and do. Put yourself into situations that place you outside your comfort zone, like taking on unfamiliar tasks that require you to do new things with new people. Teach yourself to be more open-minded, more flexible, and more of a sponge. Soak up as much knowledge and learning as you can, apply it vigorously, and watch as (just like the results you produce) you begin to sparkle and shine. The more you do so, the more you'll put yourself in opportunity's path and the greater your chances of finding it will be.

- **Always be learning.** The age of specialization is dead; choosing a niche and achieving mastery can make you singular, but it can also pigeonhole you. Likewise, if you're going to dive deep into an industry or topic, it pays to shore up the tunnel as you go, and dig alternate passageways that run parallel to it, increasing your chances of transitioning to more promising routes in case the walls ever threaten to cave in. Today's most effective leaders are eternal students, constantly seeking to expand their knowledge base, skill sets, and support networks. They're also continuously searching for opportunities to apply talents in new and novel ways. Going to night school to grab that MBA may take two years and $50,000, and building that awesome new app may eat up evenings and weekends for six months running, but if either puts you in a viable position to get the experience, capabilities, and contacts you need to catapult your career to the next level, it's probably a sound investment. Note that to overcome career-related fears and challenges, you must pursue breadth as well as depth. Education still matters, but experience is equally vital. It's imperative that you always look to grow your learning and your list of contacts, prizing talents and connections applicable to numerous contexts above all else. And, of course, you must come to see the unknown not as a challenge but rather as an opportunity. Then, as you learn more about a potential problem, steadily play smart bets around the opportunities it presents.

- **Embrace the difficult, don't fear it.** You must seek out tasks and problems that others avoid. By training yourself to overcome obstacles that others shy away from, you heighten your tolerance for pain and position yourself to reap the rewards that lie beyond it. As we saw in Chapter 6, rivals' willingness to turn away tips the odds of success in your favor and creates more opportunities to build competitive advantages. Likewise, mastering tasks they can't gives you skills that hold greater worth and further increases your odds of success. Just as an athlete works varying groups of muscles to achieve whole-body strength, so too must you guard your skills from atrophying when you exercise only limited insights and talents. Training provides the knowledge and self-discipline needed to achieve and to overcome your reflex for pain avoidance. By accepting the short-term discomfort associated with your fears, anxieties, and challenges, and ultimately surmounting them, you set yourselves up to become braver, stronger, and more capable in your life and career over a lasting, long-term horizon.

- **What you do in the off-hours matters as much, if not more, than what happens on the clock.** Employers need replaceable, easily regimented pools of manpower to keep the wheels of commerce running. But more crucially, they need leaders to guide teams and steer contributors' efforts toward more efficient, effective, and positive outcomes. Your choice is simple: Accept the decisions made and instructions that others give or elect to be the one making them. Take a moment to assess what you're doing with your life before and after work. What activities are you pursuing? Are they aiming you at the bull's-eye of your ultimate career goal? If not, identify and add activities that will exponentially increase your odds of hitting it. For example, join Toastmasters to gain public speaking skills or join a mastermind group. Going forward, your work, your reputation, and your contributions will be your résumé—otherwise, you'll be lost in the system. How do your talents apply in a world that rewards the extraordinary, not average? And, if millions possess like talents or could do the same job, what's to set you apart or make you irreplaceable? If you want to be scared of anything, with so many others competing (and going to such great lengths to do so), make it participating in a race to the bottom. Stand up, take action, and show them what you can do. Force others to stop and look; don't wait for someone to come looking for you.

- **Carefully weigh your chances, assess dangers, and then act sensibly on the information presented.** If every choice is a risk, it's simply a question of which risks to take. Actively choosing to take risks doesn't mean being reckless, either. Rather, it means being sensible about where you place your bets. Every choice comes with two expenses (hard and opportunity) attached, so make every decision count. By prioritizing economy of action, and turning away opportunities that produce lesser or less-desirable outcomes, you significantly increase your odds of success by spending time on long-term investments. Common wisdom says that busy is good. Not so, as unless you're actively channeling energy toward larger long-term goals, you're merely fueling a treadmill or siphoning power and using it to help drive others closer toward achieving their goals instead. You must tirelessly work toward creating lasting bonds, positive outcomes, and tangible assets that create enduring worth for yourself as well as those around you. Take the risks that put you in opportunity's path and put you in a position to succeed.

Why Adjust Your Strategies?

Regardless of how successful you may be personally or how entrenched your company is in its market, it doesn't mean that you or your company will be in the future. If you don't believe that, then consider the many jobs that have been outsourced, never to return again. Or, for that matter, consider businesses that have vanished without a trace just in the world of dotcoms alone: a living example of Darwinism at work, where competition is fierce, consumers fickle, and technology ever-advancing.

Remember Kozmo.com, or Pets.com, or Flooz.com? All gone. Each disappeared because they didn't keep up with changing times, they became too complacent, or they didn't take aggressive steps to course correct or sometimes they did all three. If all we do is sit still or repeat the same choices over and over, all we do is produce the same outcome, either magnified or diminished. To get different results, we have to fundamentally change the formula.

In recent years, well-established companies as diverse as Yahoo!, Best Buy, and Blockbuster have all allowed change to overtake them, leaving them struggling to compete. Similarly, millions of skilled workers have failed to keep up with changing industry times and trends, sleepwalking through life until sudden wakeup calls hit. The better choice would have been to regularly program their alarm clock.

But despite these looming threats, there is clear and compelling hope for the future. People can change their behavior, as can organizations—all it takes is a willingness to take smart risks. Most important, both can learn to overcome and even productively channel concerns associated with taking risks (such as fear of failure, change and uncertainty, and losing control) toward better outcomes.

Mind you, no one ever said that change is easy. Nor is playing the odds. But it's also not rocket science. Anyone can take more and smarter risks and profit as a result. Get to know your chances of success, and make smart bets. You can do this by:

- Rethinking the problems that confront you
- Reassessing risks
- Revisiting strategies
- Reinvesting in yourself

- Revising your bets
- Readjusting your tactics
- Repeating this process on an ongoing basis

You can keep playing the same hand, even as others at the table and the rules you're playing by constantly shift, or you can readjust your strategies in tune with the changes, and give yourself a fighting chance.

How Daredevils Do It

At pharmaceutical giant Merck, maker of medicines like Claritin and skincare products such as Coppertone, new lessons in leadership are already being written.

When Merck creates teams to steer cutting-edge projects, its management selection process often defies established convention. Sanjoy Ray, director of technology innovation, says that in an organization replete with talented overachievers "there's no point in choosing the person who is the most accomplished or highest performer because the difference between that person and most others in the organization isn't that great, on a global scale."[12]

So when creating teams to spearhead certain forward-thinking programs (not concocting drugs; don't worry—that's still left to world-class scientists) the business frequently doesn't assign tasks to the most obviously qualified candidates. It assigns them to the most excited and enthusiastic employees capable of fielding the job, often seen as—compared to more decorated candidates on paper—smarter, safer bets.

"One of the lessons that we learned was [to ask employees]: 'If you could do anything you wanted, what would it be?'" he explains. "What you do is file those [thoughts] away and you make them into opportunities as they come along. If you can do that, the performance you get is extraordinary."

Clearly, risk takers are a valuable commodity in any modern organization; they're the men and women who aren't afraid to question the status quo, to innovate, and to fix what's not broken. As with self-made successes, their creativity, capacity for problem-solving, and ability to break the mold are vital attributes that help fuel growth and momentum. That's why so-called daredevils (in actuality, relentlessly resourceful and practical thinkers) have begun to outstrip traditional standouts, such as class valedictorians and seasoned executives. By pairing street smarts with critical thinking and book smarts with ingenuity, they stack the odds in their favor to create a winning business combination.

Poker pro Phil Gordon says he calls this process *selective aggression*. In life and business, as at the Vegas tables, you must make small, probing bets designed to test the viability of potential choices and opportunities. Only then, when you're sure that the odds favor you, should you start slinging chips.

Gordon, owner of Seattle-based app maker Jawfish Games, applies this principle to his own enterprise. When he thinks about building a new smartphone application, for instance, he assigns two workers (say, one programmer and one brand manager) to research the project. In effect, he'd rather spend $5,000 to $50,000 testing an idea than make a $500,000 mistake. By collecting and analyzing the feedback gained and systematically applying this learning toward improving future efforts, he loses a few occasional bets. But statistically, he becomes far likelier to succeed with bigger gambles in the end.

Whether we're talking about your career or your commercial ventures, the system is equally applicable. Expect to be doing a lot of playing and folding as you explore potential avenues of opportunity. But at odds with Gordon's insights to take small risks, learn, improve, and keep looking out for opportunities, many of us strictly play defense.

It's one thing to excel at current strategies (which hold decreasing value in the face of new advancements) and maintain pace with competitors (hold the line). It's another to play offensively by studying your situation (surveying the market and competitive landscape), changing (adapting to better serve others' needs), and innovating (circumventing rivals and moving the line so far forward that they struggle to catch up). Both strategies are required to succeed in your life, your career, and your business. Don't just mitigate risks but make smart bets as well. Be *selectively aggressive*.

The secret to winning this game is no longer about being perfect, but about being flexible, adaptable, and objective, plus remaining competitive at something that still commands relevancy and value—and value and relevancy are moving targets. To hit the bull's-eye, you've got to keep aiming carefully and throwing darts at the board.

Want to become more successful at changing, adapting, and reinventing yourself and your organization? As poker pro Phil Hellmuth and our friends with the World Series of Poker bracelets remind us, play the hand you're dealt, and don't stop playing intelligently until your bets pay off.

"It helps," Hellmuth says, chuckling, "to be in constant practice."[13]

How the Most Innovative Companies Succeed

Today's most successful market leaders see business as a game of chance and constantly make smart, measured, and changing bets. Call them daredevils, mavericks, or visionaries if you like. In reality, they're fiercely practical. By relentlessly and systematically placing smaller, smarter wagers, they operate far more conservatively and prudently than you'd think.

For example, at personal finance software maker Intuit, leaders say their role is "to remove the speed bumps" (such as lack of support, resources, and permission) that get in the way of innovation and make cost-effective experimentation available to all. Employees have created dozens of revenue-generating ideas by suggesting and testing concepts, which are quickly translated into real-world trials and rollouts.

At online lodging service Airbnb, workers are encouraged to ship new features on day one. A designer who changed one icon from a star to a heart increased customer engagement by 30 percent and inspired the creation of a "Wish List" product.

And at digital news service Flipboard, products are never considered finished. Teams are constantly visualizing what users need from its publications before they realize that they need it.

From global IT leader EMC's annual innovation contest (where employees love ideas so much that they independently team up to bring even losing ventures to life) to Qualcomm's online network for peer review of concepts, popular approaches to innovation are myriad. But those organizations that empower employees to speak up, share ideas, recruit help, and learn by making mistakes are all winning at the game of business.

Offense and Defense:
Running a Complete Game

Gamblers, risk takers, and forward thinkers—today's mavericks—understand the importance of making safe bets. But they also realize that big wins come from playing the long shots that smaller, smarter wagers subsidize. As in baseball, base hits can add up to a win, but if you don't swing for the fences, it's hard to hit home runs.

As with professional poker players, organizations can play an endurance game, steadily building up their stacks of chips before using them to bluff, bully, or control big hands. And when opportunity presents itself and the time comes to wager, they don't hesitate to push these stacks into the pot. The difference is that instead of playing with dollars alone, organizations also do the same with ideas and with resources, like time, effort, and manpower.

There's just one difference between average performers and daredevils. Despite feeling the same worries as the rest of us, daredevils are able to set aside emotion and objectively scrutinize challenges and opportunities. They then intelligently gauge odds, manage a portfolio of risks, and make decisive bets. Given enough time, and enough tries, these bets inevitably pay off and can pay off on both an individual and organizational basis.

The best business leaders comprehend that fear is the only thing holding us back. For them there is no concept of stop or start. The game is always in progress.

Faced with opportunity or setback, daredevils find inaction unacceptable. The only choice is how to proceed logically, and course correct if necessary.

Call today's most triumphant leaders daredevils, mavericks,

innovators, or entrepreneurs as you wish; in reality, they're simply highly resilient realists.

What can we learn from them? Don't give up just because your efforts haven't succeeded thus far, and don't be fooled by fear or misconception into making bad bets. Given the speed at which change now occurs, a willingness to be flexible and selectively aggressive are now among tomorrow's most crucial talents.

Play the game, play it intelligently, and change up your strategies and styles as you go, and anything and everything is yours to attain.

Play the Odds Smarter

As you've seen here, to survive and thrive, we must be wiser about the risks we take and how we take them. It may seem like a scary prospect, but there is no single road map to success anymore. The straight and narrow has suddenly become broad and winding. To find success when playing the odds, you can't pounce on every opportunity—you must pick and choose, weighing the potential costs against the potential benefits. To find your own true path to achievement take note of the following:

- **Don't be afraid to chart your course.** You can't afford to stand idly by and hope chance plays in your favor. Instead, create your own opportunities by considering when, where, and how to most effectively wager your time, money and effort. Then don't hesitate to put your bets on the table when opportunity presents itself. It's *your* course and your life, after all—seize it. Own it. Be it. Make chance play in your favor, and make things happen.

- **Avoid sitting still.** Like a Ferris wheel or merry-go-round, the world is in constant motion, and it's going to continue its orbit through space with or without you. Keep the fear of being left behind as the world moves on in the front of your mind. You can't win the game if you don't play, and you're gambling at a disadvantage if you're not constantly watching and actively responding to how the game unfolds.

- **Create more opportunities to win.** Daredevils win because they create more opportunities to win and put themselves in the path of success more frequently. You may not hit a homerun the first time at bat, or even the third. But you can always score game-winning runs by making numerous base hits in the form of small bets that move you ever closer to achieving greater goals.

Tomorrow's leaders now possess just two talents: solving problems and creating meaningful results. Call them daredevils if you must. But in doing what may seem hazardous to most and by changing with a changing world, the irony is that they're actually making less risky and frightening decisions. They're playing the odds, and they're playing to win.

Action Steps

The future really does belong to daredevils—the individuals and organizations willing to make taking risks their permanent hallmark. You can take smart risks and get in touch with your inner maverick, starting today, by keeping a few simple principles in mind:

- **Get to know the odds.** And once you know the odds, make smarter and smaller bets.
- **Always be taking calculated risks.** However, if the risks are too high or the cost–benefit ratio is not in your favor, find another opportunity.
- **Be prepared to take a winding route to success in your career.** This may mean circling around obstacles and doubling back when necessary, if that's what it takes to put you in chance's sights.
- **Play the hand you're dealt.** But don't stop playing intelligently until your bets pay off.
- **Chart your own course in business, career, and life.** Don't let others chart it for you.
- **Create more opportunities to win.** The more opportunities you have to win, the greater your chances of winning.
- **Solve problems.** Forget fear, and consistently focus on making the right calls needed to produce meaningful results.

Chapter Nine

Rule 7: Experiment Constantly

Artist and songwriter Dave Stewart is one half of the Eurythmics (the other being famed vocalist Annie Lennox), among pop-rock's most successful duos. But when the group's run of hit singles (including "Sweet Dreams [Are Made of This]" and "Here Comes the Rain Again") petered out, Stewart also became a film director, author, producer, and multimedia creative agency owner, all in a quest to remain relevant.

Later, Stewart would return to his roots, becoming part of rock supergroup SuperHeavy. But for more than thirty years, he has successfully navigated the entertainment business, an industry overflowing with has-beens and one-hit wonders. According to Stewart, he doesn't do this by spending big bucks or leaning on celebrity connections. He does it by continuously adapting and switching up styles; times and tastes change too fast for him to remain static.

Too many things are happening too quickly out there, he says, not to be a go-getter, even if it means routinely forcing oneself to take huge risks. Had Stewart not stayed in motion and continuously challenged the status quo, he admits that "I'd probably be on an '80s rock tour with a synthesizer. I'd probably be really unhappy too."[1]

The process of constantly running, bobbing and weaving, and changing tactics and tracks, isn't without pain, he notes. But what other choice do we have but to consistently be reevaluating and responding to the shifting terrain in front us? When the road we're traveling or obstacles we're facing suddenly take a jarring turn, all we can do is shift strategies accordingly. Even if, Stewart says, this means having to pick ourselves back up and continue the journey after an inadvertent stumble.

"All the people I've worked with that are really successful have that trait . . . from the Mick Jaggers to the Richard Bransons, they'll just immediately get up," he points out. "They also have a lot of ideas. A lot of people put their eggs into one basket, and the idea doesn't work, and they never do anything again."

Besides, Stewart says, if your approach *does* work, even on the scale of success that he has enjoyed, there's no promise it will work again as successfully tomorrow.

Rule 7: Experiment Constantly

Do you ever get the feeling that the comfortable groove you're in is a little *too* comfortable? Start thinking like Stewart and cultivate another important habit: Constantly tinker with ways to expand your horizons, grow your skill set, and disrupt your career or your organization.

As we saw earlier, self-imposed roadblocks like insecurity or fear of failure and rejection want to hold you back in life and business—a big problem because the world is constantly moving forward. But there's always a simple way to overcome these obstacles, and it's the same way you can solve any problem. Give yourself permission to poke and prod at the ceilings and barriers that bar your way onward until they collapse or you discover a more efficient way around them. (See Chapter 2, more on how to do so.)

Players of popular sci-fi run-and-gun video games such as Halo or Gears of War understand this principle well; they are frequently finding nasty surprises waiting for them. When a giant, mechanized worm large enough to swallow a small tanker suddenly rears up ahead, they don't sit still or keep targeting the same spots and blasting away with the same strategies to little effect. They carefully maneuver around the beast searching for signs of weakness, systematically aiming and firing until vulnerable chinks in its armor present themselves. Then, once spotted, they concentrate their firepower on them until the challenge is overcome.

If you've ever watched a small child explore her environment, pausing to examine and interact with various objects and items, then you've seen this principle in motion in a real-world environment. Try, learn, try again . . . the formula for finding success is surprisingly obvious, and one we inadvertently forget over time as anxieties and fears limit our horizons. (Fears like embarrassment, insecurity, and isolation being especially notable.) It's the very same formula today's most-lauded market leaders use to produce breakthroughs at every level.

In the olden days (OK, the 1940s and 1950s), companies like 3M and HP famously institutionalized employee experimentation. While HP allowed employees to tinker on Friday afternoons after lunch, 3M had an unwritten rule that engineers could spend up to 15 percent of their working hours exploring their own projects. According to the companies, this tinkering time led to the invention of Post-it notes and laser printers.

Many of today's best and brightest companies (Salesforce, Foursquare, and Meetup) are leveraging similar principles to change, innovate, and build game-changing advancements. Numerous organizations are even institutionalizing the process, through routine hackathons (informal brainstorming and creation sessions), all in hopes of spawning profitable new ideas.[2] Purina has held programs dedicated to building pet-friendly apps,[3] and Bloomberg Ventures used such initiatives to find potential investments.[4] Even Campbell's recently held a "Hack the Kitchen" contest that awarded winners $25,000 plus a $25,000 contract to develop a market-ready application, among the most novel ways to drive creative breakthroughs while slashing R&D costs seen yet.[5] Countless firms now place a premium on tinkering programs precisely because of the innovations they produce and the ability they provide to spotlight talented individuals who'd otherwise go unnoticed. (And unhired.)

If you're interested in tinkering, there's no barrier to entry, unless it's one you've chosen to erect. To succeed, merely approach every challenge like a computer programmer would: Key in actions, observe how systems respond, and then react until you get the desired result.

Innovation isn't about being more talented or high-tech, it's about being more resourceful and creative. Instead of watching your prospects for advancement or strategies begin to short-circuit as they wear out over time, wipe your memory clean and start keying in new alternatives. Like electronic devices, we can all benefit from regularly giving our mindsets a fresh reboot, reinstall, or upgrade.

If one approach doesn't get you around an obstacle standing in your way, then quickly try another. If your organization isn't achieving the results that you expect with its current strategies or programs, then do something different. Just don't do nothing or repeat the same actions to diminishing return until fast-changing markets and business conditions render you and your approaches obsolete.

Try to begin with destinations, not routes, then start working backward, creating shortcuts and solutions that move you past intervening roadblocks. Like a scientist, start with a hypothesis, and assume it can work until proven wrong. Approach every day and every task as if anything were possible, and test your hypothesis. You'll never know what's possible until you try. If the experiment doesn't pan out, try a new one. Every time you do, you're creating opportunities to learn and hone your technique—and when you're constantly learning and improving, you can quickly dispense with dead ends and discover more promising avenues to get ahead. In doing so, you bend odds and opportunity in your favor and can achieve your goals the same way globally renowned innovators do.

We may not be able to see where the future is headed, but we don't have to dangerously fumble around in the dark, either. Tell the status quo to stick it, flip fear the finger, and *start trying today.* Life's one big experiment: Keep one foot anchored in what's working for you, and take the other and carefully feel around, dipping your toes into the unknown and playing the odds until you find a safe way forward.

What Does Failure Mean, Anyway?

If you and your organization aren't experimenting and innovating already, odds are fear of failure weighs heavily on your decision making. Let's pause here for a moment to examine why this fear may be holding you back and why today's most successful organizations and individuals say you're not avoiding mistakes but rather making huge ones by not embracing it.

Competitive as business landscapes have become, they're now cluttered with winners and losers alike, including contenders that are easily categorized as both, depending on their current operating reality. While we can't all be winners all the time, research shows that as many as nine in ten start-ups actually crash and burn—we can certainly win *sometimes*. Moreover, the occasional stumble doesn't necessarily signal the end. Many companies, from Groupon to Zynga, may skyrocket out of the gate, only to find themselves fighting for life mere months later and then suddenly find their prospects buoyant again.

Just because we may have failed before doesn't mean we are a failure. Success often depends on your perspective: A 10 percent market share may represent a dream for some but crushing defeat for others. It's all in how you look at it, and what you choose to take away from the experience.

At any time, you have the option to rethink your position and, in similar fashion, retrench, regroup, and bounce back. Keep trying, failing, and trying again (that is, experimenting), and you'll be succeeding in the same way world-famed businesses, thought leaders, and industry titans have for decades.

Maybe failure by traditional definitions seems a poor precedent to set for yourself. Let's redefine it as *education*. Failure is inevitable, but failure is a learning experience—nothing more. And in the same way you can decide how much to invest in academic learning, you can also choose how extensive and expensive this education will be, including the cost of your experiments. Failure can now be seen as an investment of sorts: a fundamental process through which people and organizations learn and make more informed decisions.

Ben Huh, founder of $37 million online humor blog empire Cheezburger Network, understands this principle well. He and his team are constantly experimenting and failing with new products, websites, and social media strategies, being in the hyperkinetic business of online memes, which change at breakneck speed. What attracts audiences today seldom works tomorrow.

As a result, Huh doesn't mind failure. It's only the big ones he detests.

"We talk about scaling the size of the risk," he explains. "Failure with a capital F is always scary. But when you scale down the size of the risk, you actually enable the company to take more risks. Lowercase f's are culturally important to any organization."[6] For him and his colleagues, experimentation isn't just a routine part of day-to-day operations: It's a business necessity.

"Taking risks and trying new ideas are part of the growth process," Huh says. "[At Cheezburger,] we do not reprimand employees for taking risks and failing. We reprimand them for not taking action at all."

In fact, it's not uncommon for leading organizations like AMD, Adobe, and Hubspot to publicly release work-in-progress hardware or software versions (so-called beta editions) to the public, specifically to sniff out problem spots. Why? So they can find these deficiencies, correct them, and retool products, messages, and marketing strategies to improve on them, failing early, before they go to market and really get clobbered.

Consider every failure one step forward toward the success you seek, meaning that in life and business, the concept should be embraced instead of feared. And if you're a leader, you shouldn't be punishing your people for experimenting, as long as they're not making the same mistakes twice, you should be rewarding them for it.

Of course, embracing experimentation isn't always as simple and painless as it sounds. To tinker, we must naturally overcome many common concerns, including not just insecurity and fear of failure but also every other fear introduced in Chapter 1. However, for individuals and the companies they work for to move forward with changing times and expectations, experiment constantly they must; otherwise, their competitors may quickly leave them in the dust.

Be grateful for these experiments and associated failures. Discovering them allows organizations to fine-tune and improve products to better meet users' needs before formally debuting. The faster these enterprises try and/or fail, the faster they can fix drawbacks or readjust capabilities, features, or interfaces to better serve customers; they may even discover features end users love that could have been overlooked. Google's famed Gmail actually remained in beta form for five years, allowing for plenty of experimentation, redesign, and rollout of new versions along the way. If it weren't for tinkering, testing, and tweaking (including the inevitable failures), some of the good things in life wouldn't be so good.

You can let your failures define you or you can develop an appetite for them, knowing every attempt brings you closer to success and that experimentation is essential to the change, growth, and future-proofing process. But the more bites at getting ahead you're willing to take and more you slowly, steadily nibble away at the odds by trying, failing, and then conducting more informed experiments, the closer you'll come to finding success.

Rethinking Failure

So if the key to successfully changing and innovating is simply trial and error, why all the focus on failure? What's the big deal?

That's exactly the point. Most of us make failure out to be way too big a deal in our lives. We fear it, we obsess over it, we avoid taking chances, and we allow ourselves to settle for mediocrity because of it.

Wake up and smell the java! Failure is a part of life; if you're alive, then you're going to experience failure, no matter how hard you try. But even more than that, failure is just one rung on the ladder to success. Think about all the people who failed but who refused to let failure stop their ultimate success:

- **Steven Spielberg** applied for admission to the University of Southern California film school three times. He was rejected three times as well. (He was eventually awarded an honorary degree by the school in 1994.)[7]
- **Thomas Edison** failed numerous times before he hit on the right combination of materials and construction to create a commercially viable incandescent light bulb. Said Edison, "If I find 10,000 ways something won't work, I haven't failed . . . every wrong attempt discarded is often a step forward."[8]

- When asked by a reporter about the grade he received for the paper he wrote as an undergraduate student that described his idea for an overnight delivery system, FedEx founder **Fred Smith** replied, "I don't know, probably made my usual C."[9] Today, FedEx delivers an average of 3.5 million packages daily.[10]

- **J. K. Rowling**'s first book, *Harry Potter and the Philosopher's Stone,* was rejected by twelve publishers before finally being accepted by Bloomsbury.[11] She now has a net worth of more than $1 billion.[12]

- **Dick Cheney** flunked out of Yale twice before eventually earning his BA and MA degrees at the University of Wyoming and becoming a congressman, secretary of defense, and vice president of the United States.

According to Alan Kuyatt, assistant professor at the University of Maryland University College, "When management does not accept failures as part of the innovation process, fear of failure will cause [an] organization to focus on incremental innovations that are safer and have less risk. The more radical innovations that can change the industry will be avoided because of fear."[13] Experiment at all levels and experiment often, rewarding those who tinker and take intelligent risks: It's the surest way to drive innovation and drive huge breakthroughs.

In a similar vein, Eric Ries developed the philosophy of the *lean start-up,* which comprises a set of principles for launching a new product or business. These principles—based on validated learning, experimentation, and frequent releases—can be boiled down to five steps:

Step 1: Build fast.

Step 2: Release often.

Step 3: Measure.

Step 4: Learn.

Step 5: Repeat.[14]

Not only are experimentation and failure inextricably intertwined in this model, but the more difficult a task is to achieve (and potentially the greater the reward it offers), the greater the chance of failure. Therefore, the more you experiment, the faster you fail, and the more diligent you are about bouncing back and trying again, the sooner you'll find the success that you're seeking. It's a strategy that works for the world's most advanced start-ups and biggest corporate behemoths, and one that can work for you and your organization as well.

Tinkering with Your Career

It's not just operating strategies that need to constantly be mixed, matched, and reconfigured, we also need to relentlessly tinker with our careers. In the same way that business solutions are constantly being realigned and readjusted to future-proof ourselves, so too must our livelihoods be constantly pulled and kneaded in different directions more frequently going forward.

Under the current system, we rely on predictable jobs and predictable industries; we rely on them for our daily bread, our well-being, and the future of our careers and families. But just as markets and job opportunities can shift on a dime, so too can others' interests. These interests may not align with our own or further the goals we've set for ourselves both personally and professionally tomorrow, let alone do so over any long-term horizon.

Consider that tomorrow's working professional will hold ten to fifteen jobs over his or her lifetime.[15] Those under the age of thirty are expected to switch positions as frequently as every eighteen months. (*Forbes* actually calls constant career shifts the new normal for millennials.[16])

In addition, reorganizations now strike businesses as frequently as once every seven months. Average job tenures are a fraction of historical values. Outsourcing and virtualization are on the rise. And organizations are increasingly turning to freelancers, contractors, and temporary solutions.

The same way organizations must tinker with new innovations to stay ahead of changing markets, you must therefore start experimenting with your career today, expanding your experience, skill sets, and professional horizons to increase your professional versatility and cultivate the talents and backgrounds that will be in demand tomorrow. Granted, you can wait to do so later, when you may be backed against a wall and stuck playing catch-up with others. But at some point, it's all but certain that you're going to have to reinvent yourself anyway. Why not bridge the gap between the future and present by naming yourself VP of innovation of your own life and career this very instant and immediately begin tinkering and expanding your résumé?

The more you fiddle with your career, try new things, and invest in yourself—whether by taking classes, attending networking events, or simply reading up on new trends and technologies—the more wiggle room you'll create in your career. The more you develop novel areas of expertise and work to gain influence (whether by becoming your company's resident subject matter expert or go-to problem solver) the less expendable you'll be, and fewer compromises you'll have to make.

Set aside obvious reasons for experimenting: Future-proofing your résumé by gaining additional experiences and skills to demonstrate or ways to reposition your background and expertise. There's also added incentive in the growing value, leverage, and lasting benefits you'll create for yourself.

Consider the choice we get when we decide how to interact with employers, one that's simple but crucial. We can look at them as *patrons*, and act as dependents, waiting for them to drip-feed us opportunities, or we can choose to work with them as *partners*, symbiotically striving toward shared goals to the benefit of all but also knowing that each of us is ultimately responsible for taking care of ourselves.

Buy back your time or use off-hours more effectively and put some effort into personal and career development. The more you're willing to experiment and learn, the more your wings will spread and higher your stock will soar. A little insurance never hurts. It's your career, your life, and your well-being, after all. Ultimately, you're the one responsible for your own fate. If you've been busy tinkering, experimenting, and seeking out requisite insights and experiences, you'll be far better equipped to function as a free agent.

But most important, when you're courageously tinkering and experimenting with your career on an ongoing basis, the more opportunities you'll find to do work that matters and work that you adore.

Consider the case of Anita Crofts, who voluntarily put herself— and her job—out on a limb by proposing to leaders at the University of Washington Communications Department that they allow her to experiment and create her own position within the college. No longer would Crofts be a lecturer and communication leadership associate director. Instead, she would become the Communications Department's flight instructor. (No, not the aerial kind, but rather the teaching-students-to-lead kind of flight instructor.) This new position served to stitch together the school's undergraduate, master's, and doctorate programs, while bridging the classroom and community.

While Crofts was fully committed to the idea, she knew that she would have to sell it to her department chair. And given the sticky office politics characteristic of many university workplaces, this was no slam dunk.

Says Crofts: "I didn't have the courage to actually talk to the Chair about it [for months]. I knew that given the traditions in universities, this was going to be a radical ask. It was so far outside of the box. I felt very strongly about it though, and I wanted to think in an expansive and exciting way to make my dream job."[17]

Eventually, Crofts did manage to gather the courage she needed to make her pitch. Instead of being thrown out on her ear as she feared, her boss agreed to support the experiment. Today, Crofts is no longer just any educator, she's a flight instructor.

What she learned from the experience: "Keep your eye on the prize for being better and bigger. Don't imagine that a career is linear. See it as having cycles and phases. Approach your career as having agency to it. My career is like parkour."

Croft's process is easily replicable and adaptable for repeated repetition. Inspired by Crofts, her friends Jessica Esch and Rachel Gold both took similar leaps and approaches to readjusting their career trajectories and saw equally pronounced results from these retoolings.

Esch, a United Way employee working on community impact initiatives, used her film-editing skills and, after a fifteen-minute conversation with her boss, parlayed a series of videos she made into a new gig in communications and public outreach. ("United Way was a great, natural platform ... but if they didn't want to go forward with it, I knew I'd go somewhere else and do it on my own."[18]) Gold, a former bluegrass band player who got a PhD and became a researcher for Kaiser Permanente in her forties, successfully asked her boss to let her work half-time at Kaiser and half-time at an organization for which she'd been acting as a go-between. ("I read *Lean In*, which said 'women don't ask'— so I took the book to my boss and said, 'OK, Steve ... I'm asking!'"[19])

If you're not happy with your job, your career, or where you're headed in life, maybe it's time you started out with a new hypothesis. Tell yourself: *I can afford to try new things and take chances*; then start asking as well.

A Work in Progress

Think of your organization and career as start-ups, each of which are constant experiments and works in progress. Very few businesses achieve massive success on day one, and you shouldn't expect yourself to, either. Successful companies and individuals set a big goal, they point themselves toward it, and then they chip away at it, little by little, day by day, experimenting and learning as they go. In the end, by breaking big challenges into small parts, doggedly working at them, and course correcting as needed, they keep tinkering away at problems until all the pieces of the puzzle finally come together.

Very early in the company's history, Airbnb—an online service that helps travelers find people who have a spare room or other living quarters to rent—was faced with a problem. The service wasn't catching on in New York City. So Joe Gebbia and Brian Chesky, the company's founders, flew to New York and checked out a sampling of the properties for themselves. They quickly realized that the photographs of the listed properties were terrible. So the pair tested a hypothesis: changing how well they presented the lodgings would change people's perceptions, and by creating more positive impressions through higher-quality snapshots, they would increase the likelihood that the accommodations would be booked.

So the pair rented an expensive, high-quality camera and took photographs of the listings themselves. Within a month, bookings doubled. They then applied this same solution to other cities, with similar results. Says Gebbia, "Rinse and repeat. When we fixed the product in New York, it solved our problems in Paris, London, Vancouver, and Miami."[20] All it took was one simple experiment to arrive at a powerful solution.

As with Airbnb, the key to achieving your goals and always staying ahead of the curve is evolution, never cease the process of self-improvement.

In their book *The Start-Up of You*, LinkedIn cofounder and chairman Reid Hoffman and his coauthor Ben Casnocha say that if you want to achieve success in your business or career, it's critical to adopt a new mind-set: business and career as *permanent beta*. The term refers to thinking of yourself or your organization as a constantly evolving entity.

The authors define permanent beta as follows:

To always be starting
To forever be a work in progress

Hoffman and Casnocha argue that companies and people are always evolving and never truly finished. They suggest, *"Finished ought to be an F-word for all of us. We are all works in progress."* Hoffman and Casnocha continue, "Keeping your career in permanent beta forces you to acknowledge that you have bugs, that there's new development to do on yourself, that you will need to adapt and evolve."[21]

Doing so requires you to kick fear in the face and find the courage to constantly tinker and experiment: a business concept that is becoming increasingly celebrated and increasingly common among leading organizations and experts.

But experimenting one's way to success isn't just for the world's leading high-tech innovators. SolarCity has grown into the largest installer of solar panels in the United States, not because it has invented a better solar cell but because it has invented a better business model.

SolarCity was one of the first solar companies in the country to offer residential consumers a leased financing option or the option to simply pay for the power that is produced on their own property. (At a rate that is typically about 10 percent less than they pay for regular commercial electrical power.[22]) As a result of this and other innovations, many developed through a process of trial and error, the company was named one of the world's most innovative companies by *Fast Company* in 2012.

Of course, trial and error requires a hefty dose of failure.

In fact, in a recent study of Inc. 500 companies, 61 percent of businesses surveyed said that creating an environment in which it's OK to fail directly contributes to their ability to innovate. Likewise, 38 percent say that they get their best ideas from customers, but only about 33 percent have a formal method for collecting these ideas or bouncing them off clients to see which are viable.

That's an important point to note, given that nearly 66 percent of firms surveyed (including many competitors) can go from idea to market with pilot programs and experiments in one to five months—some, within as little as thirty days. We must be open to trying and failing. The more we take risks, the more we experiment, and the more feedback we get along the way, the more innovative, effective, and successful we can be.

Action Steps

In this fast-changing world, nothing lasts long, least of all the products, approaches, and processes that virtually guaranteed your success a decade ago or even a year ago. Companies today must become hotbeds of innovation and creativity, and new ideas must be thought up, tried, and then quickly discarded, implemented, or retried, depending on the results. This process of experimentation is essential in every business today, and everyone—from the top of the career ladder to the very bottom—must be willing to take risks, put themselves on the line, and even fail because failure is but one stop on the road to success.

In the wake of change, professionals cannot be afraid to tinker and must be innovative when it comes to their careers. If you want to stay future-proof, you've got to be able to reposition and restructure your skill sets, education, and experiences and position yourself to create opportunities today that can pay off tomorrow.

Take the following steps to start putting yourself at the head of the line, rapidly moving onward and upward to success:

- **Experiment constantly.** Question everything, especially the status quo, and try new things. Assess the results, adjust your approach, and try again and again.
- **Embrace uncertainty.** This means accepting change and then facing it head-on: But do so carefully, one step at a time, learning as you go until you're prepared to make greater leaps of faith more forearmed and forewarned.
- **Rethink failure.** Failure is a natural part of the experimentation process, and it gets you closer to achieving your goals. Accept failure, learn the valuable lessons it offers, and then apply them. Above all, don't let fear of failure dissuade you from your path.
- **Work like a lean start-up.** Build fast, release often, measure, learn, repeat.
- **Future-proof your résumé.** Do this by tinkering with your own career aspirations and pathways, gaining additional experiences and skills, or experimenting with new ways to reposition your background and talents. All it takes is one slight tweak to change your current trajectory.
- **Stay in constant motion.** Never stop trying or doing; then, based on the feedback you get, continue to try and to do, now better informed and well equipped.
- **Be a work in progress.** Set big goals for your career or busi-

ness and then chip away at them, little by little, day by day. Never stop setting more goals for yourself either, as new times and trends beget new needs, and there are always new goals and aspirations to consider. Your potential becomes limitless when you keep learning, evolving, and pushing boundaries.

Chapter Ten

Rule 8: Pick Your Battles

Despite being the CEO and owner of a major NFL football franchise, the San Francisco 49ers' Jed York cares surprisingly little about winning games or even winning this year's Super Bowl. Even more so, for someone whose first business decision (the hiring of Mike Singletary as head coach) ended in a disastrous 2010 season. But York would still prefer to take chances and sign unproven players, make dicey plays, and even gamble on incensing fans if it meant chasing permanent success over instant gratification. Some battles, he says, are worth fighting.

"A lot of teams say their goal is to win the Super Bowl," he explains. "We want to be competing for it year in and year out as opposed to one season. You have to look at the long-term view, and be able to make some mistakes in the short run to have the overall success you want."[1] This means picking his battles, tackling some opportunities and challenges head-on, while giving others a pass or leaving still more to be fought another, more advantageous day. Fans may not agree with every decision he makes, but York knows just how important it is to fight for something you believe in and when, where, and why it's important to say screw it and make hard calls.

When $8-million-a-season star quarterback Alex Smith was injured, York didn't hesitate to put new, untested recruit Colin Kaepernick (then around a $300,000 investment) into the game. He wasn't necessarily pundits' first choice. But York didn't waste time going back and forth with them: He had bigger battles to fight. "We [felt] Kaepernick could be our quarterback for the next ten to fifteen years," he explains. "If you're looking over that time horizon, you're not really worried . . . you want to make sure you have the best opportunity to win over the next decade."

So when he and his coaches go hunting for talent or craft a new playbook, York doesn't worry about whose ego gets bruised or who disagrees with the strategies. Rather, he and his team always focus on making the right call, even if it means having to fight to do so over the objections of fans, critics, and colleagues.

With that attitude, confrontation is inevitable for York and his coworkers. So they don't try to *avoid* confrontation, they try to be smarter about how they address it. According to experts, he and his colleagues don't always make the correct choices or even the smart ones on paper. But to succeed in the face of changing competition and make the right calls more often, his team knows that it can't keep making the same plays. So rather than go with the flow, it constantly defies convention and is highly strategic about the battles it chooses to fight as it goes about doing so.

The atmosphere and attitude York promotes throughout the franchise to support this approach is one that may seem familiar: "We want a culture that embraces failure . . . that's what creates the best companies and innovation in the world." The strategy he embraces is pretty straightforward: Fight the battles that count the most in the long run and leave the rest for another day, or skip them entirely.

Because innovation flies in the face of established norms, by definition, the process intrinsically invites friction. But in the same way that its wide receivers are constantly looking for open lanes to effortlessly dash through when trying for touchdowns, the 49ers know that when it comes to effecting positive change, you also don't have to confront every 300-pound linebacker head-on. Moreover, when you concentrate on fighting the battles that count and stay laser focused on making the most effective calls, you can avoid wasting effort and resources on less productive and often more trying concerns. (Hint: More football games are won by prioritizing playbooks, not politics.) Doing so not only keeps you from running headfirst into every painful scenario, it allows you to bring every possible resource to bear where it matters most and against what truly counts: the bottom line.

Battles aren't easily won, on the gridiron or off. Some can take years of careful study and adaptation to emerge from victorious. But as York knows, they're eminently less difficult to fight when you dictate their terms and consistently channel time, effort, and energy toward the most productive fronts.

As a child, York remembers sitting on the lap of Jennifer Montana (wife of legendary Hall of Famer Joe), bawling his eyes out when the 49ers lost the playoffs to the Minnesota Vikings. But when the team bounced back the following year to win the Super Bowl, he learned a vital lesson: Anyone can stage a second-round comeback and successfully storm the battlefield again, provided they're willing to strike forewarned and forearmed and be more strategic about where they strike. "Knowing what is right to do is not difficult," he asserts. "Executing and following through is difficult."

When York makes decisions today, he asks himself: "What would that kid say? What decisions would you make when you're not cynical, not worried about what other people think? What is right and wrong is always right in front of your face—it's a very easy answer. The question is: Are you willing to live with the criticism at the time you make those decisions?"

If you're ready to change and innovate, understand that confrontation is unavoidable. But as York points out, it's far easier to face when you decide where, when, and how conflicts will be fought.

Rule 8: Pick Your Battles

As we learned in Rule 6, Play the Odds, overcoming fears becomes simpler when you see risk and uncertainty as a game of chance. To win more often, stack the odds in your favor. This means having to pick and choose our battles. More specifically, it means having to objectively and intelligently define viable strategies to confront them and deciding when it's best to cut losses and fight another day.

When it wanted to dethrone the popular erectile dysfunction drug Viagra, pharmaceutical maker Lilly ICOS (maker of rival drug Cialis) didn't attack Viagra and its maker Pfizer head-on in terms of safety, where it enjoyed a slight advantage. Rather, Lilly ICOS marketed the drug's greatly enhanced duration (it lasts thirty-six hours as opposed to Viagra's four or five) and *raised* prices to reinforce its strategy of promoting superior efficacy.[2] By 2012, Cialis came from nowhere to surpass Viagra's $1.9 billion in annual sales.

Similarly, software start-ups don't confront corporate giants like Microsoft or Sony by competing on economies of scale. They do it by solving problems that are too novel or fast moving for the behemoths to effectively tackle or that have escaped the giants' notice. Neighborhood retailers don't go toe to toe with Walmart, Costco, or BJ's by competing on price, either. They do it through locally geared promotions, greater community support, and more personalized customer service.

Whether you're talking about the commercial market or the hiring market, you can go head to head with others with less likelihood of success and at greater expense. Alternately, you can look for gaps in the field and strike where your rivals are weak and dramatically enhance your odds of getting ahead.

As Stephen Denny, author of *Killing Giants*, points out, large corporations often develop cultures that believe certain ideas to be unwanted or undesirable. These are exactly the areas where enterprising organizations can most effectively play. Professional reality is no different.

Pick up skills, experiences, learning, and contacts that others don't have, and you've leapfrogged to the top of HR's stack. Solve problems without being asked to or having to rely on others, and you'll catch senior leaders' eyes faster than will the brownnosing careerists. Create a work portfolio that reflects your talents and show prospective employers what you're tangibly capable of doing, and you'll be far more memorable than most candidates.

Take a minute to stop and think about it, and you can find a thousand other measures you can take.

We must be both strategic and smart about the day-to-day wars we fight and not let our emotions overrule reason when deciding to engage in battle or back away. To make sound decisions and pick the right battles to fight, you must:

- Strive to collect facts upfront.
- Understand scenarios objectively and holistically.
- Comprehend your goals.
- Strategize how to achieve your objective.
- Prioritize supporting tasks.
- Apply these strategies and take action.
- Learn from the results.
- Constantly reassess scenarios and challenges and adapt accordingly.

Accurately gauge and interpret the opportunities and obstacles presented. Respect the chances of each coming to pass. Understand what it is that you're after, what it takes to get there, and what you'll do if your tactics don't meet with success. Survey the battlefield, understand the players involved, and choose where to strike. Then go ahead and strike decisively.

Every business decision is a battle to be fought. Know how, when, and where to deploy your resources most effectively to get what you want. By being calmer and more calculated, you can make better decisions, avoid potential pitfalls, and steer toward safer bets.

Deciding Which Opportunities and Issues to Focus On

Developing the ability to identify the opportunities and issues that deserve your attention, prioritizing them, and then deciding which ones to tackle and which ones to put on the back burner or discard altogether are tremendously important skills to have in life and business. In fact, I believe they are absolutely essential for successfully future-proofing yourself or your organization. While every choice has two costs (hard and opportunity) attached, deciding which battles to fight doesn't require you to be a master strategist. Merely look to the horizon to anticipate coming trends in the business or job market and then prepare yourself to be at the right place with the right capabilities, resources, and contacts at the right time. How?

- **Focus on existing, emerging, and future trends, and gauge the impact and staying power of each.** By seeing the bigger picture, and tracking larger trends as they evolve, you'll be able to identify pressing changes in your environment and determine whether to take action. Learning, contact, skills, and capability updates or strategic realignments made now, in advance of these changes, will pay dividends tomorrow.

- **Be curious, keep an open mind, and ask questions.** Curiosity doesn't kill cats. But it does give many business professionals and organizations a very real edge. Most important, by providing fresh viewpoints and spurring you to action, it can give you an edge as well.

- **Avoid fads.** Fads are just that—temporary crazes—thus they aren't the right place to hang your star or stake your future. Fads are bright, shiny, and addictive, but they just don't last. Ask yourself, Does what's in fashion have long-term potential? If not, make the most of it while you can, but also prepare yourself to make more from opportunities that do.

- **Familiarize yourself now with talents, tools, and insights that will be in demand later.** When a significant trend does hit, you will need to be in a position to leverage it to your advantage. This may require acquiring new skills, capabilities, connections, resources, or training. Get these now, *before* you need them, not after. The best time to buy a fire extinguisher is before the house starts burning down around you.

- **Be in the right place at the right time.** Suspect the future will make a juke move in a few years away from the business, industry, market, or role you're currently in? Adapt your approach and pursue a strategic position where you'll instead be able to capitalize on the coming shift. Relevancy makes a great insurance policy.

Seize every opportunity to expand your experience, skill sets, capabilities, and contact networks . . . and prioritize those most readily adaptable to varied contexts for the battles ahead. Also recognize the value gained when others are willing to underwrite the opportunity costs associated with such endeavors. If an employer's willing to send you to MBA school (that is, make you more valuable) or give you the chance to spearhead innovation in new areas, ride that interest-free self-reinvestment straight to the bank.

Above all, play chess, not checkers. Instead of focusing on day-to-day minutiae, think several steps ahead and look for chances to build long-term learning and assets that create lasting returns. Tomorrow's leaders recognize that the world is constantly changing, and take pains to constantly grow and change as well. When you're strategic about your fights and think ahead, others are already three steps behind.

Dealing with Overwhelming Odds

Granted, fighting battles isn't always simple, especially when chance doesn't seem to play in your favor. Sometimes we know that the odds are weighted against us, and we find ourselves mired in the fear that we are about to be overcome (fail).

Although we can't outmaneuver every challenge or avoid every opponent every time, we can always try to pick the time, place and condition under which we fight our battles, and greatly improve our odds of success by doing so. This may mean having to press forward ahead of schedule, reposition products and strategies, and rethink target audiences, even potentially delaying or trashing our plans until a more opportune moment arrives to strike at rivals.

For instance, in the 1970s and 1980s, John Sculley, former VP of marketing for PepsiCo, brought the world the famous Pepsi Challenge—a blind taste test in which shoppers sampled two colas (Coca-Cola and Pepsi) to see which they preferred. But the marketing campaign, which naturally favored Pepsi and put the brand on the map, never began as a direct assault on its rival. Rather, it was more akin to a guerrilla campaign.

"In those days, Coke was number one, and outsold us nine to one," recalls Sculley.[3] So Pepsi began by rolling out the challenge regionally to Coke's top markets.

Why? "Because we had a competitor who didn't think they had anything to worry about [in these areas]," recalls Sculley. Despite Coke's strongholds in their best markets, Pepsi knew that its rival's distributors weren't expecting competitors in their own backyard, where they felt most comfortable. So PepsiCo stealthily rolled its campaign out right beneath Coke's nose and carefully kept a lid on the taste tests, so as not to alert Coke's bottlers.

By the time PepsiCo decided to make noise, the campaign had begun to roll out regionally, backed by millions of dollars in TV ads; it was too late for Coke to counter. The upstart PepsiCo quickly boosted its market share, and went from underdog to heavyweight contender.

Consider taking the following approaches to achieve similar results when faced by what appear to be challenging odds:

- **Constantly weigh the chances and odds of success for reaching the goals that you've set for yourself.** Run the numbers to determine your real chances of achieving victory. Do your homework, and research choices extensively. When introducing new products, first conduct focus groups. When applying for a job, study your prospective employer and what most rival candidates will have to offer them. When facing new competitors, first conduct extensive research into their strengths and weaknesses.

- **Choose your engagements.** Strike where competitors aren't— that is, by pitching or packaging products to better meet the needs of an underserved and lucrative niche audience. The less competition you face and less frequently you face it head-on, the likelier the odds of success and skirting trouble will be. The harder you nip at rivals' Achilles' heels, the greater the impact you'll produce. Similarly, prioritize opportunities most likely to play in your favor with the biggest potential long-term payouts. Tempting as chasing short-term gains can appear, when you factor in associated opportunity costs, the numbers ultimately may not add up in the end.

- **Pick your battlefield and scout it out in advance.** If you're going to confront competitors, then be the one who decides where the battle will be conducted—at what time, via which medium, and in front of which audience. Look for times when you know your competitors are preoccupied, areas of business where they're weak, and markets in which they've yet to effectively play. For example, rather than engaging a larger competitor in pricing wars via TV ads targeted at mainstream shoppers, you might choose to battle on online forums populated by social influencers.

- **Know when to cut your losses, double down, or try another tack.** If a sales, promotion, or operations strategy isn't working, don't be afraid to speak up and try alternatives. You can't win every confrontation, but you can learn from all of them, and use new insights to improve your strategies as the fight continues. Become wiser through experience and don't repeat past mistakes, and you can still win the war, even if you lose the battle.

Strategy Begins from Within

Of course, when planning which battles to fight, and how to fight them, you have to look internally as well as externally; you can control your actions and decisions but not unexpected shifts in competitors' strategies or changing business environments. If the terrain you face is unpredictable or uncertain, or rivals respond by adjusting their own tactics, as we learned in Chapter 7, all you can do is improvise. If you can't change the way the world works, then strategically change how you respond to it, a far simpler and more effective approach than trying to change your actual operating environment.

Like many millennials, Andrew Stinger has already enjoyed his fair share of employers and professions. Since graduating in 2006, he's been a paralegal, customer service rep, and online marketing specialist. But unlike many peers, he's not worried about constant career upheaval. Because he employs a flexible strategy that involves taking on a progression of carefully chosen job roles that provide compounding experience and education and act as springboards to further opportunity, he's never concerned about remaining relevant.

Early on in his career, Stinger says that he learned an important lesson by watching high-tech entrepreneurs: Given how fast the world must change, we must adapt equally fast, and the only sure way to do so is take smart risks. In a world of endless disruption, ambition can take you only so far in your career unless it's backed up by real-world learning and experience. So Stinger created a PowerPoint presentation of his own skills and experiences to determine where he was lacking in skill or capability.

Then he began taking on full-time roles that would help add to his professional strengths and help fill in the gaps. Stinger's so confident in this strategy that he abandoned a job at Google to join a small, unproven start-up offering him more challenging roles and responsibilities in a more demanding environment. (Going from "a cruise ship to a Jet Ski," as he puts it.)

The only way to succeed now, he says, is to make tactical choices that consistently keep you at the forefront of your field and to expand your abilities to adapt with changing environments. Stinger explains that to win today, you can't just exercise the same skills, make the same choices, or defer to past experience. You've got to purposefully cultivate flexibility and resilience, abilities gained only over time by patiently and consistently stretching yourself. "More and more," he says, "everyone is looking for a generalist."[4] To get ahead, learn as much as you can, as fast as you can, he counsels, and be highly strategic about the opportunities you pursue.

When it comes to careers, there's a big difference between *development* and *advancement.* You can keep pushing forward aimlessly to greater financial reward. But at some point, as markets realign or shift, disruption is assured, changing the skills or services that will be in demand. To address these sea changes, Stinger insists, you must prepare for them by equipping yourself with the resources and training you need to adapt well in advance. If you've had a plan in place and been strategic about gathering ways and means prior to their arrival though, you'll be well equipped to work through these shifts.

"One of the key things, especially as an entry-level employee today, is to jettison any sense of entitlement," he counsels. "Learning how to learn is vital. Front-load your time in a new company or role with learning and mastering knowledge."

On an organizational level, strategies for successfully adaptation can be as simple as providing ongoing opportunities for employees to learn, get additional hands-on training, and brainstorm new ideas. But on a personal level, says Stinger, education needn't be so formal or extensive. You can purposefully grow your capabilities every single day at work as you take on new projects, shadow colleagues in other departments, and familiarize yourself with emerging technology platforms. Off the clock, you can pursue personal hobbies and interests. Either way, it's essential to identify overarching goals, pick your battles, and execute on action plans that help you achieve your larger objective, and then consistently revise your tactics and revisit plans as situations unfold.

The strategy you'll engage as you pick and choose your battles in business, career, and life originates from within you. Instead of trying to change the world, focus on the things you can change to tip the balance of the battle in your favor, including your own decisions, actions, and the way you respond to the world around you. Specifically:

- Keep pace of shifts in your industry by constantly broadening your experience and perspective.
- Cultivate flexibility and resilience in your life.
- Be a generalist, and learn as much as you can. Learn how to learn.
- Assume that disruptions will occur, and prepare for them in advance.
- Equip yourself with the skills and resources you need to improvise.
- Be purposeful and forward-thinking about the choices you make.

Seek out the tools, training, and expertise both you and your organization need to succeed long before you need them. Knowing is half the battle. If you're adequately prepared, the rest is all about being ready, willing and able to change as situations dictate.

Being More Resourceful in Business

Picking and choosing one's battles is a constant process of assessment and reassessment; it's a fine balancing act. But just as important as deciding when and where to strike and what personal and organizational capabilities you'll need to cultivate to effectively do so is the ability to craft a clever plan of attack.

This frequently means having to think fast on your feet and invent solutions on the fly, using whatever professional resources come to hand. As we discussed earlier, though, building a game-changing strategy doesn't necessarily mean having to raise vast amounts of capital, convince high-level business leaders to explore new business directions, or galvanize hordes of colleagues toward a common goal. Sometimes, it just takes a little ingenuity and elbow grease to succeed and become successful faster than better-equipped, better-staffed, and better-experienced rivals.

Innovation doesn't have to be a fancy, complicated, or costly process to be wildly effective. Provided you know your customer, your strengths, and your industry, cunning ideas and executions can readily outshine even splashy product launches or extensive R&D investments.

Just ask Sara Blakely of Atlanta, Georgia, a former door-to-door fax machine salesperson, who's seen firsthand just how far shrewd strategies can vault you past competitors, and closer toward achieving your goals.

One day Blakely decided to cut the feet off a pair of her panty hose so that she would (in her words) "look smashing" in a pair of slacks. She filed for a patent for her footless body-shaping panty hose, and with $5,000 in savings started her own business: Spanx, a company that today sells more than 200 different kinds of products and is worth more than $1 billion. But Blakely did much more than think of a good idea and file for a patent. She also used cost-effective guerrilla sales strategies, which rapidly kick-started her business, enabling it to grow faster than her rivals' companies, which were spending millions of dollars on marketing.

Back when Spanx was still unknown, Blakely had managed to place products in Neiman Marcus department stores. But they weren't selling as fast as she hoped because these products had been given little in-store space and promotional exposure. So Blakely bought cardboard stands at Target, stocked them full of Spanx hosiery, and set them up as kiosks in local retailers. Employees naturally assumed that these displays were approved by store managers. When customers kept coming to the register to buy Spanx in increasing numbers, and cashiers couldn't scan the product, stores didn't toss out the stands. Instead, managers specifically ordered that Blakely's promotional kiosks be left up. It was an incredibly resourceful and gutsy move on Blakely's part, and it was immensely successful.

Likewise, back in 1999, Jack Ma, a thirty-five-year-old English teacher and Internet entrepreneur living in Hangzhou, China, also had a dream: to connect the nation's rapidly growing economy with the global business-to-business (B2B) marketplace. He hoped to do this by using the power of the Internet to link small- and medium-size enterprises to customers and suppliers all over the world. Because the new venture would be dedicated to opening the doors of the global bazaar to Chinese companies, he decided to call it Alibaba.

But opening those doors wouldn't be simple. A decade ago, the Chinese business market—thanks to its mammoth-scale, unprecedented rate of growth and sudden unpredictable shifts—was little short of bewildering. The entire world wanted to do business in China. But very few companies knew how to make the contacts they needed within the country, much less speak the language or understand the business culture.

Brainstorming a clever way to parlay this situation into a sustainable business, Ma decided Alibaba would play the role of online matchmaker, pairing Chinese businesses with foreign companies seeking to buy Chinese products. Realizing that Western business models predicated on taming uncertainty would not work in China, Ma resourcefully poised Alibaba to successfully traverse a chaotic marketplace by helping *other* businesses navigate its turbulent waters. Today, the Alibaba Group is a multibillion-dollar corporate giant that employs more than 24,000 people worldwide.

Many times, a simple shift in thinking is all it takes to turn a seeming black hole in the marketplace into an open door of opportunity or turn an ailing strategy into a successful one. As before, the more objective you are about the challenges before you, the more deliberate you are about picking your battles; the more creatively you're willing to fight them, the more anything and everything becomes possible.

When McDonald's Canada wanted to connect with customers, it didn't carpet bomb them with surveys or badmouth competitors. It created a YouTube channel where anyone could ask anything and get a video response. Over 2 million interactions later, viewers were watching its clips an average of four minutes apiece (as opposed to the thirty-odd *seconds* most businesses hope for), with Big Macs and Chicken McNuggets top of mind.

When young adults in Australia stopped drinking its soda and began getting together more often online than in real life, Coca-Cola didn't introduce new flavors. It printed the 150 most popular Australian names on Coke bottles and invited citizens to share these bottles and strike up conversations around them. Within just ninety days, young adults' consumption of its beverages had increased by 7 percent.

You can see this pattern of resourcefulness in the face of disruptive change, or mounting challenge, repeated across hundreds of examples in every industry. And it all comes back to the same formula: If you want to be more resourceful about picking your battles and going about fighting them, don't make assumptions—apply the FEAR model. Focus on the challenge before you and the many potential options you have for addressing it. Engage with it by deploying novel solutions. Assess how well your efforts were received, and retool less well received ones. Respond by coming up with even more wildly original workarounds—you'll discover many ways to overcome challenges, if only you can see the problems from the right angle.

Reconsider the obstacles that you think lie before you, and the many plans of attack at your disposal: What would you do if time and resources were no object, and is that time and are those resources truly needed? Contemplate if there's a more clever way to plow through hurdles or if there's another way to simply leapfrog over or steer around them. Most important, view anything and everything as possible until proven otherwise.

As you pick and choose the battles you will fight in your own business, career, and life, remember that none of us has an unlimited ability (much less the time or the money) to act on every single opportunity that comes our way or to surmount every challenge that lies in our path. We must be strategic and smart about where we concentrate our efforts, choosing courses of action that offer the most lucrative and likely returns. Focus your attention on those; don't let yourself get stretched thin or get diverted.

Bringing Your Strategy Together

Of course, as you set about the process of innovating and outpacing competitors, don't expect rivals to sit still, either. Take pains to guard your flanks. The entire executive team at the fast-growing organic restaurant chain Freshii consistently gathers on a running basis to ask themselves: "If we were our competitor, what would we do to beat us at our game?" These leaders are constantly looking for something to fix, even if it isn't broken. As founder Matthew Corrin told me, rather than patting themselves on the back for a job well done, they're focusing on "the bad stuff first, good stuff last."[5]

On the first Monday of every month, all fifty employees at ad agency Conversation shut off their phones, inboxes, and computers and lock themselves in a room to discuss and review current business challenges.[6] The company's strategy sessions, dedicated to keeping it innovative and on top of rising concerns, have helped it create better systems for addressing pending threats, provided deeper insights into emerging trends, and increased productivity.[7] These get-togethers have also streamlined workflow processes, helping make the business more nimble and responsive in the wake of impending challenges.

While time away from customers may cost the company in the immediate, by reinvesting that time in the business itself, executives say it helps the enterprise stay ahead of the curve. Setting aside time to pause and review your business environment is vital to spotting potential stumbling blocks, they say, so you can steer around them, or identify and seize on more promising avenues of growth.

To summarize: Clarity is crucial when crafting a business or career strategy, and picking and choosing your battles is vital to ongoing success. But so is the ability to create clever defenses, and resourceful plans of attack. Carefully assess your professional environment, and any challenges or windows of opportunity it may present. Decide which to act on; but before acting, put a system for readily detecting threats, executing backup plans, and performing strategic shifts in place. Set a goal, study the challenges before you, and review your options. Pick the most practical and powerful of all your clever ideas, the one that offers the biggest possible impact and return on investment, to act on. Then pick ways to begin executing it.

As you go about this process, keep an eye on the horizon, watching for emerging trends, but avoid those bright and shiny fads and fleeting diversions that can steer us off the most-direct path to success. You can do this by thinking several steps ahead and dealing with even the most challenging odds by picking the time, place, and condition under which you'll fight your battles. Remember: Strategy begins from within, and while you can't control rivals' strategies, competitive landscapes, or unforeseen events, you can control how you respond to them. Be resourceful, be innovative, and be agile. Force others to fight on your terms, and succeed by staying on your toes, constantly pushing forward and keeping your competitors off balance.

Action Steps

First, the bad news: You can't win every battle that you fight in life and business. Now the good: You can absolutely win some, including those that count most, by being more strategic. You will be far more effective if you pick your battles—that is, dictate the terms under which they'll be fought and relentlessly focus your energy and effort where it will most meaningfully affect positive change. Here are some action steps you can take right now to be more successful about choosing which battles to fight, and when, where, and under which conditions:

- **Stack the odds in your favor.** Do this by picking and choosing your battles. This means objectively and intelligently defining the challenges before you, seeking out opportunities, and then deciding on a promising means of advancement, including knowing when to proceed, when to hold the line, and when to retreat. Once you've settled on a strategy and have fully studied the obstacles and choices before you, move forward at the time and place that best suits your purposes.
- **Prioritize your attention.** Every choice comes with two costs attached: hard and opportunity. Look ahead to coming changes and decide which you can leverage to make the biggest im-

pact, knowing that your time, energy, and resources are finite. Don't hitch your wagon on fleeting developments, and remember to align where you're heading with where things are going. Do today what it takes to succeed tomorrow, positioning yourself to be in the right place at the right time with the right tools in hand.

- **Ask many questions.** The more questions you ask, the better able you will be to decide which battles to fight, and which to decline or avoid.
- **Weigh the odds and challenges before you.** Pursue the opportunities that offer the best payoffs, while passing on those that don't add much to your capabilities, assets, or bottom line.
- **Play only where you think you have a reasonable chance of winning.** Instead of tackling bigger competitors head-on, find ways to sneak by or run rings around them. Make them fight on your terms, and in ways that allow you to exercise your own unique competitive advantages.
- **Change your tactics to match your environment.** You have a limited ability to affect things in your environment, so focus on ways you can change your own actions, decisions, and strategies to adapt to your operating reality or respond to new developments. In doing so, you'll more capably deal with the challenges or opportunities presented.
- **Be more resourceful.** Craft clever plans of attack, think fast on your feet, and invent solutions on the fly, using whatever resources you have at your disposal. Be creative, audacious, and bold.
- **Bring your strategy together.** Play both offense and defense and keep a close eye on your competition. You can't expect

competitors to remain still while you move forward. Constantly look for ways to improve your approaches and your products and services. Make them better by thinking about how and where opportunity may present itself, potential challenges may arise, or competitors could strike next.

Chapter Eleven

Rule 9: Keep Forging Ahead

Things weren't going well for Genevieve Waldman. A successful public relations pro known for her winning attitude, she'd found both her confidence shattered and status quo upended following a nasty divorce.

"I'm working full-time," she recalls. "I had a dog and a mortgage . . . a very active social life. But I just wasn't prepared for what happened."[1] Shocked, saddened, and deeply frightened by the sudden change, she took time off from work, avoided family and friends, and found herself trapped in a painful cycle of depression.

Then, one day, at the deepest point of her downward spiral, a strange thing happened: Waldman's professional instincts suddenly began to kick in. Gripped by cold rationality, she asked herself what would happen if she continued to follow this path. Scared of her current situation, but more frightened of where she was heading, she carefully studied her situation and, after weighing potential solutions, made herself a promise.

Not only would she pick herself back up by her bootstraps, as she'd always done in her career, she'd also lay her fears and insecurities to rest forever. The plan: For one full year, every time the word *can't* came out of her mouth, she would turn it into *can*.

When a colleague suggested joining an office ski-racing team, Waldman's immediate thought was, *I can't*. She hadn't skied since childhood. That same Friday, she found herself hurtling downhill. When she wanted a new car, she told herself "I *can't* get a Porsche." She didn't even know how to handle a stick shift. When she went into the dealership to buy one, after the salesman stopped laughing and realized she was serious, he took the afternoon off and gave her a lesson. She drove the car home that same day. And when a job opportunity presented itself in Europe, she said I *can't* live overseas: I don't have friends, family, or a support system there. Shortly thereafter, she moved abroad and found herself heading a market-leading software company's entire PR division.

"You can say I was fearless," she points out. "But does that mean I'm not scared? Absolutely not—it just means I put challenges into perspective. You can tell yourself *I choose not to*. But understand that that's a very different sentence than *I can't*."

Having found success by conquering her fears, she offers the following advice: When confronted by a problem, don't be afraid to ask questions. Prod at it to gain insight. Dive in headfirst. Don't be afraid to seek assistance. Analyze your fears methodically and act on the insights you gain. Understand the messages being sent and learn how to capitalize on them. Then, most crucially, take action; you've got to keep forging ahead. By consistently and capably dealing with any issue at hand, you can dispense with it and even transform it into a source of opportunity.

Rule 9: Keep Forging Ahead

Whether we're speaking of business or career-related concerns, the game of life looks much like a game of football. Ground will constantly be gained and lost, hopes lifted and crushed. To allay fears, and produce more positive outcomes, keep moving the ball downfield. Every inch counts, so make the plays that deliver the most yardage fastest, and don't stop your forward momentum, even when you encounter pushback.

From the perspective of those who are insecure or intimidated by the challenges they're facing, forging ahead may sound like a grandiose concept and the epitome of wishful thinking. From the perspective of those who choose to act more courageously, it's merely a process of taking action. The secret to getting ahead, no matter the obstacles you face, isn't that much of a secret. Merely start or embrace the new ideas, projects, and activities that most rapidly or profoundly enhance your learning, capabilities, and connections and provide more pronounced opportunities to innovate, differentiate, and expand your horizons. Or if you're an individual looking to create change in your life on a personal level, simply try new things and take more chances and make a point to raise your hand, volunteer, and contribute.

Whatever you do, be proactive, and keep trying. Don't allow a knockdown to turn into a knockout, and don't remain static: If you stumble, stand back up, and keep forging ahead until you find the success you're seeking.

This means adopting an action-oriented stance and being in a constant learning and growth mode. Those who keep playing the game, and keep playing persistently, are the essence of what we call go-getters. Anyone, or any enterprise, has the ability to become one. The best way to do so: Never stop changing, adapting, or plugging away at success and you'll never stop finding ways to get ahead.

However accomplished or successful you or your organization are, never forget that you are a work in progress. To keep yourself moving forward, you must:

- Perform your work with energy and drive.
- Exercise your unique skills and talents.
- Expand your comfort zone.
- Weigh every opportunity objectively.
- Take decisive action when opportunities (or challenges) present themselves.
- Dive into new initiatives or roles with relish.
- Consistently find ways to connect people and organizations.
- Learn from your mistakes and try again.
- Reprioritize and realign strategies as new information is gained.
- Be brutal with your schedule, but generous with others.
- Look for ways to help, assist, and pay it forward.

The more you dive in, volunteer, or go out of your way to create opportunity, the more rapidly you put yourself in a position to achieve success. The more you bounce back from adversity, the stronger you emerge from having weathered it. New challenges present new chances to better ourselves. Simply maintaining the status quo or holding the proverbial line is merely a sustaining activity. To stay ahead in life and business, you've also got to be willing to move forward without hesitation when opportunity presents itself.

You cannot afford to remain static or rigid in your thinking. Sure, you or your business will undoubtedly take a few hits as you go about this process. But it doesn't mean you can't get back up and right back at it, ready to adapt your strategy and address any areas where improvement is needed.

Revisiting the football analogy, don't be intimidated by the challenges (or challengers) that stand before you. Instead, constantly look for gaps on the playing field to sprint through and ways to steer past potential setbacks; then keep pushing for the end zone. By charging onward to the point where proceeding is less painful than falling back and constantly moving the ball forward, we can build courage and resilience while increasing our chances to succeed and put points on the scoreboard.

Remaking Our Attitudes and Approaches

Tomorrow may be unknown and uncertain, but we can always prepare ourselves to face it. Moreover, the future is ours to shape when we keep forging ahead and doing so with an eye toward those aspects of the future over which we can actually exert a positive influence.

Want to put yourself in a position that puts you in constant forward motion in your life, career, or business? Start thinking about how you can actively steer toward more positive outcomes. Instead of trying to remake the world in your own image and responding with concern when it fails to comply, remake your own attitudes and approaches to fit the reality of the scenario. As we first saw in Chapter 2, observing, reacting, evaluating, and responding are the keys to successful future-proofing and sustaining forward momentum.

Getting ahead isn't just about energy and drive, it's also about routine reassessment. Wherever you are in your career or your business, regularly stop and reconsider whether you're still working most effectively toward the results you're seeking. The way forward is ever changing and so are the challenges we face; therefore, if we want to keep triumphantly forging ahead, we must be ever changing too.

New competitors may arrive on the scene, old competitors may be reenergized by the injection of new talent and ideas. Similarly, our careers can take unexpected twists and turns as we navigate rapidly shifting industries and markets. In any case, we must be ready to quickly pivot, lest we be overtaken by rivals or undone by our own unwillingness to course correct. You've got to be ready to keep moving forward, but as we've seen in earlier chapters, not necessarily by moving in a straight line.

To fruitlessly preoccupy ourselves worrying over the unknown and uncertain factors that change heralds is akin to running in place, leaving ourselves woefully unprepared to greet the obstacles and outcomes such sea changes will inevitably bring. That's why it's important to keep our eyes open, keep adapting, and keep seeking out the opportunities that push us farther along the road to success. You must always be creating forward momentum.

We can, for example, embark on new corporate initiatives, develop new product ventures, and create new personal or professional development programs. We can also decide how much time, effort, and resources we want to invest in these tactics and influence the quality of our output through skilled planning, hard work, and diligent execution.

We cannot control, however, whether consumers or colleagues will warm up to our new choices, and we can't control our efforts' ultimate success. But by trying, we've done everything we can to influence scenarios for the better and to influence outcomes so that we can always recover from any hurdles or setbacks.

Even better, as we keep diving in and taking more risks and notching up an increasing number of successes, we also cultivate growing awareness and the ability to discern what is the most promising path when faced with forks in the road. As a result, we further gain the clarity needed to strike where impact can truly be made, so we know when and how to best take action, allowing us to continue pushing forward more capably as time passes.

Herein lies the difference between those who are able to success-fully forge ahead on a consistent basis and those who are not. When confronted by the strange, unknown, or unfamiliar, the former takes calculated action, whereas the other reacts out of emotion or instinct.

So, what are some ways to remake your attitudes and approaches to ensure that you are ready and willing to be bold and to consis-tently forge ahead? Give these a try:

- **Accept what you can control and what you cannot.** Realize that while you can't control actions that other parties take, or un-expected twists of fate, you can control your response to them. In his book *Leading Through Uncertainty*, Umpqua Bank CEO Ray Davis says, "While you must be prepared for the uncertainties you can't control—with a plan in place if they come to pass—you can't dwell on them."[2] So while Davis doesn't spend much time worry-ing if a financial disaster is going to devastate the bank, he *does* spend time working with his staff to make plans for such an event. Being prepared for an uncontrollable event is something he *can* control, and he does just that, allowing Umpqua Bank the opportunity to keep forging ahead, even when faced with difficulty.

- **Don't chase ghosts; dive in with senses attuned, find the opportunities, and avoid or (better still) *solve* the problems.** Today, you are flooded with information, incoming data, and any number of potential problems and opportunities on a routine and recurring basis. But not every apparent problem is a real problem, and not every apparent opportunity is really an opportunity. The secret to addressing these challenges, and continuing to move forward in your life and business, isn't to sweat the unknown, but to take the time to examine each issue or scenario you face closely and assess if it's truly an opportunity or a problem. And, if you think you've got a problem, then take an even closer look to see if there's some way to convert it into an opportunity. When Amazon.com announced in 2013 that it had partnered with the U.S. Postal Service to initiate Sunday deliveries of orders for its Prime members starting immediately, this opportunity caught FedEx and UPS (not to mention Amazon's many competitors) flat-footed.[3] Amazon saw both an opportunity and a problem. The opportunity was the ability to serve customers faster and better than ever by initiating Sunday deliveries for repeat customers, which no one else was doing. The problem was that none of the major home delivery companies operated on Sunday. Amazon converted this problem into an opportunity by talking the Postal Service into using its employees and facilities specifically to deliver Amazon's packages on Sunday.

- **Don't try to remake the world; adapt your attitudes and approaches to fit reality.** In career and business, 99 times out of

100 it makes far more sense to adapt your own attitudes and approaches to fit the reality of what the world has given you, rather than to waste time and energy trying to change the world. According to a survey conducted by Harris Interactive for talent solutions company Glassdoor, in fact, 61 percent of employees polled said they found aspects of a new job different from the expectations that were set during the interview process. The most common differences were in the areas of employee morale (40 percent), job responsibilities (39 percent), work hours (37 percent), supervisor's personality (36 percent), and career advancement opportunities (27 percent).[4] So, if it were your new position, and you arrived to find a far different workplace scenario than promised or that your job responsibilities were not what you expected, what would you do? You could try to remake the working world by demanding that corporate culture shift, work hours change, or your new boss assign you the responsibilities you expected. You could find a more suitable job. Or you could adapt your attitudes and approaches to fit the reality that exists, work within the system to create positive change, proactively seek out the opportunities needed to excel, and create your own vehicles for upward momentum.

▪ **Course correct and refine when things don't go as planned.** No matter how many plans you make and how much data, people, or cash you throw at a business problem or opportunity, things may turn out quite different from what you imagined possible. This is also true in your career, which may require recalibration along the way to stay on track. That's why, as before, it's vital to constantly reassess and continuously ensure you're moving forward. Not sure if your career is on the right course or not? According to top authorities, answering no to the following questions means you're probably overdue for a career course correction:

- Am I happy with where I am in my career?
- Do I like the work that I'm doing?
- Am I getting appropriate recognition?
- Am I leveraging the skills I have or learning new ones?
- Am I rewarded for what I do?
- Am I swimming upstream in this career?
- Do I feel passionate about what I'm doing? About how I spend my day?

Uncertain if your business is on track? You can ask yourself similar questions, such as:

- Are we satisfied with our current strategy, message, and market position?
- Do we feel that we're creating high-quality, meaningful work?
- Are we serving customers in the best ways possible?
- Are we successfully expanding our capabilities, connections, and learning?
- Are we both meeting and surpassing industry standards?
- Are our market and sales potentials growing?
- Are we operating most efficiently, cost-effectively, and productively?

If you find a course correction is, in fact, needed, then make it. By taking action, you'll give yourself the flexibility you need to always be steering around potential stumbling blocks, and consistently forge ahead.

- **Pivot and shift as needed.** Sometimes, you need to make more than a simple course correction to succeed; you need to take an entirely different course. Before Walt Disney launched his successful film studio and amusement parks, he was a newspaper editor. Ellen DeGeneres was an oyster shucker. Kitchen impresario Julia Child was a spy, actor Harrison Ford a carpenter, and musician Elvis Costello a computer programmer. Companies pivot and shift, too. Such was the case with Hewlett-Packard, which pivoted from its late-1940s origins in engineering and electronics test equipment to electronic calculators in the 1970s, to personal computers for home use in the 1990s. YouTube was originally a video-dating site, and Twitter a podcasting operation. Each pivot took these companies closer to finding new customers, new revenue streams, and greater profits. Says Kevin Systrom, whose mobile photo app company Instagram—purchased by Facebook in 2012 for $730 million—started out as a check-in service by the name of Burbn, "[Changing stride] is a hard decision to make. But you have to be flexible enough to give yourself the opportunity to fall into these other opportunities."[5] Individuals and businesses seldom succeed on their first try: Despite associated fears and discomforts, keep pushing forward until you find what works.

Lessons in Modern Leadership

This brings us to an equally notable point—as we mentioned in Chapter 7—that improvising and making it up as we go is a vital skill we must regularly exercise if we hope to consistently get ahead.

You don't need an advanced degree or fancy job title to excel at improvising, either: Just start thinking like a leader.

But a contemporary leader doesn't have to be a great intellectual, orator, or politician, simply someone able to solve problems and create results—in other words, just make and do. In the absence of progress, leaders don't wait for instruction, they keep pushing forward and build, observe, refine, and react, using whatever insights and resources are available to address the situation at hand. Regardless of your experience level, job position, or background, you can succeed by constantly moving forward and acting like a leader too: Consider this your official promotion.

Given the power to put forward out best efforts that instilling a sense of accountability, ownership, and leadership in ourselves provides us, you'd think that many organizations would celebrate this quality. But Bing Gordon, head of venture capital firm Kleiner Perkins Caufield & Byers (a $250 million investment initiative from Comcast, Amazon, and Facebook), says that not all enterprises encourage workers to think and act like leaders. In fact, many operating in the modern workplace actually train professionals to do just the opposite.

According to Gordon, "When I taught at the University of Southern California, I found that students could do almost any assignment in a week, so long as it was clearly stated, and they had the ability to ask clarifying questions. Give them two weeks to do the same work, and they'd start a week in advance anyway."[6]

"When these best and brightest get into a big company, though," he notes, "I saw them take twice as long, and actually resist weekly goals. They wanted the second week to check that they weren't going to embarrass themselves. When people like this got their first promotion, they took even longer. And at VP level, longer again. Same amount of work hours, but logarithmic increase in CYA (cover your ass) hours."

Or, as educator Jake Breeden told Southwest Airlines' *Spirit* magazine, "Collaboration is successful when individuals with the courage to commit to their own work bring ideas to the table. Fish school together to protect themselves from predators. Similarly, people seek safety in numbers to hide from the shark of accountability. Collaboration fails when it becomes a habit."[7]

To get ahead in life and business, you've got be courageous, self-sufficient, and willing to speak up and take action—that is, constantly moving forward and thinking and acting like a leader. It's the surest, simplest way to keep victoriously forging onward.

At instant messenger software maker Xfire, traits like leadership, accountability, and quick decision making are intrinsically baked into corporate culture. Employees are expected to show up to meetings having conducted research, being game to present innovative ideas, and being able to back up their arguments. By turning every member of the organization into leaders and outspoken contributors, the business is able to make smarter decisions, react more quickly than rivals, and launch products at record speeds.[8]

In the words of educator John Holt, "Leadership qualities are not the qualities that enable people to attract followers, but those that enable them to do without them. They include, at the very least, courage, endurance, patience, humor, flexibility, resourcefulness, stubbornness, a keen sense of reality, and the ability to keep a cool and clear head, even when things are going badly. True leaders, in short, do not make people into followers, but into other leaders."[9]

Writing about successful baseball managers (among the most resilient and experienced of team captains), author Buzz Bissinger further says that they must possess the skills of a tactician, psychologist, and riverboat gambler:

- Tacticians because they must sense developing currents, predict competitors' actions, and plan responses to rivals' impending countermoves
- Psychologists because they must provide clear goals, encouragement, and feedback
- Riverboat gamblers because they must understand probabilities and be able to read opponents

But you don't need to have an MLB franchise at your fingertips for these principles to apply.

To keep pushing forward, you've got to be able to make clever, creative, and courageous choices, and then keep making them again and again. Decision makers must ultimately develop two vital skills, says Phil Rosenzweig, author of *Left Brain, Right Stuff: How Leaders Make Winning Decisions*. Specifically, they need the ability to discern the facts of the decision at hand and offer an appropriate response. "They require a seemingly contradictory blend: a talent for clear-eyed analysis and the ability to take bold action."[10] Put simply, despite the challenges they face, leaders must move forward relentlessly, with their senses sharp, if they want to keep winning and making good decisions.

Today's leaders must also doggedly channel actions into end results, whether by constructing from scratch, brainstorming new solutions, or serving as connectors that help others act more effectively in concert. Invent or innovate: Either way, they're constantly seizing emerging opportunities to remix, repurpose, and recycle the old into new, generating forward momentum by doing so. And you can easily become a leader as well.

Stop seeing absences or lack of activity as causes for doubt. Look at them as signs of potential opportunities instead. Fill in the gaps by being a leader and pushing onward to provide solutions, and you've got all the qualifications you need to succeed.

Action Steps

To future-proof yourself, you must be willing to continuously forge ahead, adapt, and explore new areas of personal and professional growth, even while suffering from the distorting effects of the seven fears. You've also got to be able to handle setbacks and adversity as they come, learning from these experiences to keep pushing onward more effectively. Here are some actions you can take to continue to move forward in your life and business, regardless of what the future hurls your way:

- **Know what is within your power to control.** Quit trying to control what you cannot. You're just wasting your time, energy, and money. Focus on the action steps and decisions you can undertake to help propel forward momentum. Be proactive, not reactive. Put plans, programs, and/or platforms in place that allow for constant, ongoing change, growth, education, and experimentation to help you address potential problems or make course corrections long before they ever become concerns.
- **Remake your attitudes to match reality.** Don't expect to remake the world in your image; it's not going to work. Instead,

work with what you've got. To quickly leapfrog ahead of the pack and find success, start searching where others have yet to look, and make ever-deeper forays into such unknown and promising new avenues of exploration.

- **Be ever changing.** The world is constantly changing, as are markets, customers, and businesses. Keep evolving and seeking out opportunities that will lead you to the success you desire. Update, keep trying, make prototypes, and react. Don't stop or accept the status quo; success is always temporary.

- **Don't hesitate to adapt.** When the world changes around you or when obstacles can't be surmounted no matter how hard you try, pivot to an entirely new or different course to sustain forward momentum. The key is to plan several steps ahead, while your house is stable, that way you'll be well-equipped to keep moving forward and handle any changes if the structure ever threatens to collapse.

- **Build and maintain relationships.** To remain relevant, you must forge a direct and ongoing relationship with your customers. Of course, recognize that customers are suddenly everyone (for example, supervisors, peers, colleagues, and vendors) you deal with, not just those who buy items or services from you. By proactively taking steps to understand their needs and the specific problems they're looking to solve, you gain the insight needed to do what it takes to stay current, create a leading solution going forward, and maintain a perpetual growth mode. Likewise, their partnership and feedback can provide precious assistance and insights that can help you fill in the blanks and fuel the rapid repetitions which will help you keep ahead of changing organizations and business environments.

- **Make continuous self-reinvestments.** Before you give yourself to others (which you certainly should do when it makes sense to do so), reinvest in yourself first. Obtain the skills, contacts, capabilities, resources, and opportunities needed to drive your future growth and advancement. Put time into building your own education, learning, and networks of relationships that will pay dividends to you in the future.
- **Never stop moving forward.** To forge far ahead of competitors, it pays to take a leap and look for places to soar where there are no ceilings, recognizing that singular achievements point out a flaw with perfection; once there's nowhere else to go, things cease to be remarkable. Keep your eyes on the changing environment around you, and constantly update your strategies, approaches, and perspective to match. Success may be fleeting, but it's easier to latch onto when you're constantly nipping at its heels.

Chapter Twelve

Rule 10: Stay Relevant

L&T General Insurance is a full-service health, property, and casualty provider. Part of a $12 billion business group, it's about the last place you'd expect to find executives taking risks, let alone huge ones. But recently, it decided to take a large gamble, making a run at India's nationwide insurance market.

Just one problem: Traditional strategies that worked in the West, such as one-size-fits-all insurance packages (income levels widely vary) and networks of local brokers (it's a big country) couldn't be simply superimposed on the Indian market. Instead, serving the nation's far-flung and diverse population would require a solution that offered more affordable pricing for varied customer segments and one scalable enough to reach the most remote towns and villages. This solution wouldn't just have to be accessible, reliable, and capable of working on a massive scope. It would also have to differentiate itself quickly; build trust; and most crucially, make itself relevant to one of the world's most complex emerging markets.

Luckily, all L&T had to do to solve the problem was look in its pocket.

You see, more than 900 million Indians now carry cellphones, most Internet ready. And so L&T provided a simple, straightforward solution a great deal of them could get on board with by rolling out a cloud-based online platform capable of issuing policies, handling claims, and filing paperwork from nearly any device. This system allowed L&T to pass cost savings on to customers via variably priced insurance packages and paperless transactions. Equally as important, it also allowed its agents to go to customers, smile, and shake hands in person, instead of asking skeptical customers to come to them.

Had it simply retrofitted an existing Western business model to India, L&T would've found itself out of tune with its customers, out of luck in terms of implementation, and most likely out of business. Instead, with a simple tweak to an existing formula, and strategic repositioning, in less than two years, L&T went from operating just 10 branches to issuing over 100,000 policies worth more than $28 million.

The company didn't just do this by putting itself closer to Indian customers and offering policies at every price level, though. It also did so by making itself nimbler and more responsive and by offering a more viable solution for serving shoppers in every region. Put simply: L&T made itself a workable and sustainable choice and, most important, up and down the line, made itself more relevant to its end users.

The company combined tactics with technology in such a novel way in an emerging market that it actually leapfrogged many well-established ones, potentially making itself relevant to other evolving markets as well. In several years, as smartphones and tablets become more ubiquitous in other nations, and healthcare regulations change, perhaps L&T's solutions may be headed your way as well.

But that's the beauty of innovation: As we touched on earlier, it's not rocket science, and the secret to remaining relevant is simply *reinvention*. See opportunity. Study opportunity. Customize solutions. Assess responses and adapt. Keep doing that, and not only will you remain relevant on a running basis but the future will always be what you make of it.

Rule 10: Stay Relevant

More than ever, given today's frenetic pace, everything is evolving, and at a faster, more far-reaching clip. From careers to commercial markets, operational planning to organizational priorities, everything around us is in a state of perpetual flux. If you want to remain relevant, you'll have to keep course correcting to follow this winding road and keep adapting to stay in tune with its ever-changing environments.

Across the full spectrum of life and business, *change* is the only constant. The jobs we hold, the colleagues and collaborators we pal around with, and even the people we date or marry are seldom those we initially envision. In fact, most shift with surprising frequency. According to researchers at Utrecht University, half of even our closest friends are replaced every seven years.[1] Is it truly so strange and frightening that we must change personally and professionally to keep up with shifting topics and times as well?

Doing so is critical to advancing in today's fast-moving business environments and getting ahead when the time comes to make a move.

Realize that relevancy isn't a permanent state; it's a condition. And as in healthcare, the best medicine for dealing with changing conditions, whether acute or chronic, isn't necessarily the one you've been taking for years. Rather, it's the one that best cures the problem at hand. When you consistently strive to make yourself relevant and reinvent yourself with each passing season, you'll never fall behind or out of fashion. Moreover, when you always keep an eye on where things are heading, you can strive to be in a position to arrive at this destination before the world catches up, putting yourself at the forefront of emerging opportunities.

Do you feel like your business or career prospects are suddenly ailing, and in ways that are uncomfortable or unexpected? Next, we'll dig deeper into why you should be concerned about losing relevancy and value and then discover several ways you can move beyond such complaints and restore relevancy, using a few simple strategies and techniques.

Losing Relevancy and Value

No one wants to be left behind in this fast-changing world (read: isolated and rejected), but that's exactly what can happen if you don't make a near-constant effort to keep up with rising competitors. Fall behind in your skills, training, market knowledge, contacts, capabilities, and other business necessities, and guess what? You'll lose relevancy to your company or customers. And if you lose relevancy, you'll lose *value*. And when that happens, don't be surprised if key clients (including, potentially, your employer) go looking for someone new who can provide *more* value.

Just as workers can lose relevance and value by failing to maintain adequate knowledge and training, businesses can also lose relevance and value by not keeping up with customer needs. Long before Saab Automobile went bankrupt in 2011, the brand had lost relevance for the vast majority of U.S. car buyers, who bought 39,479 of the cars in 2000, but just 5,446 in 2010.[2]

The good news? Only *you* get to decide when to slam on the brakes in your career or enterprise.

As you might imagine, fears related to losing relevancy and value (including very real concerns such as loss of control and subsequent failure and embarrassment) can be important drivers of motivation and success. When you're worried about losing relevancy and value, you can expect the following good things to happen:

- **Fear will alert you to potential concerns.** Among such concerns are not knowing how to use new technology tools effectively, exercise cutting-edge methodologies, or reliably respond to new products and services being introduced by competitors. Once you detect any shortages, however, you can immediately begin taking steps to remedy them.

- **Concerns will prompt you to put proactive solutions and safeguards in place.** On a personal level, safeguards can be as simple as exploring multiple career opportunities simultaneously, experimenting with side projects, and attending social functions to expand your network of professional contacts. From an organizational standpoint, precautions can take the form of branching strategies, pilot programs, forays into new markets or industries, and other forward-thinking solutions. In all cases, when you're worried that you may fall behind, guess what? You'll quickly find yourself prodded to do whatever it takes to make sure that you *don't* fall behind, the best insurance policy against an uncertain future that you'll ever enjoy.

- **Worries will continuously motivate you to keep pressing and taking action.** The fear of losing relevance will propel you to keep seeking out new education, experiences, and opportunities, and remain constantly on the lookout over the horizon for the next big thing. Want to avoid falling behind in your chosen field or profession? Make a point of staying abreast of its changing landscape and pursuing the consistent capability, learning, and resource refreshes it takes to remain ahead of the curve.

To counter the underlying fears associated with losing relevancy and value, you must constantly:

- Challenge yourself to stay up to date with most current tools, trends strategies, and information available.
- Become fully plugged into your organization in ways that ensure you aren't left out of vital information and decision-making loops.
- Pursue ongoing skill and talent refreshes.
- Rethink your perspectives.
- Go from thought to action.

What can you do today—right now—to channel your anxieties into action? Here are a few simple suggestions:

- Pursue continuing education.
- Volunteer for new roles and responsibilities.
- Expand your network of contacts.
- Explore new business opportunities.
- Incubate and prototype new ideas.
- Research and take original approaches and angles.
- Expand your comfort zone through small acts of bravery.

Becoming Redundant

Because it can trigger any or all of the seven fears and applies universally, concerns that we may feel about becoming redundant often impact us deeply on both an individual and organizational level.

When a financial powerhouse like TD Ameritrade, Wells Fargo, or Bank of America acquires a small chain of community banks, it may no longer need all of the acquired chain's accounting staff; it may already have enough of its own. And when a company like Groupon, which was for a time a huge hit, loses its mojo with mainstream shoppers, it can quickly find itself replaced by a competitor such as LivingSocial. Faced with these prospects, we can retreat into a false cocoon of safety, trying to fall back on the strategies that brought us success thus far. Or we can respond to these fears of becoming more redundant by becoming more productive and using them to strive to boost our performance, differentiate ourselves, and make it difficult to easily duplicate or replace us— that is, to prevent us from becoming outmoded. The more singular and irreplaceable we make ourselves, the better branding, recognition, and perceived worth we enjoy and the more relevant we become.

Given the level of competition out there, it's completely understandable that many would experience the fears associated with becoming redundant quite keenly. But when we embrace these fears and own them, there are many welcome things that these concerns can (and should) induce us to do, including the following:

- **Plan for tomorrow today.** Instead of waiting to be made obsolete or redundant, you can plot how to adapt to changing environments and map out a strategy for doing so. Likewise, you can also research which capabilities will be required to thrive in future environments and determine the simple action steps that you can take to gain those skills, talents, tools or training. Make plans for the future that will enable you to stay relevant.

- **Acquire learning opportunities, experiences, and capabilities now that will be in demand later.** Determine where gaps in the marketplace or job market can and will exist and then look to fill them. To future-proof yourself, don't just stay up to date with the latest technologies, trends, business practices, and industry landscape. Plan several steps ahead and consider which routes present the brightest potential pathways to opportunity. Gain the capabilities, contacts, experiences, and resources that allow you to effectively pursue them. The most valuable will translate well to multiple industries and roles, so they'll serve you well in any capacity.

- **Bet against multiple outcomes and then hedge your bets.** Unless you've got a crystal ball that actually works, then there's no way to know which choices or decisions will provide you with the best future outcomes for certain. Because this is the case, research

possible alternatives, weigh the odds associated with each decision, and pick out a handful of the most promising to pursue.
Maximize your efforts by allocating them to a mix of activities
that sit at the cross-section of the most desirable, most lucrative,
and most likely opportunities to materialize; play a balanced and
diversified portfolio of bets.

- **Plot a business and/or career strategy that goes beyond
simple income-building activities to include a mix of educa-
tional and experiential opportunities.** The insights, opportunities, resources, and contacts gained from associated efforts can be
every bit as valuable as actual financial gains. You can't always predict the future, but you can certainly see many beginnings taking
shape at present. And, of course, take the necessary steps to expand
your capabilities, connections, and resources to remain relevant as
each story unfolds.

Ultimately, as with relevancy, only you can decide if you will
become redundant in your industry or enterprise. It's your choice
whether to keep your capabilities, contacts, and insights up to
date, and your skills current. If you feel a twinge of fear at the idea
of becoming redundant, consider why the many underlying causes
of these worries are present, and what you as an individual or enterprise need to do, build, or acquire to counteract them.

Staying Relevant in Your Career

Because relevancy isn't a permanent status, and one that's directly
affected by rapidly changing times, trends, and situations, it can

be a difficult state to maintain, especially in topsy-turvy professional environments. A fast-moving target, it's one we've always got
to keep our eye on and be aiming for to succeed, however. Therefore
it's vital to train ourselves to keep relevancy in our sights and perpetually strive to sustain it.

To maintain relevance, successful professionals must be committed to:

- Rethinking challenges
- Reconsidering goals and objectives
- Reexamining strategies and solutions
- Experimenting and failing
- Incubating new ideas
- Implementing flexible approaches
- Learning and adapting

How many app developers do you think existed twenty years
ago? Zero. How about Millennial generation experts? You're
right—zip. What about a chief listening officer (CLO)? Nope. That
one was invented in 2010 by Beth LaPierre at Eastman Kodak,
whose job it was to monitor the thousands of mentions of her company each month on blogs, forums, and social networks, looking
for emerging trends.[3] Internet data miners, social media managers, and cloud computing experts did not exist just two decades
ago. However, fast-changing times and technologies have brought
them all into being.

But these changes in careers cut both ways.

The U.S. Bureau of Labor Statistics' "Occupational Outlook
Handbook" provides projected growth rates for a variety of different occupations. While growth rates for veterinary technologists

and technicians, marriage and family therapists, medical assistants, glaziers, and audiologists are all positively bullish at 29 percent or higher, estimated growth rates are negative for air traffic controllers, file clerks, millwrights, and power plant operators.[4]

In all cases, the skills needed to succeed in each of these professions three years from now, let alone five or ten, will be vastly different from those required today.

"All the rules have changed," explains Randy Gage, bestselling author of *Risky Is the New Safe*.[5] "We're quickly approaching the time where a six-month certification will be more valuable, lucrative, and useful than an MBA or PhD." Why? Because it provides practical everyday job skills that pros can draw on when things inevitably change. In today's unstable environment, you can count on only one source of continued relevancy: the value of personal skills and experiences that can be leveraged to produce tangible results and that directly align with current and emerging needs.

Pointing to today's most successful entrepreneurs, Gage notes that precious few went to school to get degrees. Instead, they went there to acquire specific knowledge and, when academia could take them no further, went elsewhere to further their education.

"An employee who thinks like an employee is worthless," argues Gage, explaining that to stay relevant in your career, you'll have to think less linearly. "The people who want to stay employed and want to prosper will have to think like entrepreneurs. Critical thinkers are the ones who will write their own ticket and survive downsizings."

Now, countless substitutes all look and perform similarly to you and are easy to come by, especially from an employer's perspective. Unless you're a highly specialized or niche worker, the value you bring to the table is plummeting. And as even today's brightest stars warn, people are quickly becoming commodities.

Social media guru Gary Vaynerchuk is a poster child for online success. His Internet video series single-handedly took his website, WineLibrary, from $3 million to $45 million in business and paved the way for bestselling books and successful speaking tours. But even for proven standouts like Vaynerchuk, success is far from certain. Whether or not you're a celebrity, you can't afford *not* to take risks.

The Internet, Vaynerchuk notes, is among the fastest-moving and most cutthroat commercial landscapes today: a sign of what happens when competition in any field balloons to staggering size and change accelerates to breakneck pace. In chaotic and tumultuous online environs, even standouts such as Vaynerchuk constantly struggle to stay ahead of the curve; the next big sensation is just a single click or YouTube video away. The only cure for this condition, he says, is to be constantly seeking ways to change, innovate, and regain relevance. Unfortunately, most people don't think that way, he explains—a fortunate coincidence for those that do: "I'm successful on the back of people who are risk-averse, cozy, or comfortable," he says.[6]

If you want to stay relevant in your career, you've got to stay on your toes and stay creative.

Fictional spy MacGyver, star of the eponymous 1980s TV series, was renowned for his resourcefulness, using whatever materials were at hand to solve pressing dilemmas. You can continue to get ahead in your career by becoming the MacGyver of your own life and constantly seeking ways to expand your toolbox of talents, insights, and experience and then applying such skills creatively to solve problems and demonstrate your capabilities. As noted earlier, members of Generation Flux will be best equipped to succeed and stay relevant in today's era of uncertainty. The term, according to *Fast Company*, describes working professionals for whom adaptability, flexibility, openness to learning, and decisiveness in the face of ongoing change is the norm. In fact, the descriptor has nothing to do with age. Rather, it's a psychological designator: Anyone can belong to this group—all that matters is mind-set.

These individuals can be defined by the nature of their most prescient insights:

- The most important new survival skill today is the ability to acquire new skills.
- Multiple types of intelligence (emotional, social, practical, and so) and multiple types of skills (including soft skills, such as communications, empathy, and teamwork) will be required to succeed going forward.
- Real-life experience will hold greater value than classroom training.
- Rules will be constantly rethought, as will business models and best practices.
- Perspectives must be regularly reconsidered and recalibrated.
- The best approaches are those that work, whether or not they have worked in the past.
- Hierarchies and silos must be overcome: Successes will find ways to work inside and outside systems and inside and outside teams as well.
- Changing and adapting are our only options if we want to stay relevant and ahead of the curve.

The faster you start applying these principles in your career, the faster you'll start succeeding and the faster that you'll make yourself future-proof.

Of course, all of this change is also impacting our organizations, sometimes vaulting us ahead of our competition and sometimes kicking us into the ditch. Where we ultimately end up isn't a function of change itself, though, it's a function of how prepared we are to greet change and respond to it when it arrives, so we can take the steps needed to help ourselves remain relevant.

Keeping Your Business Relevant

While we can control to a great degree how relevant we remain in our personal lives and careers, when we look at an organization—particularly a large, well-established one—the task becomes much more difficult. The larger the organization and the more comfortable it is with success, the more likely it is to resist change and lose relevance.

The only truly sustainable method for keeping up with changing times and tastes—continuous adaptation—often directly flies in the face of established convention. (Especially in businesses that boast a long and proud legacy of successful processes, systems, and cultural norms.) This strategy requires us to shift in time with our environments and pursue constant growth and evolution. Doing so inevitably invites change, change that can be at odds with everything an efficiency-minded organization strives to achieve, prompting many of the fears discussed in Chapter 1 to come calling.

Luckily, the process of change doesn't have to be as painful or far-reaching as you suspect: If your enterprise isn't ready to think big, start thinking small. As we've seen throughout this book, slight adjustments to strategy or positioning can produce significant windfalls. Moreover, anyone can make these changes and steer themselves closer to finding success by continuing to adapt and innovate, no matter the scale at which these principles are applied. All you need to do is start thinking about which changes you can make today that will allow your capabilities to continue growing, stay in tune with others' needs, and maintain relevancy and value tomorrow.

Run regular systems checks to reveal whether current activities align with larger goals, and if shifts in strategy are required. Being relevant means staying on target and focusing on a target that's constantly moving. So to stay productive and stay relevant, tactics must change as well as attitudes and approaches. To effect positive change, you must make sure you're tying actions to outcomes in tangible ways that make the most sense given the situation you're facing.

Contrary to popular belief, busy isn't always good. When it comes to changing, adapting, and remaining relevant, busy is good only if you're pursuing tasks that bring you closer to hitting this target and directly applying effort toward driving positive results. Otherwise, you're simply spinning your wheels. To stay relevant, stay focused on the bottom line; if not, you can fill entire weeks, months, or even years with busywork, yet still accomplish nothing.

All of these principles aren't applicable just to organizations; they're also applicable to life and career on an individual level. Take a moment to stop and look ahead at where you need to be, where you are, and what you're doing to span the distance on a routine basis. Afterward, realign efforts and rethink your strategy to make sure you're still on the road to remaining relevant and remaining most productive. If you can get in the habit of making routine readjustments and realignments on a consistent basis, you'll save yourself from having to make more sudden, drastic ones going forward. Even for the world's largest, most successful enterprises, little changes can exert a big impact both today and tomorrow.

When restaurant chain Hard Rock Cafe wanted to add $150 million to its revenue, it didn't tell employees to grow quarterly sales targets or market share by a percentage.[7] As *All In* authors Adrian Gostick and Chester Elton point out, it asked employees to make 50¢ more on every check. When Blue Cross and Blue Shield wanted Minnesota mall shoppers to get fit (and slash healthcare costs), the company didn't ask them to avoid the food court, it asked them to take the stairs instead of the escalator, improving health one step at a time.

So, what's the best way to keep up with change—or get ahead of it—and keep your relevance meter set to high? Follow these simple steps:

- **Scan your environment for changing paradigms.** Some minor changes are simply noise and can be ignored. However, others are major and will permanently change the way business is done or the course of your organization and career. Constantly scan your workplace and industry environment for signs of change, and then determine which are important enough to be acted on.

- **Pick two or three simple goals to focus on.** Less is more. Simple, achievable steps are easier to pursue than broader strategies and can carry you and your organization farther in the end. You can't do everything at the same time or expect your organization and/or colleagues to, either.

- **Pursue the goals with the greatest import.** Certain tasks will take you farther down the road to attaining your goals. Concentrate your efforts on those that deliver the greatest and most direct long-term payoff the fastest. Focus on objectives that tie most closely to your mission. Defer those that are less promising.

- **Periodically revisit your goals and update them as necessary.** Change is constant. Regularly review your goals and ensure that they are still relevant to meeting your objectives. If not, revise your goals and your approaches for achieving them.

Also important to note if you want to change and remain relevant as an enterprise: To *really* make an optimum effort toward moving forward and achieving your business's goals, everyone has to have a voice in developing its stratagems. Speak up, speak often, and speak openly together about where you see yourself today and tomorrow and where you see the future heading. Work with teammates to develop shared goals, clearly defined approaches for getting from here to there, and accomplishing intervening tasks, then collaborate to create a system for making sure your objectives and approaches remain in tune with current or upcoming needs. Give yourself and give your team the gift of awareness, a voice, and the ability to problem solve.

When you, your organization, and your peers are all part of the change management and goal-setting process, all will work harder to make sure that the job gets done and done correctly, on time, and far better than expected. When you do so, it'll help speed you along as you pursue your goal, and steer you closer to maintaining a state of ongoing relevance.

Always Be Creating Worth

Another key part of remaining relevant in a world of rising competition and shrinking visibility is consistently finding ways to differentiate, demonstrate our capabilities, and show why we're impossible to replace. With dozens or even thousands of rivals to face, any one of which can offer similar benefits cheaper, faster, or more effectively, what's to set us apart from the competition? If you can't answer that question, others won't be able to, either. More important, they'll be unable to see why they shouldn't simply turn to another solution in your place.

Commanding and illustrating value is a vital piece of remaining relevant. Blaine Loomer, CEO of Green Tower Energy in Cincinnati, Ohio, says, "The best way to keep your job in today's economy is to be so valuable to your employers that they simply can't do without you."[8] Loomer goes on to describe creating worth in terms of ROI (return on investment). The company measures its ROI on you, so you should measure the ROI on yourself as well.

Look at your salary and benefits as a fixed cost. What are you doing to provide employers significant gains on this money and justify why it isn't better spent elsewhere—say on hungrier, more affordable workers that may possess more varied or up-to-date skills?

Customers are asking the same questions. What makes you so special, let alone valuable? Focus your efforts on answering these questions quickly and visibly demonstrating the answers, and you'll always remain future-proof.

You can create lasting worth for yourself and your organization by

- **Being a part of the solution instead of the problem.** It's easy to be the one who is constantly pointing out what's wrong. It's much more difficult to be the one who is constantly making things right.

- **Adding more to the bottom line than your company pays you in salary and benefits.** If you aren't already doing this, then you need to be creating more value to demonstrate how the numbers add up.

- **Focusing on long-term opportunities.** Long-term opportunities are the future of your business, and if you make a habit of capitalizing on them, then your capabilities, resources, and value will increase significantly. Likewise, you yourself need to pursue long-term opportunities that allow you to increase your learning, experience, and expertise. Each ultimately makes you more valuable and provides lasting worth that's far more lucrative than any individual sale or paycheck. Whether you're an individual or organization, time, not money, is your most finite and valuable asset; be careful where you spend it.

- **Innovating, creating, and taking risks.** Every organization needs people who can come up with new ideas that can save money, improve processes, enhance productivity, and boost the bottom line. It needs even more people who can successfully execute them. Be one of those people.

Through regular and strategic investments (including not just financial investments but also personal and professional investments), we can build a sturdy framework and safety net that helps us stand out and achieve lasting success. These choices not only help us accumulate precious resources, create more successful action plans, and make wiser decisions, they also provide us with the insights, assets, and assurance we need to take risks. In doing so, we can find the courage needed to remain relevant by constantly cementing personal, professional, and organizational value and changing with the times, innovating all the while.

To Succeed, Innovate

According to XPRIZE Foundation founder Peter Diamandis (whose organization is charged with producing radical breakthroughs), advances in technology are driving exponential change in our world today. And all this change is making it harder for both individuals and organizations—who naturally favor the static and predictable—to stay relevant, let alone get a leg up on the competition. Coupled with our inborn resistance to the unknown and unfamiliar, this rapid rate of change can quickly spin us around in circles, rather than provide the clarity and courage we need to constantly evolve.

Moreover, Diamandis explains, you can't simply research or plan your way out of this pickle. All you can do is navigate it in real time. It's no longer business as usual in modern enterprise. Like Harvard business professor John Kotter explains, "As things speed up and more stuff gets changing out there, to prosper, organizations have to react. You can't still do things the way you've done in the past and grab opportunities or avoid hazards that come at you."[9]

If your enterprise is too slow, or too hesitant, to relentlessly push forward in the face of change and uncertainty, there's still hope, however. Plan. Prepare. Put the processes, people, and systems needed to handle these shifts in place long before these changes ever arrive. If you need to buy yourself time to respond, don't sit still. Have a framework in place that will buy you that time and give you the means to smartly react. But to successfully innovate, as discussed in the previous chapter, we need to remake our own attitudes and approaches to productively fit the context and scenario before us.

Consider that hundreds of firms can now go from idea to market in as little as one month. Even multibillion-dollar global giants suddenly have teams to introduce apps every six weeks for less than $25,000 apiece. To compete in incredibly fast-moving, competitive, and unpredictable environs such as these, we must be clever and resourceful, and we must *improvise*, changing strategies to suit changing scenarios.

For example, in America, national drugstore chain Walgreens faced a challenging market. After a public dispute with a prescription partner, tightened consumer spending, and growing competition caused prescription counts to fall, the company didn't bump up ad spending. Instead, it reinvented its approach to customer care by the following measures:

- **Bringing pharmacists out from behind the counter** to provide more clinical and counseling services. This allowed Walgreens to create added value for shoppers, new income streams, and more growth opportunities.
- **Building an online "Find a Pharmacist" search tool** to

match customer needs with pharmacists' areas of expertise, clinical backgrounds, and spoken languages, boosting trust and convenience among its buyers.

- **Creating a** mobile app and pill reminder with prescription refill and transfer abilities, to drive more business and stay top of mind.
- **Building software tools** that let third-party developers create new ways to let patients order refills at its 8,000+ pharmacies, driving more interest and foot traffic with minimal expenditure.

But Walgreens didn't stop there. To capitalize on growing urban markets, the business has also completely rebranded flagship stores in major cities. Instead of places to simply get meds, they're hip, one-stop shops where you can go to be well, live healthy, and grab sushi, a smoothie, or even get a bottle of wine and manicure during your lunch hour.

Same company. Same business model. Entirely different approach to retail design, marketing, positioning, and support services—one that's designed to provide greater convenience, a deeper sense of community, and more accessible care. As a result of the changes it made, Walgreens has not only begun to post record sales but also made itself more relevant to modern customers in every age group.

Again, innovation isn't rocket science, and keeping up with change isn't always as difficult as it seems; sometimes, all it takes is a simple repositioning or rethinking to make yourself more relevant, more future-proof, and more successful. And you can absolutely put the same strategic principles that today's most successful innovators use to work for yourself or your enterprise at every level. As we've discussed, relevancy is simply a function of reinvention, and you always have the power to reinvent yourself.

Creating Competitive Advantage

If you want to go from simply being relevant to being ahead of the curve, there's also another crucial piece of the puzzle to be aware of: cultivating your competitive advantage.

To do this, get to know and embrace sources of pain and discomfort, as discussed in Chapter 6. By pushing past the most challenging obstacles, which others balk at, we enjoy greater chances of gaining singular skills and opportunities that command more worth—the essence of competitive advantage. Strive to create knowledge, experience, and talent or contact gaps that others cannot easily replicate. The more valuable and unique your skills or business benefits, the harder others will find it to easily mimic or abandon them and the more indispensable, beneficial, and future-proof you'll be.

As Georgetown University professor Cal Newport points out, if all we do as enterprises or individuals is clock in and clock out, never deviating from our daily routine, we eventually plateau. His best advice for enterprises and workers looking to remain relevant and to vault themselves to the front of the pack: Seek out crucial capabilities and competencies and hone them to a razor-sharp point. Then have the courage to capitalize on your points of singularity to chart your own path.

How can you create personal competitive advantage on an individual and corporate level?

- Offer unique capabilities, benefits, or resources.
- Have one-of-a-kind contacts or connections.
- Master singularly challenging skills or tasks.
- Know more about the competition than your colleagues and more about the market and customers than your rivals.
- Anticipate coming trends better than your colleagues or competitors.
- Solve hard problems and create singular worth for customers.
- Establish visibility and value and instantly differentiate in audiences' eyes.
- Serve your coworkers—and bosses—better than your colleagues, empower the best and brightest talent, and encourage these creative minds to innovate.
- Be self-sufficient and able to perform tasks without support or instruction by stockpiling the resources and leverage needed to become self-reliant.
- Have a positive instead of negative attitude; look for opportunities, even within the most difficult challenges.
- Don't be afraid to make decisions, to take risks, and to put yourself out there.

Not good at something? *Get* good at it. Scared that the farthest you can go isn't far enough? Push yourself or your organization until you truly find out. But also, understand where your talents are lacking, realize the importance of becoming conversant in those subjects, and know whom to call on for aid when needed. To do otherwise is to provide others with an unacceptable advantage. Instead, put these suggestions to work for you by leveraging them to remain relevant, remain invaluable, and remain ahead of the curve.

Action Steps

We cannot always predict the unknown or change the world, but we can always research the unknown, get to know it better, and adapt in turn—changing and evolving to remain relevant and increasingly valuable in our companies and careers. Work past obstacles to find growth and opportunity by pursuing the following action steps:

- **Stay alert for shifts in your environment.** Some changes are major, others minor, and many of little consequence—still, few should be ignored. Identify the changes that will have an impact on you, your career, and your business, and create a list that divides the changes and overarching trends you've identified by immediacy, impact, and import. Then determine which ones are most pressing—and which ones to do something about or temporarily defer. Revisit this list often: Over time, new trends and developments will emerge, and priorities will need to be reconsidered.

- **Relentlessly reinvent yourself.** Don't expect the world to change for you, and don't expect it to sit still. As times and trends evolve, constantly evolve along with them—never stop innovating, and you'll never lose relevancy. Make sure to plan in advance as well. Adapt your perspectives and strategies today with an eye toward providing skills, services, or solutions that will be critically in demand tomorrow.

- **Create a list of your own action steps that bridges the present and the future.** Once you've got an idea of where the future is heading, create a list of tangible achievements you must accomplish to successfully greet it when it arrives. Then break this list down further into specific tasks you must complete, deadlines to complete them by, and action steps you can pursue to immediately begin working toward these goals. Regularly reassess if your strategies are still in tune with them and readjust as needed.

- **Always be creating worth.** You are relevant to your employer and customers only if you are providing them with value. Be someone who creates value and worth for your company and colleagues, not someone who sucks it up and offers little or nothing in return.

- **Don't stop innovating.** Constantly pursue change and evolution by rolling out new strategies, solutions, and approaches that challenge conventional approaches, perspectives, and thinking. Changing times and trends demand changing responses and tactics, changes you can constantly be deploying and experimenting with and using to prepare for impending shifts long before they arrive. Note that innovation doesn't always have to be about invention. Sometimes a slight repositioning is all it takes to reestablish relevancy on an immediate and long-term scale.

- **Pivot or shift as needed.** Do this when a simple readjustment just isn't enough to respond to changes in the business environment. Sometimes a leap of faith is needed to go from failure to success; others, a quick spin on one leg. If a pivot is required, keep one foot in your core competencies (that is, what's working) and the others' toes constantly dipping into the unknown (that is, potential areas where you can leverage those compe-

tencies in new and more advantageous ways) until you find a
promising way forward.

- **Create competitive advantage.** Offer your customers, employers, or end users unique capabilities, benefits, or resources and
  anticipate and quickly adapt to future trends: The more helpful you are, the harder you will be to replace and the more
  relevant you will be.

Future-Proof Your Life and Business

So is it really possible to future-proof yourself—to possess the high level of agility and flexibility needed to continually succeed, regardless of the uncertainty we all face in our careers, lives, and businesses? As we've seen throughout this book, on both the individual and organizational level, the answer is an emphatic *yes*, absolutely.

At its core, every story, every example, every chapter of this book comes back to the importance of four simple principles and rules, which allow us to both positively enact and react to change:

F—**Focus** on the problem at hand, and objectively study it to create a plan of attack.

E—**Engage** it by taking action and testing these theories.

A—**Assess** the response you get as a result of the actions you take.

R—React based on the insights gained, and refine your future approaches accordingly.

Or, put even more simply: *Think. Act. Observe. Respond.* Then rinse and repeat. The key differentiator between those we quantify as successes and failures today is their own attitude toward common fears and their approach to tackling adversity.

Strategic innovators use these principles to deliver game-changing breakthroughs. Executives use them to lead through times of great uncertainty. Individuals use them to plot a career path and sustainable future, despite growing risk and unfamiliar challenges. In all cases, the only thing that qualifies all is a willingness to steadily move forward, learning and adapting as they go—the very essence of demonstrating and exercising courage. Relentlessly practical, leading individuals and organizations let logic, not emotion, rule their decisions—and, instead of avoiding risk, make calculated gambles.

Change is natural. Uncertainty is everywhere. And risks? You're taking them every day, even when choosing to read this volume over another book. The smartest time to take these chances: While your stock is hot, while your prospects are booming, and while you're at the top of your game.

When times are good, double down on change and innovation, reinvest in yourself, recalibrate your plans, and then put your plans in motion. When times are bad, put all the resources and leverage you've been steadily amassing—say, all those skill refreshes, pilot initiatives, and professional development programs you've been pursuing—to work, fueling further growth and evolution. Change and adaptation are the surest ways to ensure a promising future.

Why wait until competitors are circling you like sharks in the water before you plug the holes in your leaking strategy or steer your business plan toward brighter shores? Why hold off until near retirement to reach the peak of your skills, achievements, or earning potential or to reap the benefits you could enjoy today?

The best time to change, innovate, and stockpile assets such as fresh capabilities and resources is while the market (whether it's the financial market, job market, or commercial market) is on an upward swing. And the best time to leverage and spend all that intellectual, experiential, and material capital you've been amassing? When it's on a downswing, so that you've already got a firm safety net in place (you *were* putting some away for a rainy day, weren't you?) and (because each resource goes further) all this capital can work harder for you when tapped. Change your perspective, change your approach, and change your future: It's all in the mind's eye.

Innovation and disruption aren't rare or inborn talents, reserved for a select few, or the province of technology giants and leading manufacturers alone. They're simple, quickly applied strategies that you can exercise on a daily basis and apply to every aspect of your life, career, or enterprise.

However, becoming a force for positive change and becoming a courageous leader—whether you're a thought leader, team leader, or executive leader—is not a circumstance that happens to us. Rather, it's a shift that we must actively bring about by taking accountability, and taking action. Doing so doesn't just take concerted effort, focus, determination, hard work, and the ability to counter uncertainty and fear of the unknown with bravery, persistence, and perseverance. It also takes forethought, planning, execution, and follow-through.

In this book, we have considered the stories of numerous individuals who have effected positive, lasting change and in doing so future-proofed themselves; we've also discussed many companies that have done the same. In each case, uncertainty was looked dead in the eye and sized up and action was taken to create success in its place. The moment was seized and firm decisions made. These individuals and businesses made the best of their circumstances by changing and adapting to the challenges at hand. And all did so without knowing with absolute certainty what was going to happen next.

In the very first chapter of this book, we met Vermont restaurant co-owner Melissa Kirmayer Eamer—a twenty-six-year-old who was sick and tired of her intellectually unchallenging job serving up bowls of clam chowder to an endless parade of customers. Despite the fear she felt about making such a momentous change in her life, Eamer decided to find a new job that would be more personally rewarding. She ultimately went from slinging chowder to landing a high-ranking leadership position at a major online retailer.

As she says, the secret was simple: Learn to deal with ambiguity and dive headfirst into any given challenge.

We also saw just how seriously the bigwigs at FedEx take driving fear out of their organization to get the best out of their people. Longtime marketing and sales executive Michelle Proctor decided that she could make a difference by helping find ways for FedEx employees to embrace the idea of taking chances and pursuing game-changing opportunities. Proctor's solution was to create a forty-person-strong team of traveling FedEx employees whose job it is to get the company's people to speak up and take action without fear of reproach, reprisal, or being ostracized. The experiment worked: by driving fear out of the organization, Proctor's team turned everyday employees into bold, forward-thinking visionaries.

And we met Gerry Graf, who was faced with the job of telling his top-shelf client (consumer products giant Unilever) that the approach it had taken to marketing its popular Ragú pasta sauce was no longer relevant to consumers and needed to be abandoned.

Steeling his courage, Graf spoke up and confronted his customer with the bad news, while suggesting a better, more timely and relevant approach. The client agreed, new ads were created and run, and suddenly, shoppers started to develop a taste for Ragú again.

For each of these individuals, and their careers, all's well that ends well. But it also ends well far more often than you think.

Consider some of the many other change leaders and comeback stories that you haven't yet met:

- **Mari Smith**, an otherwise nondescript Canadian with no college degree, who transformed herself from a hobbyist to a social media powerhouse whom *Fast Company* calls "a relationship marketing whiz" and "the Pied Piper of the Online World."[1] "Take smart risks," she says. "Stop waiting for permission."[2]

- **Calvin Smith**, principal manager of global innovation and marketing for big data leader EMC, coaches employees up and down the organization, from accounting managers to software engineers, in entrepreneurship, communications, and marketing abilities. "We fill in skills gaps . . . ask them to think like a project manager," he notes.[3]

- **Wiz Khalifa**, the chart-topping rapper who uses small shows as prototyping laboratories to test new songs before playing larger

concerts and managed to spin a relentless barrage of bootleg mix-
tapes and guest verses into multiplatinum success after being
dropped by Warner Bros. Records. "A lot of people get comfortable, and let fans move on," he says. "I move on with them."[4]

More important, what will *your* story be?

The point is simple: You and your organization cannot afford
to do nothing. In an ever-changing world, doing something is what
it takes to future-proof yourself and the company for which you
work. Overcome the sources of anxiety and fear that blind us to the
reality of the situation, and challenges and problems will simply
become puzzles to be solved. You can always steer events toward
better outcomes and, in doing so, regain control of your future.

Put yourself back behind the dashboard. It's far easier to navigate changing environments when your eyes are on the road,
hands on the wheel, and your butt's in the driver's seat.

You now understand that the sun always rises, no matter how
dark the night before it may be, and that anyone can find personal
or business success despite the great uncertainty that surrounds
us. The old saying that nothing is certain in life except death and
taxes is not really true. As you've seen here, with rigorous planning, intelligent decision making, and a little bit of both elbow
grease and perseverance, *everything* becomes virtually certain in
time.

We can and should choose to become alchemists of certainty,
actively mixing and matching ingredients and combining insight
and intelligence to transform the unknown into a source of opportunity. Using the numerous tools, strategies, and stories of success
presented here, you now have all the knowledge that you need to
tamp down fear's inhibiting effects.

So here's the challenge:

- Step outside your comfort zone.
- Take risks.
- Do things differently.
- Speak up.
- Make leaps of faith.
- Keep the ball moving forward.
- Think differently.
- Be your own champion.
- Qualify yourself.
- Embrace the change that is needed for you to succeed today and in the future.

Remember: Change happens whether you decide to get on board with it or not. So why not lead change instead of be led—or even be run over—by it?

The moment is yours to seize. Now, go make a change.

Acknowledgments

For twenty years, life has been an endless series of unexpected new detours and adventures. Despite unrelenting change, however, the support and goodwill of countless friends, family members, and colleagues has remained an ongoing constant. Decades of experience have helped inform this book. But many others' insights have helped shape it: My eternal gratitude—this would be a far lesser work were it not for their boundless wit and wisdom.

Special credit must be given to Z, who never failed to improvise, adapt, and forge ahead, despite the endless disruption taking place around her. My deepest thanks to publisher John Duff and editor Amanda Shih as well, for their invaluable insights and input, and Celeste Fine, for her expert eye and feedback. All gratitude further goes to Florence de Martino, the Grassiano brothers, Chris Zimmerman, Paul Scigliano, Marc Saltzman, and Mark Fusco for believing from day one and to Kris Ramac, Bjorn

Larsson, Nrupesh Gajjar, Eric Knipp, and Fab Furlough for helping translate belief into action. Also, I am very appreciative of the
contribution of Perigee's art director, Lisa Amoroso, for her eye-
catching jacket design.

Richard, Karen, Jamie, and Lisa: Thank you for standing behind
this work every step of the way and thank you to Calvin Smith,
David Droga, Jessica Esch, and Paul Lester for helping speed it
down its path. Susan Bisno, Joel Massel, Cesar Bittar, Katie Hal-
lahan, Richard Flores, and Vitek Goyel's ongoing support has made
all the difference as well.

In addition, all appreciation goes out to the following individ-
uals as well: Joseph LeDoux, Martin Paulus, Sharon Wong, Justin
Kan, Jack Bogle, Ari Wallach, Barry Schwartz, Beth Blumenthal,
Bob Mendenhall, Christine Costello, Ingrid Vandervelde, Oren
and Ariella Gonzalez, Dick Bolles, Raina Kumra, Matt Ployhar,
Saras Sarasvathy, Sridhar Balasubramanian, Johner Riehl, Rusel
DeMaria, Trip Hawkins, Nolan Bushnell, Warren Spector, Damon
Brown, Will Wright, Amy Gahran, Andrew Grochal, Brian Meece,
Dan Nainan, Greg Gillis, John Bordeaux, Joshua Dzabiak, Linda
Lombri, Matt Grigsby, Brian Fargo, Rachel Orston, Sarah McDer-
mott, Allison Graham, Rue Phillips, Ken Levine, Scott Gerber,
Brian Solis, Chris Klaus, Raina Kumra, Deborah Shlian, Jim
Schleckser, Kenny Beck, Kevin Thompson, Scott Young, and Tim
Hwang.

As for the innumerable others who've never hesitated to open
doors, or provide fresh perspective, as the years roll on, a hearty
cheers for making this possible as well. Everything has, and continues to, change for the better because of you.

Notes

INTRODUCTION

1. http://www.houdini.org/interior-harry-houdini-attractions-pocono -poconos-scranton.html.

CHAPTER 1

1. Phone interview, June 2013.
2. Joseph Ledoux, "Searching the Brain for the Roots of Fear," *New York Times*, January 22, 2012, available at opinionator.blogs.nytimes.com/2012/01/22/ anatomy-of-fear/?_r=0.
3. https://www.youtube.com/watch?v=j1O2DuNS69w.
4. Phone interview, May 2013.
5. Phone interview, September 2013.

CHAPTER 2

1. *Engadget*, "Podcast 235—04.08.2011," available at www.engadget.com/ 2011/04/08/engadget-podcast-235-04-08-2011/#disqus_thread.
2. Email interview, April 2013.
3. Leading Innovation Through Design, conference hosted by the Design Management Institute, August 2012; see www.dmi.org/?page=Journal, http:// sloanreview.mit.edu/article/the-evolution-of-the-designinspired -enterprise/ and http://onlinelibrary.wiley.com/doi/10.1111/j.1948-7169.2002 .tb00294.x/abstract.

4. Jake Swearingen, "Great Intrapreneurs in Business History," CBS Money-watch, last updated June 17, 2008, available at www.cbsnews.com/news/great-intrapreneurs-in-business-history.

5. Phone interview, May 2013.

CHAPTER 3

1. David Martin, "The Truth About Happiness May Surprise You," CNN, November 20, 2006, www.cnn.com/2006/HEALTH/conditions/11/10/happiness.overview/index.html.

2. Phone interview, May 2013.

3. http://www.researchgate.net/publication/232442435_The_construct_of_courage_Categorization_and_measurement.

4. "Highlights: Workplace Stress & Anxiety Disorder Survey," Anxiety and Depression Association of America, available at www.adaa.org/workplace-stress-anxiety-disorders-survey.

5. G. Jeffrey MacDonald, "When Courage Is Encouraged on the Job," *Christian Science Monitor*, January 26, 2009, available at www.csmonitor.com/Business/2009/0126/p13s01-wmgn.html.

6. http://www.apa.org/helpcenter/road-resilience.aspx.

7. "Resilience Training," U.S. Army, available at www.resilience.army.mil.

8. http://hbr.org/2011/04/building-resilience/ar/1.

9. Phone interview, April 2013.

CHAPTER 4

1. Damian Kulash Jr., "The New Rock-Star Paradigm," *Wall Street Journal*, December 17, 2010, available at online.wsj.com/news/articles/SB10001424052748703727804576017592259031536.

2. https://www.youtube.com/user/OkGo.

3. Phone interview, May 2013.

4. Phone interview, May 2013.

5. Cheryl Conner, "Who's Starting America's New Businesses and Why?" *Forbes*, July 22, 2012, available at www.forbes.com/sites/cherylsnappconner/2012/07/22/whos-starting-americas-new-businesses-and-why.

6. Mark Harrington, "Countering the Growing Social Threat of Brandjacking," Business2Community, September 26, 2013, available at www.busi

ness2community.com/social-business/countering-growing-social-threat
-brandjacking-0627443.

7. Phone interview, June 2013.

8. Ibid., 104.

CHAPTER 5

1. Phone interview, June 2013.

2. Kate White, "How a Little Career Paranoia Can Pay Off Brilliantly for You," available at katewhite.com/resources/how-a-little-career-paranoia -can-pay-off-brilliantly-for-you.

3. A. G. Lafley and Roger L. Martin, "What P&G Learned from the Diaper Wars," *Fast Company*, February 8, 2013, available at www.fastcompany .com/3005640/what-pg-learned-diaper-wars.

4. "Huggies vs. Pampers," Diffen, available at www.diffen.com/difference/ Huggies_vs_Pampers.

5. "Don't Rest on Your Laurels: The Secrets to Keeping Your Business Relevant," Rescue a CEO, available at rescue.ceoblognation.com/2013/06/24/ dont-rest-on-your-laurels-the-secrets-to-keeping-your-business-relevant.

6. Andrew S. Grove, *Only the Paranoid Survive* (New York: Crown Business, 1999), p. 65.

7. Jim Collins and Morten Hansen, *Great by Choice* (New York: HarperBusiness, 2011), 107.

8. Ibid., 104.

9. Michael E. Porter, "The Five Competitive Forces That Shape Strategy," *Harvard Business Review*, January 2008, available at hbr.org/2008/01/ the-five-competitive-forces-that-shape-strategy.

10. Sean Williams, "Starbucks: Keeping Its Friends Close and Its Enemies Closer," *Motley Fool*, April 9, 2013, available at www.fool.com/investing/ general/2013/04/09/starbucks-keeping-its-friends-close-and-its-enemie .aspx.

11. Innosight, "Creative Destruction Whips Through Corporate America," *Executive* Briefing, Winter 2012, available at www.innosight.com/inno vation-resources/strategy-innovation/upload/creative-destruction-whips -through-corporate-america_final2012.pdf.

12. Andrew S. Grove, *Only the Paranoid Survive* (New York: Crown Business, 1999), 3.

CHAPTER 6

1. Statistic Brain, "Startup Business Failure Rate By Industry," available at www.statisticbrain.com/startup-failure-by-industry.
2. Jim Collins, "The 10 Greatest CEOS of All Time," July 21, 2003, available at www.jimcollins.com/article_topics/articles/10-greatest.html.
3. Bill Treasurer, *Positively M.A.D.: Making a Difference in Your Organizations, Communities, and the World* (San Francisco: Berrett-Koehler, 2005), 8.
4. http:// books.google.com/books/about/Lean_and_Green.html?id= 7yfmT8BHVLcC—Page 189.
5. "Tiger Woods," Answers, available at www.answers.com/topic/tiger -woods.
6. http://www.encyclopedia.com/topic/Tiger_Woods.aspx.
7. "Mika Brzezinski: I Almost Left 'Morning Joe' Over Pay Disparity," *Huffington Post*, last updated July 6, 2011, available at www.huffingtonpost .com/2011/05/06/mika-brzezinski-i-almost-_n_858495.html.
8. https://sites.sas.upenn.edu/duckworth.
9. http://www.sas.upenn.edu/~duckwort/images/publications/Duckworth PetersonMatthewsKelly_2007_PerseveranceandPassion.pdf.
10. "Our Work," The Duckworth Lab, sites.sas.upenn.edu/duckworth.
11. American Psychological Association, "The Road to Resilience," available at www.apa.org/helpcenter/road-resilience.aspx.
12. Ibid.
13. "About Fort Jackson," Fort Jackson, available at jackson.armylive.dodlive .mil/about.
14. Brendan O'Brien, "Executive Insights: If at First You Don't Succeed," *QSR*, April 2013, available at www.qsrmagazine.com/executive-insights/if-first -you-don-t-succeed.

CHAPTER 7

1. Phone interview, June 2013.
2. Lydia Depillis, "Congrats, CEOs! You're Making 273 Times the Pay of the Average Worker," *Washington Post*, June 26, 2013, available at www.wash ingtonpost.com/blogs/wonkblog/wp/2013/06/26/congrats-ceos-youre -making-273-times-the-pay-of-the-average-worker.

3. Seth Fiegerman, "Grooveshark CEO: 'I'm Broke,'" Mashable, April 22, 2013, available at mashable.com/2013/04/22/grooveshark-radio.

4. "FIELD: Global Immersion," Harvard Business School, available at www .hbs.edu/mba/academic-experience/FIELD/Pages/default.aspx.

5. Phone interview, May 2013.

6. Charlie Collier, "How I Hire," LinkedIn, September 23, 2013, available at www.linkedin.com/today/post/article/20130923225654-255625200 -how-i-hire-you-re-not-interviewing-for-the-job-you-think-you-are?trk= tod-home-art-list-large_0.

7. IBM, "Making Change Work," available at public.dhe.ibm.com/common/ ssi/ecm/en/gbe03100usen/GBE03100USEN.pdf.

8. Michael S. Dahl, "Organizational Change and Employee Stress," July 6, 2010, available at www.wiwi.uni-jena.de/eic/files/WS%2010%20JERS% 20Dahl.pdf.

9. http://www.scientificamerican.com/author/benoit-b-mandelbrot.

10. "About," Star Alliance, available at www.staralliance.com/en/about/air lines/united_airlines.

11. http://www.hemispheresmagazine.com/2013/09/01/expecting-the -unexpected.

12. Pamela O'Leary, "From Dead-End to Dream Job," *Forbes*, April 27, 2011, available at www.forbes.com/sites/prettyyoungprofessional/2011/04/27/ from-dead-end-to-dream-job-taking-control-of-your-career.

13. Phone interview, May 2013.

14. "Is College Worth It?" Pew Research, available at www.pewsocialtrends .org/2011/05/15/is-college-worth-it.

15. Interview, April 2013.

CHAPTER 8

1. Dean Takahashi, "Is Microsoft's One-Time Star J Allard Leaving the Company?" *Venture Beat*, May 21, 2010, available at venturebeat.com/2010/05/ 21/is-microsofts-one-time-star-j-allard-leaving-the-company.

2. J. Allard, interoffice memo, available at www.google.com/url?sa=t&rct=j& q=&esrc=s&source=web&cd=1&cad=rja&ved=0CCwQFjAA&url=http% 3A%2F%2Fwww.microsoft.com%2Fabout%2Fcompanyinformation% 2Ftimeline%2Ftimeline%2Fdocs%2Fdi_killerapp_InternetMemo.rtf& ei=Y5kwUtLmJOioyAGm64DADg&usg=AFQjCNHO04HZPALsUN

9Rp4v1jKDYQ8eRpQ&sig2=9phna85Ti0RZoUj4OYM-6Q&bvm=
bv.51773540,d.aWc.

3. Interview, June 2013.

4. "Famous Names in Gaming," CBS News, June 6, 2013, available at way
-back.archive.org/web/20111126021604/http://www.cbsnews.com/2316
-100_162-1673418-8.html.

5. Jason Nazar, "16 Surprising Statistics about Small Businesses," *Forbes*,
September 9, 2013, available at www.forbes.com/sites/jasonnazar/2013/
09/09/16-surprising-statistics-about-small-businesses.

6. Deborah Gage, "The Venture Capital Secret: 3 Out of 4 Start-Ups Fail,"
Wall Street Journal, September 20, 2012, available at online.wsj.com/
news/articles/SB10000872396390443720204578004980476429190.

7. http://www.fastcodesign.com/3016310/pepsico-indra-nooyi-and-mauro
-porcini.

8. Malcolm Gladwell, "The Sure Thing," *New Yorker*, January 18, 2010,
available   at   www.newyorker.com/reporting/2010/01/18/100118fa_fact_
gladwell.

9. Michel Villette and Catherine Vuillermot, "From Predators to Icons," Cor-
nell University ILR School, available at digitalcommons.ilr.cornell.edu/
cgi/viewcontent.cgi?article=1056&context=books.

10. Heidi Shierholz, Natalie Sabadish, and Nicholas Finio, "The Class of 2013,"
Economic Policy Institute, April 10, 2013, available at www.epi.org/publi
cation/class-of-2013-graduates-job-prospects.

11. Annalyn Kurtz, "Class of 2013 Faces Grim Job Prospects," CNN Money,
April 10, 2013, available at money.cnn.com/2013/04/10/news/economy/
college-grads-jobs/index.html.

12. Phone interview, July 2013.

13. Phone interview, April 2013.

CHAPTER 9

1. Phone interview, May 2013.

2. Alec Foege, "The Trouble with Tinkering Time," *Wall Street Journal*,
January 18, 2013, available at online.wsj.com/news/articles/SB100014241
27887323468604578246070515298626.

3. Lauren Drell, "Attention Pet Owners: You Need These 3 Apps," Mashable,
March 5, 2013, available at mashable.com/2013/03/05/pet-apps-tails-rails
-hackathon.

4. Alyson Krueger, "Hackathons Aren't Just for Hacking," *Wired*, June 6, 2012, available at www.wired.com/business/2012/06/hackathons-arent -just-for-hacking.

5. See www.hackthekitchen.com.

6. Phone interview, June 2013.

7. Evan Luzi, "The Steven Spielberg Three-Step Guide to Rejection," *The Black and Blue*, available at www.theblackandblue.com/2011/04/05/the -steven-spielberg-three-step-guide-to-rejection.

8. See www.thomasedison.com/quotes.html.

9. "Online Extra: Fred Smith on the Birth of FedEx" [interview], *Bloomberg Businessweek*, September 19, 2004, available at www.businessweek.com/ stories/2004-09-19/online-extra-fred-smith-on-the-birth-of-fedex.

10. "FedEx Corporation Company Information," Hoovers, available at www .hoovers.com/company-information/cs/company-profile.FedEx_Corpo ration.e6bc953d777db293.html.

11. Alice E. Vincent, "Rejection Letters," Huffington Post UK, May 17, 2012, available at www.huffingtonpost.co.uk/2012/05/16/publishers-who -got-it-wrong_n_1520190.html.

12. "#82 J.K. Rowling," *Forbes*, available at www.forbes.com/profile/jk-rowling.

13. Alan Kuyatt, "Managing for Innovation: Reducing the Fear of Failure," *Journal of Strategic Leadership* 3, no. 2 (2011): 31.

14. James Donelan, "Do Lean Startup Principles Have a Place in the Enter-prise?" The Next Web, available at thenextweb.com/entrepreneur/2013/ 08/06/do-lean-startup-principles-have-a-place-in-the-enterprise.

15. Bureau of Labor Statistics, "National Longitudinal Surveys: Frequently Asked Questions," available at www.bls.gov/nls/nlsfaqs.htm#anch41.

16. Jeanne Meister, "Job Hopping Is the 'New Normal' for Millennials: Three Ways to Prevent a Human Resource Nightmare," *Forbes*, August 14, 2012, available at www.forbes.com/sites/jeannemeister/2012/08/14/ job-hopping-is-the-new-normal-for-millennials-three-ways-to-prevent-a -human-resource-nightmare.

17. Phone interview, June 2013.

18. Phone interview, May 2013.

19. Phone interview, July 2013.

20. Austin Carr, "Most Innovative Companies 2012," *Fast Company*, February 7, 2012, available at www.fastcompany.com/3017358/most-innovative -companies-2012/19airbnb.

21. Reid Hoffman and Ben Casnocha, *The Start-Up of You* (New York: Crown Business, 2012), p. 22.

22. Martin LaMonica, "SolarCity IPO Tests Business Model Innovation in Energy," *MIT Technology Review*, December 11, 2012, available at www.tech nologyreview.com/view/508616/solarcity-ipo-tests-business-model -innovation-in-energy.

CHAPTER 10

1. Phone interview, May 2013.

2. www.rthausler.com/wp-content/uploads/When-Marketing-is -Strategy-Harvard-Business-Review.pdf.

3. Phone interview, April 2013.

4. Phone interview, May 2013.

5. Phone interview, June 2013.

6. Frank O'Brien, "Do-Not-Call Mondays: The Perks of Being Unavailable," *Inc. Magazine*, June 2013, available at www.inc.com/magazine/201306/ frank-obrien/the-perks-of-being-unavailable.html.

7. Conversation, "First Mondays in Inc. Magazine," available at www.convo agency.com/round-the-office-3.

CHAPTER 11

1. Interview, August 2013.

2. Ray Davis with Peter Economy, *Leading Through Uncertainty: How Umpqua Bank Emerged from the Great Recession Better and Stronger than Ever* (Jossey-Bass, 1st Ed., October 2013).

3. http://www.usatoday.com/story/tech/2013/11/11/amazon-sunday -delivery-usps/3479055.

4. http://www.shrm.org/hrdisciplines/employeerelations/articles/pages/ newhiresfeelmisled.aspx.

5. http://mashable.com/2011/08/04/instagram-kevin-systrom.

6. Interview, April 2013.

7. Jake Breeden, "Make or Break," *Southwest Spirit Magazine*, March 2013.

8. Stephen Denny, "Start It Up," *Southwest Spirit Magazine*, July 2012.

9. https://www.goodreads.com/author/quotes/1792210.John_Holt.

10. http://www.thehindu.com/todays-paper/tp-features/tp-opportunities/ what-makes-strategic-decisions-different/article5370404.ece.

CHAPTER 12

1. http://www.livescience.com/5466-friends-replaced-7-years.html.
2. http://www.goodcarbadcar.net/2011/12/saab-brand-sales-figures.html.
3. http://www.forbes.com/sites/kashmirhill/2010/11/19/names-you-need-to-know-in-2011-chief-listening-officer/.
4. http://www.bls.gov/ooh/.
5. Phone interview, April 2013.
6. Interview, May 2013.
7. http://dra.gov/!userfiles/editor/docs/TomHarris-SmallWins2012.pdf.
8. http://www.amanet.org/training/articles/15-Ways-to-Show-Your-Value-at-Work.aspx.
9. http://www.forbes.com/sites/johnkotter/2011/07/19/can-you-handle-an-exponential-rate-of-change/.

CONCLUSION

1. http://www.fastcompany.com/1327156/mari-smith-pied-piper-online-worldthe-interview.
2. Phone interview, April 2013.
3. Phone interview, June 2013.
4. Ibid.

Index

Award-winning strategic consultant and professional speaker **Scott Steinberg** is one of today's most-renowned leadership and innovation experts, as seen in 600+ outlets from CNN to *Time* and the *Wall Street Journal*. The Fortune 500 call him a "defining figure in business and technology" and "top trendsetter to follow." The CEO of TechSavvy Global, a management consulting and market research firm, he helps clients create a competitive advantage and design cutting-edge programs for driving change, innovation, and growth. A business strategist for corporations, nonprofits, universities, and start-ups, he aids with change management, leadership training, and marketing and communications strategy efforts and has consulted on dozens of industry-leading products and services.

Among today's most-quoted keynote speakers and trend experts, as seen by over 1 billion people worldwide, Scott's more than ten-year track record for accurately predicting business, consumer, and technology trends has made him a fixture in mainstream media. Today's number one–ranked technology expert according to Google, he's been a syndicated columnist on change and innovation for numerous outlets, ranging from *Fast Company, Inc.*, and *Entrepreneur* to *Rolling Stone* and the *Huffington Post*. His motivational speeches, leadership seminars, and training workshops are widely acclaimed for helping tomorrow's leaders and organizations become more productive and successful at every level.

For more information, please visit his website at www.AKeynote Speaker.com. Follow him on Twitter @AKeynoteSpeaker.